GEORGE ORWELL

THE SEARCH FOR A VOICE

LYNETTE HUNTER

Open University Press

Milton Keynes

Open University Press
A division of
Open University Educational Enterprises Ltd.
12 Cofferidge Close
Stony Stratford
Milton Keynes MK11 1BY England

First published 1984

British Library Cataloguing in Publication Data

Hunter, Lynette
  George Orwell.
  1. Orwell, George—Criticism and
  interpretation
  I. Title
  823'.912   PR6029.R8Z1

ISBN 0–335–10580–7
ISBN 0–335–10424–X Pbk

Text design by Clark Williams
Cover design by Phil Atkins
Cover illustration by John Byrne
Printed in Great Britain by
St Edmundsbury Press, Bury St Edmunds, Suffolk

Contents

To Jean and Sidney Emberley

Acknowledgements

The research for and writing of this book were undertaken while I held University Research Fellowships at the Universities of Liverpool (1978–81) and Wales (1981–84). The initial typescript was prepared by Annie Davies with the aid of a grant from the British Academy; and the final computerized version was completed with help from Jennifer Ball of the University of Wales Institute of Science and Technology Computing Department, and John Henshall of the Edinburgh Regional Computing Centre. The book has been typeset by the Lasercomp facilities at the Oxford University Computing Service.

I am grateful to the Script Library at the BBC, who were most generous with their time, and to the Manuscripts Derpartment in the D.M.S. Watson Library of University College London who made available to me a number of papers from the Orwell Archive.

But I would particularly like to thank those who read the script at various stages of its progress – George Kerevan, Peter Lichtenfels, Beverley Stern and John Thompson – all of whom provided invaluable advice.

Introduction

Genre and Rhetoric : The Search for a Valid Voice

Orwell is considered one of the foremost commentators on literature and politics in the twentieth century and this is primarily due to the reputation of his writing style as clear, direct and precise. In view of this it is surprising that this 'clear style' lies at the centre of enormous debate and controversy which call into question his literary and political contributions. In effect he has been consistently underestimated in terms of his awareness of the complexity of literary and linguistic strategy. From the beginning he recognizes that the distinctions between form and content, subject and object, fiction and documentary, are all versions of the fundamental separation between fact and value that has dominated rationalist humanism since the seventeenth century.[1] And for Orwell, the final question is indeed one of value and morality: his writing career is concerned with a search for a valid voice with which to persuade others and express opinion.

Questions of persuasion, morality and value are intimately part of the study of rhetoric, and in the process of exploration Orwell drew the outlines of an understanding of rhetoric in a manner that is extraordinarily prescient of the work in this discipline that would follow over the next thirty years.[2] 'Rhetoric' is a blanket term for both persuasion and the study of persuasion. Broadly speaking, people tend to think of rhetoric as something that persuades them to do something they do not want to do. However, rhetoric has nothing to do with what you are being asked to do, but how you are being asked to do it. This may have negative and restrictive aspects but it may also have alternative, positive elements.

Rhetorical studies are made up of the strategy and stance of rhetoric. Put most simply, strategy defines the techniques that can be used in persuasion.

In literature, strategy provides an artificial divisiveness that separates out the components of writer, work and reader, and allows us to define and discuss what each does. For example, we can speak of the strategy of the writer in using a first person narrator, or the strategy of a work that moves in and out of the satiric genre. But while this can be most helpful, it can also be very restrictive and distorting of the event of reading and writing which includes writer, work and reader in their combined activity. Stance describes this combined activity; and stance, like all activity, involves morality and at root indicates the beliefs that people have about their relationship with the external world.

Rhetorical strategy can be neither positive nor negative, in the sense of opening out or limiting a text, because its techniques have no value in themselves: for example, metaphor is not inherently generative or restrictive. However, when part of an event of reading and writing, strategy is placed in a context of value by the activity of rhetorical stance. This activity can take many directions, but in general stance may take a negative path and restrict the interaction of writer, work and reader, or it may act positively and encourage and stimulate that interaction. Neither writer, nor work nor reader can alone define stance. A writer may want to restrict and impose a specific structure of meaning on the activity of reading. Depending upon the strategic skill of the writer, many readers can find themselves caught within the restriction, finding only the allotted meaning. But a particularly active reader may have strategies to perceive that restriction, pierce the structure, and in leaving it behind, may go on to read the broader implications of the work. Since stance is the event in which all three combine, any definition that is arrived at is an indication of a tendency rather than a fixed solution, and a far more precise description of stance lies within the values that its activity generates.

It is necessary to outline this briefly partly because of the common limitation of rhetorical studies to tactics and occasionally to more involved strategems which has led to the idea of rhetoric simply as a handbook of techniques. But it is also necessary because of the contemporary, widespread delusion that rhetoric can and should be avoided completely. This idea arises from the whole activity of negative rhetoric which hides its use of strategy and therefore of its stance. At the same time it insidiously attempts an imposing control, and aims toward a successful end rather than toward quality.

For the last three hundred years an epistemology that claims a neutral logic and a neutral language has been the main source for strategies of imposition, and these have concentrated on claiming access to absolute truth. A well-documented area of the history of rhetoric notes the rise during the seventeenth century of a rational, analytical logic and the idea of a univocal language,[3] which provided the perfect breeding ground for a negative rhetoric because persuasion appeared to be completely unnecessary. The very concept of stance was not just hidden but completely wiped out, and with this loss also went any concept of active value – one is left with a static morality of fixed standards. Against this background truth becomes a commodity that can be reached if you pile up enough units of information, or facts gained by sequential rational logic. Language enables the accuracy of this activity because it is exact. The process reaches its apotheosis in post-Renaissance science, in which the dominance of fact appears to bring the external world completely within mankind's control.[4] This was a brief flush of extraordinary confidence and while modern Western history may be read as a series of attempts to achieve this control, much of Western philosophy can be seen as an attempt to come to terms with its impossibility.

I would argue that Orwell is particularly sensitive to the limitations of this outlook and spent his writing life searching for alternatives through experiments with genre. Up until the writing of his documentaries Orwell is concerned more with strategy than with stance, but with *The Road to Wigan Pier* he shifts the focus. When this happens the dualities involved in the question of who controls and who is controlled which have dominated Western metaphysics, become transformed into the more profound issues of evaluation and belief. The divisions between subject and object, fiction and fact, novel and documentary, and the whole field of static genre became subordinate to stance. And at the same time that Orwell recognizes the ambivalent status of these divisions he realizes that the factual, rationalist basis for morality is not sufficient to human value.

First his novels, and then later his critical essays as well, present a recognition of the external materiality of language and literature. This becomes the basis for his separation between fantasy and allegory, the former denying materiality and the latter explicitly indicating it, which informs his search for valid stance. He was able to define the means and ends of fantasy, which maintains the dualisms of rationalist thought, in quite explicit terms; but allegory eludes attempts at strategic definition because its activity is specific to each event of reading and writing. Unlike many contemporary critics, who have followed the lead of J. Huizinga, Orwell not only appreciated the function but perceived and outlined the limitations and dangers of games within fantasy. Despite recent writers such as Colin Manlove noting and underlining these problems,[5] most critics either do not perceive them or become involved in a tortuous logic in order to evade them.[6] At the same time Orwell's inconclusiveness about allegory and its spread through the genres of utopia, satire and nonsense, reflects a problem in current criticism which has suggested instead alternative generic words such as apologue, anatomy and modern romance.[7] Yet the development of an allegorical stance within his writing indicates a resolution similar to that of commentators such as Paul de Man who, in *Allegories of Reading*, begins to look at allegory in terms of stance rather than rigid genre.[8]

Orwell's approach to fantasy and allegory as stances meant that they extended out of literature into a range of disciplines including politics and philosophy: with this approach he could speak of these disciplines both in theory and practice as analogous. But while theoretical definition was easy, it was far more difficult to pick out the practical effects. Once he began doing so he began to recognize the basis of all fantasy strategies in a rational logic that leads to limited rationalist humanism, and to perceive the vicious circle of political authoritarianism and the selfishly private individual that lies within that humanism. He became dissatisfied with nineteenth-century liberalism, which he suggested had led to twentieth-century fascism, but also with Stalinist communism which was not only the most dominant alternative in the 1930s but derived from the same rationalist grounds.[9] In Orwell's assessment of the grounds themselves he speaks not only for his contemporaries but for many people today, and reflects their desires and frustrations in his search for a valid political and literary alternative.

It may be the profoundly radical nature of Orwell's questioning that leads to an underestimation of his work, both political and literary. Although I would not agree with his conclusions, I would agree entirely with Raymond Williams's suggestion that to describe his 'paradox of Orwell we would need concepts beyond the consciousness and social structures of his period'.[10] Too many commentators read from within the very grounds that Orwell was questioning and as a result limit their readings and find themselves in contradictory positions. The critical confusion that exists around Orwell's literary work focuses on the attempt to define it in strict generic terms. From *Down and Out in Paris and London* which is both straightforward and overwritten,[11] to *Keep the Aspidistra Flying* which is not a novel but an argument, yet also a parody, a burlesque and a satire,[12] to the struggle for definition in *Animal Farm* and *Nineteen Eighty-Four*, the issue of genre appears to worry critics.

The critical comments on *Animal Farm* are linked with theoretical problems in genre theory itself and with political and moral issues. There are two primary and opposed readings: the first is that it is an allegory because of point to point correspondence with events in the Russian revolution, and the second is that it is allegorical because of the very fact that that correspondence does not dominate it.[13] These opinions are underwritten by contrasting assumptions that the book needs external events to make sense, or that, on the contrary, it is not just an anti-Soviet story but more generally applicable.[14] This leads to definitions of the book as a beast fable and therefore on the one hand a restricted puzzle, but on the other dynamic .[15] It has been called a satire and a didactic sermon as opposed to an anatomy which generates interactive readings;[16] the animals are simply types or complex humours.[17] The opposing definitions are parallel to readings of the story as Orwell's abandonment of political polemics as opposed to a political act in itself,[18] and to judgements of it as both a moral story and not really moral at all.[19]

But nearly always the possibility that Orwell is experimenting with genre, teasing out the edges so that conventional assumptions cannot be counted on, is dismissed or discounted. His skill and consciousness of writing is consistently underrated and leads to accusations of failure, of lack of logic. John Wain states that Orwell is remembered more for his ideas than his skill.[20] Zwerdling's *Orwell and the Left* notes the critical consensus on Orwell's 'failure' as a writer[21] and moves on to suggest that Orwell did experiment with genre. But he concludes by saying that Orwell's commitment to prose made him parasitic on existing trends 'rather than transforming them' (p. 144). Even George Woodcock's perceptive biography *The Crystal Spirit* claims that Orwell was not interested in experiments with form.

An important source for these dismissals of Orwell's skill is that commentators come to the writing with critical expectations that lie within the framework that Orwell came to challenge. The most common expectation is that fiction and non-fiction, the novel and the documentary are always significantly divided from each other, and this prevents the reader from appreciating Orwell's own suggestion that they can be viewed fruitfully as part of a continuum. The attitude becomes especially limiting if a critic claims to believe in the value of the overlap, but criticizes Orwell for separating them. Williams claims that Orwell fails to reshape the novel because 'he seems to have accepted the division between "documentary" and "fiction"',[22] but in fact it is Williams who distinguishes between them saying that the 1930s distinction between the two is 'evident enough'. He goes on to say that Orwell got past the division in practice, but he implies that he did not do so consciously: a judgement that restricts the scope of the rest of his discussion.

Another critical expectation that contributes to the confusion is that genres are fixed. This leads many critics to condemn any development that lies outwith the accepted conventions even though they may profess to want Orwell to be reaching for a new expression. There is, for instance, the criticism of Orwell as a novelist: he does not control his material through his plots, nor can he create rounded characters as novelists should.[23] This approach is underwritten by a tendency to take Orwell's comment that he was not a real novelist[24] as a confession of failure rather than an indication that he was trying to achieve something rather different.[25] When Zwerdling examines Orwell's unwillingness to transform genre, he suggests that it arises from a hesitation between subjective and objective forms[26] that undermines the realistic genre of novel (p. 158); and in the end he criticizes Orwell's writing for not being 'seamless' (p. 209) but has no regard for the possibility that Orwell may not have been aiming at these ends, may not have wanted seamless writing.[27] Woodcock again is more generous, and says that because Orwell is a moralist he writes fables and parables rather than novels,[28] and even notes the allegorical play around a central topic or area of content, that each work develops (p. 232). Yet he too is severely critical and asserts that Orwell was not interested in a structure for his novel-writing (pp. 269–70).

Underlying these readings are certain philosophical and critical assumptions that blind readers to alternative directions in Orwell's thought. The enormous range, diversity and contradictory nature of the criticisms and commentaries on his philosophy, literature and politics should indicate the richness of his work, the comprehensive grasp that Orwell himself had of the complexity of contemporary issues. But all too often critics place him within the grounds of the predominant dualism of rationalist thought, and appear reluctant to acknowledge the possibility that he was conscious of that dualism and purposively setting out to go outside it.

Although many writers provoke debate, few do so in terms of such diametric opposition with readers explicitly defining one side or the other of the dualism, as Orwell. Some critics have claimed religion and morality as the basis for his work, while others have stated firmly that he has no interest in either.[29] Within Christian theology itself he has been claimed for both Protestant and Catholic.[30] He has been called a rationalist and a sentimentalist,[31] he is for science and against it;[32] he is objective and subjective or both and hence a solipsist.[33] Similarly, he has at times been accused of making the individual dominant and at others of making him passive,[34] of refusing to see the 'conditioned' nature of life and of believing in a determined pattern of institutional change.[35]

In terms of literature, some critics say his readers are imposed upon, others that they are left without guidance.[36] By corollary his fictions are designed either to dominate or to evade,[37] and even his documentaries exist both to voice the subjective or to achieve objective truth.[38] All of these divisions are used indiscriminately to present the writer as either dishonest, honest or sincere[39] with varying degrees of subtlety and perception as to the 'criterion of truth' that underlies such judgements. Politically Orwell is for change, against change, or for neither.[40] He is for the oppressed then for the oppressor,[41] both of which are usually phrased in terms of the extent of his political knowledge or ignorance. This is reflected in the assessments of those who claim that he recognized the profound difficulty in changing one's class, as against those who make the romantic claim that he tried personally to be classless.[42] But at most times opinion places him in the paradox of being both, although on rare occasions he is neither and apolitical.[43]

The interesting point about the political criticism is not that it indicates a superficial division between 'liberal humanism' – a term I dislike for its vagueness but which often appears to indicate a contemporary form of

nineteenth-century *laissez-faire* liberalism – and state-centred communism, but the way that its paradoxes indicate similar divisions in each. The
positive aspect of Orwell is that he is neither for the private individual nor
for any oligarchical state, whether based on fixed ideology or rationalized
pluralism. He suggests instead another form of collective humanism but he
never fully defines it in the practical terms which he posits and discusses in
the activity of his writing.

The assessments of Orwell's politics concentrate on examining his
strategies and in doing so they restrict themselves to the superficial
'message' of his writing. On the basis of strategy many have claimed that he
fundamentally undermined the strength of the left in British politics.[44]
Reactions to *The Road to Wigan Pier* bear out this claim, not only in
Gollancz's famous introduction condemning the book for facile calls to
Liberty and Equality, but also in those who complain that it provides no
definite answers.[45] Others have noted that Orwell never wanted to provide
definite answers.[46] While he recognized that strategy influenced others, it is
not as important as stance. Yet stance is not 'the only answer of the exile
who cannot provide solutions',[47] but the response of the constructive
thinker who recognizes the limitations in all the prevailing ideologies
because of their common grounds, and who tries to indicate radical
alternatives to those grounds. The important aspect of Orwell's thought
for both contemporary socialism and liberalism is that he perceived their
common basis in humanism, and criticized their rationalist developments.
Orwell is not pro-humanist[48] but neither is he anti-humanist. What he does
is to question the attempt to make humanist values fixed standards in
themselves, in other words he refuses to accept any grounds as unalterable.
He is not questioning their quality in action but in their common use as a
means or an end.

The emphasis on stance needs a shift in attitude to politics, literature and
philosophy, by all those whose thinking derives from the dominant
rationalist logic and the dualisms it generates, and depends upon the
naïvely univocal and exact relationships between word and object that
arise from it. Orwell came to recognize that words were neither equal to
objects, and nor do the two maintain an adequate and defined relationship,
but that language and literature are part of the materiality of the world.
When readers discuss Orwell's need for a pure, clear, precise language that
attempts to reflect an external world, they tend to focus on an attitude of
dominance over an objective, physical world. There is the assertion that his
concerns with language and politics derive from a belief in objective,
discoverable truths, that solid objects are the source for truth, that the fact
and observation of the documentary fiction is a more trustworthy and
objective account of the world than 'myth'.[49]

These judgements in turn encourage opponents to stress the reverse: the
subjectivity involved in all objective statement, and the imposition of

supposedly 'free' fiction. Such accusations range from comments on the emotive organization of the documentaries, to studies of his supposed claim to put aside the aesthetic and speak authentically, whose purpose is to expose the claim as misleading.[50] Like the political divisions these conflicting critical responses result from a concentration on strategy, and too often become mutually destructive. For Orwell the external world became important for its materiality, its radical otherness and alien quality: it could never be dominated nor dominating, it made necessary the interaction of a positive stance.

Similarly, the activity of his writing was not a matter of communicating explicit messages, although throughout the contemporary debate runs an insistent emphasis on Orwell's clear, precise prose that on one level always implies that he is 'easy to read', that his 'message' is obvious. This assumption underlies many of the contradictory, sometimes superficial readings of his work. The catalogue of adjectives used to describe his prose reads like a thesaurus entry: its aim is said to be the expression of truth 'by the concrete and the simple word', to be neutral with 'cold, clear prose', 'saying straight out' what he means with a clear prose style.[51]

This leads even the most perceptive into contradiction. Woodcock starts by illustrating that Orwell's 'pure and transparent' prose in fact concealed complexity.[52] Yet he moves through the statement that in his best writing language and meaning were so close that metaphor could not intervene, to conclude that the prose was created so that reality could shine through its transparency (pp. 279-80). The implication of the statement is that we can 'have' reality exactly as it is. Others have noted that the transparent 'windowpane' of his writing was in effect personal rather than characterless,[53] and Christopher Small speaks for many when he notes that the paradoxical subjectivity of the 'dry, clear, almost flat tone . . . the effacement of the writer's "own personality" nevertheless allows what he wants to say to show more clearly and, indeed to be most unmistakably his'.[54] Small proceeds to comment on the complexity of the writing, but this tone is often simply dismissed as a 'talent' for 'lucid prose'.[55] More problematic are the misreadings that completely invert the direction of Orwell's writing by claiming that it sought objectivity and absolute truth, and that by failing to recognize the naïve implications of this stance he perverts the influence of the writing.[56] Some critics have gone further and suggested that he consciously manipulated his audience through this appearance of neutrality. There is, for example, the comment that Orwell's 'plain reportorial style coerces history, process, knowledge itself into mere events being witnessed . . . such a style is far more insidiously unfair, so much more subtly dissembling of its affiliations with power, than any avowedly political rhetoric'.[57]

On another level the misreading becomes fused with the idea that Orwell's prose 'gives' the actual human being, an event complicated by and taken up into the George Orwell and Eric Blair separation. Time and time again, Orwell's supposed autobiography is used as the primary access to his writing.[58] The comments can be revealing but as other critics have suggested they can also mislead, sometimes producing startling critical assessments.[59] None are more startling than some of the extraordinary judgements of *Nineteen Eighty-Four*. There is not only the commonly found assessment that Orwell's tuberculosis gave the book 'the gloomy intensity of his vision and language',[60] but also the 'explanations' for its negative reading in Orwell's hypothezised homosexuality or sado-masochism.[61] These are not so much odd as limiting, and obstruct broader, more enjoyable readings of the work.

The author is conflated with the characters of his novels, despite an awareness that this may be a rather limited way of reading. Take Gordon Comstock in *Keep the Aspidistra Flying* : he is continually identified with Orwell; he embodies his hatreds; he, like the author, oscillates between Romantic and anti-Romantic.[62] In more general terms similar comments on the characters in his novels indicate the restrictions of this critical approach more clearly. It is said that Orwell's lack of human understanding combined with the fact that he always puts himself forward as the protagonist, leaves all the novels the same. His business was human relationships, but because he had no resources of great depth his characters are flat and undeveloped.

The confusion of Orwell with the major characters goes hand in hand with an unwillingness to make them 'live'; they are merely types.[63] George Woodcock's assessment that the characters created from within are like Orwell himself,[64] leads him to criticize the lack of development in the others that undercuts any real 'relationships' (p. 269). Woodcock notes elsewhere in his biography the contrast of the essays where 'We no longer feel that we are inside the author's mind' (p. 261), but in practice the same conflation also occurs in criticism by others of the documentaries and essays.[65] For example, it is the accusation that Orwell is not showing the whole picture in *The Road to Wigan Pier* in comparison with his diary entries, that leads to the naïve conclusion that he is 'fixing' the evidence, defining the conclusions before he starts.[66] But as Bernard Crick acutely points out in *George Orwell: A Life*, the diary 'must have been worked up afterwards ... "The Diary" is not necessarily a more literal record of "what actually happened" than the published book'.[67] Because it is assumed that Orwell is at one with his creations, his ability to construct skilful narrator and character interaction is underestimated, whereas in effect these provide a clear indication of his developing attitude to stance and the interaction between reader, writer and text.

The assumption that in Orwell's plain writing style we can find an actual man giving us an explicit message, places a considerable amount of commentary within grounds that Orwell himself challenged and thus restricts their reading and evaluation. A case in point is a comment by Raymond Williams on that clear precise prose, ironically placed just after he has taken Orwell to task for, as he thinks, a belief that language does convey content directly.[68] He moves on to state that 'Orwell usually describes his feelings so accurately that surface analysis is hardly even necessary' (p. 35). The implication is not only that Orwell's writing is obvious, his messages easy to define, but that the text is giving us Orwell the man himself and his feelings.

Even Bernard Crick noted in 1977 that people went looking for difficulties in Orwell's writing. By 1980 he has come to emphasize the need for such explicit study, saying that the writing is indeed difficult, generating 'several different Orwells. The wielder of plain prose becomes complex and enigmatic'.[69] Here the recognition that the plain prose style is neither easy nor direct is linked to the caution that we can never 'have' Orwell the man. At least three separate critics took Crick to task for 'laboriously' coming to obvious solutions about Orwell, and for overemphasizing and overanalyzing the problem of the division between the autobiographical person and the construction of biography.[70] Yet the historical interpretations of Orwell vary so widely, all the while asserting so much authority, that Crick's painstaking method was necessary to his exemplary biography and is necessary to any study that faces the same divergences.

The assumption that one can absolutely define Orwell in biographical terms is parallel to the assumption that his writing and its message or interpretation are equally clear and fixed. But the very attempt to define and fix into stasis is part of a world view that Orwell rejected. If this is not recognized then the outcome is often the suggestion that Orwell is being inconsistent, hence untrustworthy and deceitful. And the deep-rooted desire evidenced throughout the criticism to make Orwell into a truthful, honest representative of at least two generations of English political thought, turns on its head and becomes a virulent attack on his 'character'. These readings are not only unnecessary but self-limiting. They confine themselves to strategy rather than stance. Yet it is in the questions of belief and value that inform the writing and are approached by stance that the reader can move past party ideology toward what Orwell called politics in 'the widest possible sense',[71] which was an activity necessary to any effective ideology.

In approaching Orwell's own outlook it is helpful to recognize that Richard Hoggart's description of The Road to Wigan Pier as the story of an education[72] may be seen as a suitable description for Orwell's entire writing life. All too often there is an unwillingness to accept that Orwell might learn, come to appreciate different things and change his mind, and to recognize that this apparent inconsistency overlays a fundamentally consistent belief in the need to evaluate actively, never to assume the quality of axioms and fixed standards. Because Orwell has always questioned, he has been called a revisionist as a matter of course.[73] However he is in effect engaged in a complex rhetorical activity with both positive and negative aspects. The rejection of his ability to learn results in a tendency to impose one view of the man on all his life, one aspect of his thought or writing on the whole: and inevitably this leads to charges of contradiction and judgements of weakness.

There is also too little appreciation of Orwell's own attitude to learning: that it is not what you learn so much as how you learn, and the corollary that movement from ignorance to a position of knowledge does not mean that knowledge is then something fixed and to be imposed upon others. A fundamental part of this attitude is an appreciation of the role of stance which Orwell's writing comes to in *The Road to Wigan Pier*. As the writer recognizes that moral activity is more important than techniques in themselves, he comes to outline positive and negative directions in persuasion or expression and communication of opinion. The positive directions are ones which stimulate to discussion and then further to a full interaction, whereas negative directions restrict and control by imposition.

Orwell's search for a valid voice through experimentation with genre was a search for writing that would be able to move outside the dualisms that surrounded him. The early writing explores the relationship of this dualistic outlook to a self-enclosed deluding stance in both literature and politics that he later comes to call fantasy. *The Road to Wigan Pier* is the story of a political education in this stance, and it is the danger of the extreme political fantasy of totalitarianism that alerts Orwell to the danger of this stance in literature. The structures of *The Road to Wigan Pier* provide an admittedly rough beginning of an attempt to move out of that stance through a literary voice that does not impose opinion on others but invites discussion.

The strategies of familiarization and alienation that he uses in *The Road to Wigan Pier* are part of the luggage of the 1930s. But just as he is not long a political fellow-traveller so his literary search goes on to take a rather different route. *Homage To Catalonia* tranforms the strategy into a complex writing of elusive analogy that establishes the basis for his allegorical stance: a writing that leaves the reader in little doubt as to Orwell's opinion but opens up the text to active involvement.[74] The valid voice is not a question of simply claiming good faith,[75] but of a mature and comprehensive outline of rhetorical stance, that recognizes the tendency to restrictive readings in the dualism of the time, and consciously moves past discussion to explore alternatives that make possible interaction with the text itself.

By the time Orwell writes *Animal Farm* he has developed his grasp of stance into a formidable presentation of the activity of reading. Through fantasy it can be read as a simple, rigidly moralistic comment on the events and consequences of the Russian revolution conveyed through animal emblems. But through allegory it can be read as a perceptive invitation to discuss the responsibility of human beings to take up their political destiny because they, in contrast to the animals, do have the ability to communicate. *Nineteen Eighty-Four* may also be read either through the stance of fantasy or through that of allegory. Read as the former it appears to be a perverse, neurotic, depressing and limited view of an extremist politics. But read as the latter, as an allegory of a political fantasy, it is not only more enjoyable but the writing enacts the possibility of a political alternative. At the moment that Orwell's life is interrupted by death, the earlier analogy is reversed and it is the literary that informs the political.

I Documentation and Early Novels

CHAPTER ONE

Stories and Voices:
The Early Novels

Down and Out in Paris and London : Stories

The movement of *Down and Out in Paris and London* (1933), provides an analogy for the overall movement of Orwell's approach to writing in the 1930s as it moved away from an authoritarian stance of information and fact toward a stance of interactive discussion. The narrator of this novel-documentary moves from a single dominant control of narratorial perspective to a split narrative of presentation and comment. He also shifts from a confidence in his judgement to a recognition of his own ignorance. At the end of this particular work, the process of learning that has been followed leaves the narrator with a new confidence in his objectivity which is the result of an improved method of observation and reporting. But if one is reading the movement of the book in detail one recognizes an illusion bound up with the new 'objectivity'. This development is apparent in the changes that occur in the stories told by other characters, and these changes also indicate why the stories are told in the first place. Both the characters and the stories cast back on the narrator and comment on the changes in his expression, and as the stance of the narrator shifts, so does the basis for the reader's evaluation of his judgement.

The first part of *Down and Out* recounts the narrator's experiences in Paris at a time when he has suddenly lost his normal means of financial support. Initially a detached observant outsider, he moves toward an understanding of the inhabitants as the financial problems he encounters plunge him into their way of life. The part concludes with specific questions as to the value of this life, and it is in order to arrive at a suitable or valid position for commenting on it that the narrative progresses as it does.

The narrator attempts to speak in the urbane, lightly humorous 'gentlemanly' tone of the literary magazines. He presents his readers with the clichés that a middle-class public of the early 1930s would know and expect, commenting on the 'typical' French street scene and the 'representative' Parisian slums (p. 6), in a manner that assumes that he can 'type' them absolutely and that they will be instantly recognized. For these expected readers the narrator is acceptable; he can be trusted to come to the kinds of conclusions that they would themselves. He is initially external to the situation, handling it with the ironic mastery of superior knowledge, the stiff upper lip of the comfortably off among the unfortunate poor. Yet even for an audience with different expectations he is made appealing by force of his detailed observant mind as well as the very earnestness of his naïvety. At the same time, reading this first chapter alone a reader might well conclude that such a narrator was blinkered, ignorant, prejudiced, sentimental, clichéd or worse, snide and supercilious. Any judgements he made on poverty would be invalid, coloured by his irrevocably narrow perspective.

Orwell is making both points about the narrator. Any observer is governed by the conditions of his background, yet all observers have a responsibility to attempt to see, to assess, to find out where they stand in the situation. The narrator's ensuing description of Paris portrays him learning, finding the people behind the types, realizing the truth of his observation that a biography of the inhabitants would be 'fun' but limited and invalid. By contrast, his account of them in his own story always keeps them in the context of his restricted personal narration. The story presents not a movement to full knowledge, but one from the narrator's ignorant generalizations on type to an understanding of his limited view of the people.

The detachment of this initial narrator continues through the early chapters by way of a static presentation of external accounts resembling little magazine pieces. It is only when he is thrown into action by necessity, when he has no money, that the expression changes and with it the stance. As the narrator and his friend Boris become involved in looking for a job, the internal fears and anxieties that close upon them and restrict their horizon to the next meal are never spelt out. However they are nevertheless there in the curious sense of enclosure produced by chapters 5 to 9, a sense that results from the repetitive structure of vocabulary and event. But once he has a job the narrator expands, observes, indulges in humour and the generalizations about the earlier comments become more specific. Chapters 15 to 18 return to generalizations of the hotel life with which he is involved but this time they are always from personal experience.

By the time the narrator comes to comment on his experiences at the end of Part One, he has come a long way from the external, snide, rather superior observer of the opening chapters. The conclusions he now reaches are specifically presented as his own opinions. They are divorced from the middle-class magazine reader initially associated with the narrator, yet they carry the implication that just as he was once one of them and has learned, so too should they. The tone of these opinions is reasonable, not rebellious or revolutionary but questioning earnestly why the life of the *plongeur* or dishwasher should go on as it does. He even turns to examine why he is questioning in the first place, and brings it down to a distrust of the uncritical acceptance by most people, their 'way of taking it for granted that all work is done for a sound purpose' (p. 158). What he tries to do is to fuse an initial identification with himself as a middle-class narrator into the fact that he has changed and learned.

At the same time as these fluctuations in personal expression guide the reader to an assessment of narratorial stance, the movement through the plot of stories told by other characters provides an external index to stance. And it is in the way the various individual stories of the text are re-presented by the narrator that one learns how to read the larger story of the entire work.

Charlie is an important character accorded three individual and substantial stories. Each is completely different in writing and narration from the rest, and why they are there is initially baffling. At the start of the first story Charlie is introduced as an eccentric character of the neighbourhood, and the tone of the narrator's introduction is still one of superiority. His attitude is indicated by the opening sentence, 'I give you Charlie, one of the local curiosities, talking' (p. 12). The proprietory sense of 'giving' a character, and the implication that we shall 'have' him in his entirety, points to the total control that this speaker assumes. Charlie himself does not speak for several sentences. Before he does so the narrator provides a history, which clearly defines and controls the reader's reactions; and we are also told that Charlie likes to talk about himself. The narrator's build-up with its disgusted tone of voice is presumably to prepare the audience for the semi-pornographic story to follow and to dissociate himself from it.

Only after this introduction does the narrator allow Charlie to begin. The melodrama of it comes across as the most important factor: 'Alas, messieurs et dames, women have been my ruin, beyond all hope my ruin. At twenty-two I am utterly worn out and finished' (p. 13). What follows is once more a crude stereotype of the 'blue' Frenchman, the originator of pornographic books filling the English market.[1] Charlie is portrayed as a hypocrite. He dines with his brother to please his parents, only to rob him in order to enjoy himself by beating up a girl in a whorehouse. He is totally without sensitivity. For him the 'true meaning of love' is sadism. The scene of his story is blatantly set, with all the stage machinery of a gothic porno book, raising a thrill of terror at the 'narrow, solitary street with a single gas-lamp flaring at the end', the 'stone passage', the 'great, rich garish bedroom, coloured blood red from top to bottom' and the prototype innocent, shrinking with her 'whimper of fright' (p. 17).

The point is that this writing is also a stereotype. But the initial narrator, from his viewpoint of disgust, presents it almost as if he believes it. He pretends to be objective by failing to comment, trying to indicate his *savoir faire* if not *savoir vivre*. It is also fair to say that unless alerted to the artificial melodrama of it the majority of his audience will probably also be disgusted. Only if one recognizes it for the generic stereotype it is can one position the narrator with respect to it: that he is taken in means that he is untrustworthy. Yet for the reader there are few hints about how to read the tale. Perhaps Charlie's sarcastic comments would alert one, and it might also be possible to realize from the self-dramatization involved. But one could only know for sure if already acquainted with the genre, and such recognition is essential to an adequate understanding that at this time the narrator is still ignorant. He, like many of his audience, cannot understand the conventions being used nor the humanity that lies beyond them.

Charlie's second story, in chapter 18, is presented in a far different tone. While it begins in a similar histrionic manner, this time the reader is left in no doubt that Charlie is ironic in many of his comments. The narration is straightforward, explanatory, interjected with humorous comments and contains a great deal of reported speech. It is not melodramatic at all. There is an exaggeration of his role, but it is obviously for humour not for self-aggrandizement. The details of his story also reveal a considerable number of aspects about his character. He condemns the 'peasant girl' he lives with, yet cares enough for her to think of a trick of deception that allows her to get food. Even the overall situation reveals his character. She can eat fully, and he simply gets some 'bread and cheese' (p. 133). But the point of the story is that he can tell his audience about the witty remark that he made, which saves the girl from discovery when she is met by someone involved, a year later. The unspoken evaluations are clearly there. First, he is still with this girl a year later, and second, while there was no need to protect her, he does so anyway. Charlie may be self-glorifying but it is now difficult to take his egoism seriously.

The divided reaction that Charlie's first story receives indicates the self-deception of the narrator of *Down and Out*. As the stories progress, the narrator becomes more distanced; he is able to separate out his assumptions with greater clarity, and examine his preconceptions. This activity becomes the aim of the penultimate chapter of Part One, chapter 22. Here the narrator straightforwardly tells the 'educated' reader that ignorance breeds fear and sustains a deplorable class system. Implicitly, he has indicated this in the progress of the narrative, specifically in his reactions to the stories he hears and recounts. This chapter is presented by the later narratorial voice commenting on the earlier; and the 'average' reader, the middle-class magazine consumer who was led initially to identify with the former voice through vocabulary and received idioms, is now asked to distance himself from his own background and examine it.

Charlie's third story, told in chapter 23, provides the denouement to Part One of the book. It moves one step further than the previous two, from direct speech, to reported speech within direct speech, to reported speech by the narrator. By now the reader knows enough of the narrator to be able to evaluate the extent to which he is interfering with the report. He prefaces the story with the remark, 'Very likely Charlie was lying as usual, but it was a good story' (p. 165). There is no doubt about how we are to read it. Unlike the first tale which took the narrator in, and the second, which was descriptively presented, this tale is retold by the narrator specifically as a story. He begins by downplaying the extent of its eccentricity, and provides a list of stereotypes in a repetitive, additive manner alerting the reader to its artificiality. The entire tale may be seen as formal and conventional, beginning with the traditional 'One day . . .'

Whereas the first story was a stereotype whose ambivalent status indicated the ignorance of the narrator, the second story was character-revealing, recounted by a more understanding, less prejudiced narrator. The third story can be read as a parable of being taken in by something that appears to be the real thing but is not. In this the narrator makes clear not only that he has learned about the dangers of observation, but also that he is beginning to recognize the use of convention and fiction in expression.

It is significant not only that the argument of Part One concludes by indicating the fictional, the personally controlled nature of any retelling of events, but also that it cannot be satisfactorily concluded in any other way. This more experienced narrator makes it quite clear that the story is a story; it is a personal opinion; it is at second-hand. The reader not only watches the narrator weighing and balancing the probability of its implications, but weighs and balances them himself. We have to make the same distinctions as he does, and apply the techniques of evaluation that we have been taught. At this stage, however, these are fairly thin. It is the development of the presentation and status of the 'story' in the second part of the book that expands on them.

The change in the status of stories in the second part is again presented through a change in narratorial expression and stance. Just as his changing reaction to Charlie's stories exposed his learning process, so the changing reactions to these later stories indicate the narrator's personal techniques for reassessment and evaluation. Many of the changes arise from the new situation, for the narrator is now in England. Several of the strategies previously employed lose their effectiveness because his readers have a different knowledge of the topic under discussion. It is far more difficult to try to gain acceptance on the basis of these grounds, since English readers will be more likely to have individual and different attitudes to the country they live in. Paradoxically it is also more difficult to get people to change their minds, to examine their assumptions, since being on home ground makes them more likely to 'dig in' and insist that they are in the right. For these reasons and others the narrator turns to an examination of how evaluation and assessment should be undertaken; and the narrative becomes more purposeful. The low-key narration, and the technique of a detailed gentle observation which is naturalistic and unsensational, gives the second section of the work a more serious air. The restriction on generalizations yields more specific explanation and personal opinion; but because it is personal the reader knows that he has to take it carefully, and because it is specific in its factual detail he may come to make judgements of his own.[2] However, that we are tied to the narrator's 'facts' proves in the end a restriction.

The introductions to characters also indicate the change in narratorial expression. Paddy is mentioned not because he is 'a curious character', but because 'I want to give an account of him'. Whereas earlier characters were first presented with a history, then their appearance was described, and finally their stories or anecdotes recorded, here the first thing the reader finds is directly reported observation made by the characters. Next comes a description of the situation and the appearance of the character, usually quite detailed and clear yet with some overtly personal observation, and then finally their anecdotes are presented in a private context specific to each character. In this context it is impossible not to realize the fictional and artificial nature of the construction of the anecdotes; and lest we are in any doubt at all, the narrator continually underlines the point. The result is that he gives up considerable control over the reader's direct reaction to his characters.

Soon after his introduction to Paddy who will become his tramping companion, the narrator relates the story told by the 'old Etonian', the public school boy who frequents the lodging-houses. The event proceeds with a brief introduction, followed by a report of his speech which captures his conventional verbal tics and idioms; and concludes with a few observations on his 'refined, worn face', 'his good patent-leather shoes' (p. 217), and the comment that perhaps he was visiting the doss-houses in search of 'the "nancy boys"'. This anecdote is followed immediately by one from Paddy. In contrast, it is totally exaggerated and far-fetched, telling of a fourteen-stone man lifted from his mattress 'as light as a feather' and relieved of four pound ten. Placed side by side as they are, the two stories point toward a difference in function. The first is an attempt by the narrator to present a situation that examines and questions. It tries to allow for evaluation and personal opinion by both reader and writer. The second is a fixed part of tramp mythology. It evades any assessment, functioning as entertainment, and is part of the way in which these men come to terms with their lives.

As these anecdotes illustrate, the narrator is also becoming more interested in the minutiae of speech and diction. Chapter 30, which introduces Bozo, is a case in point. He is one of the few tramps that the narrator meets who is neither ashamed nor self-pitying. One of the narrator's first comments is that Bozo 'had a strange way of talking, Cockneyfied, and yet very lucid and expressive. It was as though he had read good books, but had never troubled to correct his grammar' (p. 218). Bozo is indeed articulate, intelligent and interesting. The chapter concludes with the narrator noting that Bozo 'had a gift for phrases. He had managed to keep his brain intact and alert . . . he was, as he said, free in his own mind' (p. 227). Implied in this are at least two aspects. The first is that one can assess the state of a man's mind from his language. One can question whether he is still using the language effectively and with interest, or whether it has become a nondescript background activity. The second is that an interested use of language may actually keep one's mind alert. Attention to language may keep one reassessing, and never allow one to get into a rut.

Following soon on the study of Bozo comes the narrator's chapter on slang, swearing and insults. The discussion indicates again a curious two-way process in effect. First, words obviously define their users: '"Judy" and "bawd" are East End words, not found west of Tower Bridge. "Smoke" is a word used only by tramps' (p. 237). Not only do words define the geographic area, but also the social class of their users. Yet some words, for example swear words, are defined *by* their users: 'words, especially swear words, being what public opinion chooses to make them' (p. 240). That words define people is irrational, a 'species of magic', yet paradoxically once they do so they lose their original meaning. What the narrator is getting at here is that we may take up a choice with language. We may certainly allow language to define us, give in to its 'magical' identifying quality; but we also have the option taken by Bozo to define it, to find our own voice and resist the pressure into standard forms. The separation between the two approaches to language parallels that between the story of the old Etonian and of the fourteen-stone man. One story is told to stimulate ideas and questions, and provide personal opinions and answers, the other to preserve a fantasy, a set of accepted conventions about a way of life. As the book moves into its final chapters the narrator allows more and more of these latter stories to enter the narration.

But it is not the stories themselves that receive a critical view. It is a certain kind of story which provides an unthinking 'happy ending'; and this is contrasted to Bozo's humorous and often deflating stories against himself. But Bozo is the exception. Most tramps fall into and maintain their self-pity and shame by accepting these stories, assuming that there can be no change in the *status quo*. The recounted stories for the most part are melodramatically exaggerated, based on shared prejudices. They indicate a narrator with a stance of acceptance; one who neither questions nor contemplates. This kind of narration is like that of the initial narrator of the book, whom we have learned to distrust. In contrast the narrator has developed for himself a stance that does inquire, that compares, assesses and attempts to answer even if in a personal manner. He suggests to us in the latter part of the book that we can learn to evaluate not only from the details of dress, money and statistics, but also from close attention to language. He does so by presenting himself as learning to differentiate, learning to assess, developing new skills to alert response. The narration has progressed from control to overt personal comment, from reporting out of a context to reporting within one, from the narrator's unthinking acceptance of a 'style' and vocabulary to an attempt at his own voice.

The last tramp scene, in chapter 25, recalls the social origins of the narrator by telling a story in which they are noticed. When he then moves on in chapter 26 to his observations on the entire second part, we are prepared for it; we have been quietly reminded of the discrepancy that exists between himself and the tramps, and of our basic identification with him. The more serious tone of this part of the book is maintained in the opening remarks to his conclusions. He begins by restating explicitly the implicit ignorance of the earlier chapters saying 'one cannot even start to consider it until one has got rid of certain prejudices' (p. 271). The inquiry proceeds by examining the 'prejudices', the 'generally accepted' ideas about tramps, and showing them to be based on ignorance. The ignorance involved is far more convincing here than that of life as a *plongeur*. First, it is ignorance about one's own country and the responsibility for learning is closer at hand. Second, the narrator of this part of the book has proved reliable and has established several reasonable bases for evaluating his observation. His discussion here is a careful study of various elements including direct observation and statistics, and steering clear of the emotive association with slaves that he used previously. And third, we have been through the experiences with this narrator who has indicated the actual situation so that we can judge for ourselves the discrepancy between that and the fictional presentations.

Yet the final short chapter goes on to undermine these conclusions. He takes us back to the tramps so that, having read his suggestions, we may make our own assessments. But the repetition of 'I had news of', 'I was told that', 'I have heard', indicates the unreliable, second-hand nature of this narration. It is transitory personal opinion; he had not really understood 'the soul' of these people. Further, the chapter is a weakly constructed series of rather naïve and uncomfortable reminders of the trivial and superficial nature of the documentary. In the end the information about the tramps is not as important as the act of education. Similarly for the reader, even if he does not identify with the middle-class assumptions of the narrator, to watch the growth of his awareness to these prejudices, and follow his attempts to go beyond them is a more appropriate and rewarding way of reading the book than to say, as a number of critics have said, that his prejudices and final opinions were unacceptable in the first place.[3] To do the latter misses the main point about the book, that the narrator is exposing his weaknesses in order to show that he is prejudiced, and he can only try to reassess and understand.

Burmese Days : Voices

Burmese Days (1934) presents problems quite different to those in *Down and Out* because it is specifically novelistic and it does not have a first person narrator. But the concerns with validity are similar. A problem arises in *Down and Out* from the sense that once the narrator has separated his distanced observing voice from his prejudiced initial character, he rests there, implying that this second distanced voice is an objective and sufficiently valid stance. As an indication of the discrepancies and the possible fallibility of the narration, the separation is effective. It is helpful in understanding the process of learning being undergone, but only fully so if applied to the distanced narrator himself as well as the early naïve narrator. Almost as if having learnt once is enough, the distanced narrator does not seek to put himself in question; and the detailed factual information that he employs as the basis for evaluation discourages further questioning.

Burmese Days goes much further. Here the narrator, possibly because he is already separate from the main character by virtue of being a third person voice, sets about providing bases for the reader to assess his role through the creation of different voices. Our awareness of the contrasting voices of the narrator, points also to the restricted voice of the main character Flory and explains much about the problem involved in this novel. There is not only the main character in contrast to the narrator, but also the narrator in contrast to himself. The question of voice is paramount for all the other characters as well, and the novel's primary concern is communication.[4]

The book opens with a passage of great control, utterly unlike the brash, clumsy, naïvety of *Down and Out*. We are introduced first to an official, the magistrate U Po Kyin, and even within this brief, slightly ludicrous, officialese runs the ironic voice that will control most of the narrative. The narrator observes with precision and detail, often placing unobtrusive comments within the text by qualifying a comment or slightly exaggerating a description. The delicacy of emphasis leaves his control over our reactions to the character of U Po Kyin, nearly complete. Yet the nature of his control is clear: it belongs to an ironic voice which chooses to present the character's attitude to spiritual life in terms of success.

Irony acts by pointing out the discrepancies between an actual event and our assumptions about it.[5] With active and positive irony, the writer goes to considerable trouble consciously to demonstrate what these assumptions are and where they come from. The reader in turn is extensively involved in assessing and evaluating them. But the irony used in the first chapter of *Burmese Days* is far more restricted. It makes sure that the reader evaluates and assesses according to unspoken but understood assumptions that derive either from cultural, racial or religious conventions, or from grounds previously stated or insinuated by the writer. They allow the writer to say one thing and have his reader immediately understand something else by it. No matter how even-handed such a narratorial approach may appear, it contains within it these unspoken standards for assessment that the writer is insisting upon. During the introductory chapter about U Po Kyin the narrator's balance appears sound because, even though it is done with subtlety, he is reinforcing his expected reader's prejudice about oriental and Asian people.[6] The fact that the narrator points to his control of our reactions by alerting us to the translated status of the description and dialogue, cannot eradicate our initial evaluations made as a result of his ironic outlook.

While the narrator looks to shared norms to make his ironic voice function effectively, he also develops different voices which need other bases for evaluation. In doing so he exposes the limited extent of the initial irony and alerts the reader to the necessity of being aware of narratorial prejudice. Flory himself is also initially described in this manner. His friendship with Dr Veraswami indicates that he is unusual: a white man whose friend is a native. But having been established by this friendship as 'different', we see Flory going along with the conventional suggestions in the Club about India going 'to the dogs'; and we begin to evaluate him on the ironic discrepancy between this conservatism and the radical we have been led to expect. When the narrator weights the argument, even if it be in this friendly and indulgent manner, the characters become reduced to types and caricatures. It is an unfair judgement on the narrator's part, but it parallels closely the kind of arguments that one does often make and provides the reader with an example of the restrictiveness of negative irony.

The second kind of voice that the narrator is allowed, is one of observation. The voice extends from personal histories to the internal voices of the characters. Just at the moment that Flory appears completely compromised by our ironic knowledge, we are allowed into his mind, thrashing about and lashing out at the people around him, the civilization they represent, and their arguments which go on 'year after year, repeating word for word the same evil-minded drivel' (p. 35). Flory will not express these inner thoughts for fear of retaliation, but our knowledge that he thinks them reminds us about his standards of value. He coincides once more with the 'different' man we were introduced to.

The observing voice may include considerable irony, yet it is usually more positive than the initial ironic voice. It depends more upon the reader noticing and examining coincidences, repetitions or shifts in structure. When Flory proceeds on to a visit with Dr Veraswami, we are presented with his eloquent, voluble, anti-imperialist views in a manner which confirms again our initial sympathy for him. But there is something ominous in the regularity of his argument, in the comment that the doctor 'always interrupted the argument at this point (for as a rule it followed the same course, almost word for word)' (p. 44). The irony lies in that Flory does not recognize the similarity with the arguments at the Club. The irony of the observing voice is less sarcastic, more pervasive, and more dependent on the reader's activity than on his acceptance of the narrator's standards. While the first narratorial level of detailed irony presented the conventional 'types' and ways in which we initially see others, the second more observing level points to the mass of ambiguity and confusion that sustains a situation in experience. It further indicates the need to be able to observe and evaluate for ourselves or we shall be left, as Flory is, in ignorance of the cause of our unease and shame, providing others with an ironic perspective on our lives from which we are unable to appreciate and learn.

The third level of narration, at which the author of *Burmese Days* constructs extensive symbolic complexes, is often linked with the jungle. The character is taken out of his known and accepted civilization and can no longer depend upon the assumptions of that world. Similarly, the character loses the conventional means of expressing his experience. In many ways these movements not only complement each other, so that as the character leaves civilization he no longer expresses himself conventionally, but also make each other possible, so that unconventional expression indicates a break away from the accepted norms of the civilization. The duality functions for both character and narrator. When Flory leaves his home for a walk in the jungle after a disgraceful episode with his mistress, he works something out about his confused situation. He does not work it out in language, but in the action of going into the jungle, casting off his corrupt life and swimming in the pool. He literally loses his way, and when he returns he has regained his perspective and his ability to see outside himself and his small world.

For the narrator the episode allows him to present an experience of regeneration that could not satisfactorily be explained or analysed. It proposes a stance based on experience alone; no analysis is required to sort out the situation. The enigmatic green pigeons stir images of survival through their self-effacement, blending into the background of the jungle; yet they elude any definite interpretation.[7] The extensive prose uninterrupted by dialogue allows the narrator to slow the pace of description. It is gradually detached from Flory's frustration and moves into distanced observation of colour, shape and sound. As it does so, the reader follows Flory's own detachment, his own inability here to stand back for a moment, and view himself and his surroundings in a clear perspective. Yet the expression of this detachment is strictly the narrator's. When Flory does overtly think he says, 'Alone, alone, the bitterness of being alone!' (p. 62), the melodrama clashing with the restrained expression of images on the part of the narrator. As readers we experience the resonance of such prose passages as well as the absurdity of Flory's attempts at expression. The clash reveals both his tendency even in dissociation from civilization to draw back toward it with ludicrous clichés, and his particular inability to express himself satisfactorily.

The conjunction of Flory's sentimental and stifling tendency with the problems of expression is significant. When the narrator moves on to the final level of narration which comments on and discusses Flory's predicament, the two aspects are clearly linked. The progress into the fifth chapter follows through the other narratorial voices as if summarizing their individual effects to highlight the final element. Only the odd phrase such as 'learning to think for himself; almost willy-nilly' (p.73) toward the end of the observations indicates the personal intrusion about to be made. The narrator's rephrasing of Flory's melodramatic comment appears here entirely in context and leads into the discussion:

> Since then, each year had been lonelier and more bitter than the last. What was at the centre of all his thoughts now, and what poisoned everything was the ever bitterer hatred of the atmosphere of imperialism in which he lived. For as his brain developed − you cannot stop your brain developing, and it is one of the tragedies of the half-educated that they develop late, when they are already committed to some wrong way of life − he had grasped the truth about the English and their Empire. (p. 74)

The use of 'you' signals the presence of the commenting, discussing narrator; and that he is able to move away from a specific personal reiteration of one of Flory's exclamations indicates the importance of this element of narration. Flory is restricted to the vague means of working things out haphazardly in reaction to his natural surroundings, only voicing his problems in inadequate expression. On the other hand, the narrator can not only present that experience but move on to examine the bases of Flory's problem because he can find expression for it. Unlike Flory who is different from those around him, but still unable to concretely work out new standards or processes of evaluation, the narrator can do so. Specifically he points to the necessary reassessment of the values of society, which is something Flory paradoxically shies away from. He can neither accept nor reassess civilization, only reject it. And this is because he is caught in the clichés, the conventional vocabulary and phrasing of the world he wishes to leave.

Orwell allows the commenting narrator to place the predicament

squarely in the troubles of a totalitarian world where 'Free speech is
unthinkable'. In contrast to England where 'we sell our souls in public and
buy them back in private' (p. 75), there can be no private life in imperial
Burma. The result is that you create a whole 'life of lies', a secret world of
escape, where you no longer even care for those people whose suffering
initiated your revolt. The commenting narrator concludes that it is 'a
corrupting thing to live one's real life in secret' (p. 76); one ends, as does
Flory, living 'silent, alone, consoling oneself in secret, sterile, worlds' (p.
70). The reaction against despotism is to create one's own world for
oneself, to revolt into extreme anarchy of the mind, unless of course one
may discuss as the narrator is doing here, the issues involved. But with free
speech 'unthinkable', such discussion is impossible. Flory's talks with the
doctor are after all 'a kind of talking to himself'. One is driven inside
oneself into a private loss of perspective just as corrupt as the public loss.

The novel is concerned with what happens to Flory when he is put in a
position to discuss this private world of his. It follows his meeting and
falling in love with Elizabeth Lackersteen, his attempts to talk to her, and
his failure. He soon discovers that it is far more difficult than he had
imagined. The only contact he makes occurs when he moves into her
clichés, calling the weather 'beastly' for example, or when they go into the
jungle and the communication is through action alone. On the occasions
that he does break through to her, she rejects his private world. In doing so,
she not only undermines the bases for his escape which have been
constructed in isolation and which cannot stand criticism, but also points to
its corruption. But Flory is not completely enclosed. He recognizes this
corruption, and by the end of the novel, he is clearly in the process of
conforming to the public, when suddenly all the aspects of his private
world, his Burmese mistress and his friendship with Veraswami, rise up to
challenge him again. Unable to resolve the differences he shoots himself.

Burmese Days examines in lighter detail through all its characters and
incidents this adjustment of the private to public. Flory, perhaps by virtue
of his difference, is simply given the fullest study. The main technique the
narrator adopts for his curtailed treatment of other characters is a study of
language, of how far their vocabulary and construction measure up to or
deviate from the officialese, the slang, the conventional expression. Apart
from Flory the only characters who have specific problems in saying what
they mean are Mrs Lackersteen, Elizabeth's aunt, and Verrall, who for a
time becomes Elizabeth's boyfriend. Mrs Lackersteen's problem arises
from the fact that she restricts herself entirely and completely to public
language. Her communication becomes a standard for all public
communication that the other characters adapt through compromise to
their own mode of officialese. Verrall on the other hand uses virtually no
public language at all. It is interesting that while Verrall is as externally
anarchic as Flory is internally, Elizabeth loves him for that anarchy while

loving Flory only for his conformity. But Verrall is a member of the ruling class. Unlike ordinary members of society he can live out his fantasies in actual life for he has physical and social power. The most ominous note of the novel is that political change appears to occur only through deception by the underdog or force from the ruler. The possibility for discussion is discounted. The narrator has placed the political situation in a despotism, but is also by corollary making the remark that democratic governments should not function this way, and that if they do perhaps they are closer to despotism than one thinks.

From the political to the personal, the narrator suggests that discussion is necessary for a suitable communication between public and private lives, indeed that one has a responsibility to it or one will remain isolated, will wither and become corrupt. Language is the index to such interaction. It makes us, but we make it. Neglect of the activity implied by such interaction indicates either that we are dominating it unfairly or that we are allowing ourselves to be controlled by it. As in *Down and Out* the character has a choice. He may accept the *status quo* language as the tramps do, or he may actively use language to his own purpose as does Bozo. Those who take the second choice indicate their awareness of personal responsibility, of the need to find their own way within a common public arena. In the activity of doing so they define themselves. Flory never realizes the problem for which language provides a paradigm. He never makes those decisions and choices and is never able to define himself. The narrator by constructing his different voices, asks us to participate in a discussion about the entire situation. In this he is partially successful. However, the consistent use of the initial negative and restrictive ironic voice at the expense of the other characters militates against extending Flory's experience as an analogy for broader situations. Also, in choosing a character who finds no answers, the narrator himself is restricted to suggesting why there are none, rather than being able to indicate positive, alternative modes of action. He has alerted us to narratorial prejudice; he has posited the bases for his kind of evaluation; but in the end it is a negative evaluation, and therefore all too easy to conflate narrator and character.[8] However, the split between the melodramatic and the detailed approach that does distinguish Flory from the narrator is similar to that between the initial narrator of *Down and Out* and the second narrator who has learned. 'Why I Write' notes that *Burmese Days* probably came the closest to the early 'purple passage' aims of the young writer, yet it may also be read as self-criticism of these aims. It is a statement that melodrama, clichés, and the language of the public leave you enclosed, with ideological consistency perhaps but with no real answers.

A *Clergyman's Daughter* : Forms of Address

The early novels consistently combine narratorial self-criticism with an education of the reader. By becoming aware of the narrator's failings one also becomes aware of one's own. Flory as a character was criticized but unable to educate himself. With *A Clergyman's Daughter* (1935), the writer presents a character moving from self-delusion to self-criticism and education. Later Orwell was to call the novel simply an exercise, published because he had no money, and an exercise it is. Yet this is of great help in studying his concerns, for they are here presented in an obvious, even crude manner. The book is a discussion of the conventions within which we run our lives. It makes a statement about certain conditions which prevent one's questioning of conventions, especially those aspects of mental and physical deprivation which are allied to social problems such as the status of women, poverty and the education of children. Within these conditions neither total personal freedom nor total external dominance are portrayed as desirable. The narrator presents them as equally escapist. However, he also fails to suggest any adequate alternative for the character's way of life.

A Clergyman's Daughter follows Dorothy's education in deluding assumptions, and in the recognition of them. It is no accident that one of the closest studies of the book concerns education and the assumptions that surround it. The fourth part, specifically on education, provides an analogy of the extremes of prejudice and the process of learning in all situations. The second topic of the book concerns religion: Dorothy loses her faith, but still opts for its cultural and ideological background which proves the most appropriate to her way of life. As Orwell was to state in 'Why I Write', a person's background will inevitably provide him with 'an emotional attitude from which he will never completely escape' (*CEJL* I 3). One's past will always encroach upon one's present. Dorothy comes to understand the questionable nature of her unexamining faith in Christianity, yet at the same time feels that there is a need for some convention, some public acceptance. She returns to the Church as if it is the convention which she knows the most about and can be the least deluded by. The novel could indeed be viewed as one of the first of many future workings out of Orwell's comment that while Marx called religion the opiate of the people, he also noted that something else was necessary, that man needed some kind of external reference for his life. Orwell's entire philosophical development was concerned with an unsuccessful pursuit of this 'something else'. But here at the root of each study is a compromise: educational, religious, sexual and finally literary. The narrator himself emerges from his interaction with Dorothy appearing to condone her compromise.

Just as the two previous novels founded their presentation of learning processes on a separation between the narrator and the character, here, too, an unreliable narrator is initially established who only gains our trust as he separates from Dorothy. In order to differentiate himself he develops techniques new to Orwell's writing yet part of a straight progression from the distinction between narratorial voices in *Burmese Days*. In common with the commenting narrator of that work, the use of the pronoun 'you' alerts the reader to different modes of address; and these modes are carefully established during the first section of the work.

One distinct voice employs the descriptive 'you'. It is a colloquial technique that, from common use, could often as easily be Dorothy's. The only distinguishing devices between the narrator and character here are the sophistication of vocabulary and control of pace and phrasing. An example of an ambiguous use of this 'you' would be the comment made when Dorothy is in church, 'You could have imagined that there was only a dry skeleton inside the black overcoat' (p. 14). It is descriptive because it does not overtly address the reader, but uses 'you' in an inclusive manner in order to proceed to description. But for the measured discursive structure of the note it could be Dorothy speaking; and even then one is not sure that it is the narrator alone for, after all, the macabre observation is appropriate to her state of mind. Another use of 'you' that is more clearly the narrator's is the generalizing 'you'. Again in the church he notes 'It was not an appetising mouth; not the kind of mouth that you would like to see drinking out of your cup' (p. 14). Here it is generalizing since 'you' refers out to a common judgement that most people would make. It functions similarly in a multitude of examples, such as 'From hearing her talk you would have gathered the impression . . .' (p. 52). This use is easier to distinguish as the narrator's alone. It is often employed when he wants to connect the reader to a reaction Dorothy has, indicating by it a familiarity, a common experience. Dorothy herself does not verbalize these reactions, but they are spoken for her.

During the first section the generalizing voice becomes clearer and more separate. Gradually, the mode of address develops into a commenting voice, that makes specific evaluations, and is clearly separate from Dorothy. One example occurs when the narrator says about Dorothy that 'the beauty of the earth and the very nature of things that one recognized, perhaps mistakenly, as the love of God' (p. 63). There is no doubt in Dorothy's mind at this stage about her belief in the love of God. But the narrator, now completely separate from the character, suggests that there should be.

The narrator has from his first appearance a more straightforward sentence structure than Dorothy's abrupt truncated commands and partial comments. His vocabulary is less tied to girl's magazines and colloquiality. He also uses more similes and makes obvious and heavy-handed judgements, neither of which Dorothy has time for, and he speaks in the present tense to Dorothy's past. While the narrator builds the generalizing and commenting voice, he shifts into discursive prose, uses fewer brackets (which diminish the force of argument), developing a more complex vocabulary and distanced stance. By the conclusion of the first section he is established as a completely different figure; and in contrast with the initial voice, ambiguously linked to Dorothy's, is trustworthy and reasonable.

But there is little that asks for the reader's participation in the prose. If the narrator is not making his own judgements, he is usually reinforcing our prejudices with the presentation of accepted stereotypes. Nearly every character but Dorothy herself verges on the edge of being a caricature. Yet, whereas the reader may perceive their restrictions, Dorothy appears totally taken in by them. She accepts these cardboard characters as real, and she also accepts the way they see her. All her fears, her duties, which hover constantly on her mind, defining her, she simply takes for granted.

The narrator's separation indicates Dorothy's self-delusion, her enclosed world, and in a secondary manner also hints at the enclosure of the other characters who allow themselves to be typed in this way. Unlike Flory's distrust of the Empire, Dorothy has firm faith in the Church as the support for her assumptions. There is considerably irony in her seeming dependence on the actual physical church in which her father preaches, for it is slowly falling down about their ears. But more than this irony, there is something wrong about her faith, indicated by her apathy, and her continual need to goad herself into reaction, resorting to pricking her arm with thorns when she drifts off during service. The convention of the Church which provides the basis for her life is dead to her. This neglect of basic assumptions is not only due to an apathetic acceptance but an almost perverse disregard and evasion of the implications of her personal experience.

At the start of Part Two, it becomes apparent that all the busyness and pressure that Dorothy has been under, has enforced on her a loss of memory. Suddenly she finds herself standing on a street corner in a city she does not know. Here the narrator is posed specific problems in his interaction with her because there is nothing of the character of Dorothy left for him to act with or against. In order to present her mind the narrator has to be precise and careful. Throughout the second part the narrator assumes a factual reporting role similar to the narrator in the second part of *Down and Out*, yet also develops another, linking voice that states the new alliance between the narrator and Dorothy. He tries to speak as she sees, as far as possible without bias. He moves for the most part into a past historical tense, a reported past which clearly presents his function. It also alleviates the potential dryness of the factual account by placing it in a legitimately fictional, re-presented perspective. There is far more dialogue and use of diction to reveal aspects of character, and far less of the dominating generalized voice which controlled and spelt out the reader's reactions in the first section of the novel. The voice here dwells on precision of detail, qualification of description and explanation of situation rather than judgement.

Whereas there is little impetus for the reader's involvement in Part One, here the reader is brought much closer to Dorothy's experience than before; and is actively involved in weighing up and trying to understand the situations described. Secondly, the narrator's qualification and explanation make these unfamiliar scenes appear familiar. It ties the reader to them as if they have been directly experienced with Dorothy, and establishes the basis for future development of this identification. Throughout Part Two, both during and after the process of remembering, there is a strong commenting voice with the narrator forced to fill in all that Dorothy, more obviously now, does not know. This commenting voice fills in our own ignorances at the same time, and subtly implicates us in a greater knowledge than Dorothy has which we then desire her to achieve.

Within the story itself Dorothy moves from total amnesia, seeing the world 'cold', with absolutely no previous assumptions nor expectations of them, to a recognition and felt loss of them. For her, words make objects, and the existence of those objects in turn defines the presence of a person. Watching this occur, the reader should also note that those words are not fixed. They represent a set of assumed rules that are basic to man's concept of everything else he views; but they are not absolute, they are chosen. Dorothy has lived for a week without words and without memory. Awakening to the use of them re-establishes a past in all the assumptions they carry, yields her a memory initially of existence. Choosing to use them places one irretrievably within the bounds of the history they signify. This never need be negative, but may easily be disregarded and taken for granted.[9] Just as words re-establish history, so her face, reflected in a window, 'was appropriate. It corresponded to something within her' (p. 97); it re-establishes her past identity. Although aware that her past was somehow different from her present life on the road, she begins to take her present 'for granted', 'she accepted everything' and was 'far too tired to think' (p. 107). When she moves on to hop-picking in Chapter 3, the physical exhaustion of her life acquires added significance. It is a life of literally stupefying activity that allows her to push the question of her identity out of her mind, 'it was precisely as in a dream that she had been living – it is the especial condition of a dream that one accepts everything, questions nothing' (p. 138). The writer is noting that while previously she had been in mental enslavement, here she is in physical enslavement. In both situations the possibility of self-definition is made even more difficult by external conditions.

Dorothy suddenly recovers her memory after a disturbing incident, and she immediately attempts to return to her old life exactly as she was. The reader notes her fall back into the old patterns of thought and speech; but as it becomes clear that she will not be able to return home, she has to look for a job. After a week of no success, sinking into 'a species of miserable apathy', she is reduced to the escape of reading magazines in the library. *Cage Birds* and *The Barber's Record* 'were strangely, absorbingly, interesting' (p. 162). The situation records another type of deprivation within which it is difficult to actively examine the assumptions of one's life. Retaining integrity and establishing identity in the face of unemployment is extremely difficult.

Part Three of the book blatantly expresses this conscious lack of identity in the narrator's attempt to withdraw from the prose by presenting direct dialogue as in a play. Here Dorothy escapes into a solipsist landscape of her own mind, just as she previously escaped into the unexamined safety of the Church, then into the physical exhaustion of hop-picking, and finally, into the fantasy of magazine jargon. The scene portrayed is of Trafalgar Square at night and the tramps who inhabit it. What the reader receives is an account of the impressions entering Dorothy's mind. It has a cast made up of the characters in her past, and the themes that have preoccupied her. And here she does not react; she allows these figures to define her totally.

Throughout Part Three the reader is left alone to make personal decisions about the interaction of the relevant images and language. Each of the figures in Trafalgar Square has its own defining habits and clichés that are incessantly repeated. Just as the tramps in *Down and Out* told stories that tied them together into a community, so the people of the square mumble, sing, chant, repeat old phrases as if they magically convey a chance of survival. An examination of their identity is so far from possible that their stereotyped identities are all that lie between them and madness or death. Such destitution carries the implicit comment that for those lucky enough to be able to, there is an overwhelming responsibility to take up the opportunity of self-definition.

The author has made his point about the increasingly detrimental social conditions that induce a mental state of enslavement and apathy. In Part Four he provides Dorothy with a *deus ex machina* exit from poverty. This book is, after all, an exercise. A rich uncle appears, to find Dorothy a post with a private girls' school. Her life there experiencing different types of education, gives the writer an opportunity to summarize the different experiences of learning and their positive and negative aspects. In complete contrast to Part Three, the narrator becomes much involved with Dorothy. At the outset there is continual use of the generalizing and descriptive voices. The narrator creates characters in a heavily caricatured manner, making no pretence that these are not stereotypes. But the important point is that Dorothy now recognizes the limitation, can see and criticize the restriction herself.

Dorothy's experience at the school puts her in a new situation and in facing it she develops a voice for herself. To start, she responds actively as her attitude to the children implies. Her first reaction to teaching is that 'she must educate herself before she could even begin to educate anybody else' (p. 229), and she throws herself into her work. She soon discovers that the children 'showed more intelligence when it was a question of *making* something instead of merely learning' (p. 238). But soon enough she is told by the headmistress, Mrs Creevy, that she must educate by memorization and rote-learning, must maintain the status quo, and Dorothy capitulates through fear of losing her job. She starts the new programme 'in exactly the same spirit as one would start a brothel in a bucket shop' (p. 256). While the allusion to the 'bucket shop' lightens the comparison, 'brothel' indicates exactly her position. No longer an unconscious slave to external assumptions, she consciously prostitutes herself to fulfil someone else's fantasy of education. Memory and rote-learning do not require the persuasion of active participation, but the imposition of 'fact'. She is finally reduced to the ultimate extreme of negative persuasion, threats of force, and force itself.

The reader is asked to watch this growth of Dorothy's personal voice and identity. Yet the observing is not uncritical. By now the reader should have learned the necessity for active participation. It is at this point that the narrator begins to shift into 'one' not 'you' as if extricating himself from the implications of the situation, and he becomes increasingly ironic. The irony is based on our knowledge of Dorothy's own educational standards which she has had to drop. The irony also operates on the more fundamental standards of learning to assess oneself which Dorothy here disregards, but which the reader has come to acknowledge. The strategy allows the narrator to move away from Dorothy, and prepares us for his further withdrawal in the final section. More and more Dorothy herself takes on a detached and generalizing voice as she judges from her own experience, yet she never attains the ability that the commenting voice has, to stand right outside herself and view her ignorance.

The knowledge of her suppression leaves Dorothy with an active responsibility to redefine her identity. Creevy even tells her how to worship and it is in the comparison between religious authority and Creevy's educational despotism that Dorothy begins to understand the nature of her solution. She realizes that she has clearly lost her faith; but she sees in the Church, even without faith, something 'of decency, of spiritual comeliness (p. 266). The dangers of complete personal freedom have been underlined both by the vulnerability of that freedom – the ease with which she was forced to change her teaching methods, and by Creevy's freedom to dominate her. Dorothy comes to realize that it is 'better to follow in the ancient ways, than to drift in rootless freedom' (p. 270). The only balance of force against despotism that she perceives is further individual despotism. It appears as though the individual will always have to compromise his private world with his public, and he may as well do so by choosing the more acceptable structure or convention within which to live. For the moment, however, Dorothy again attempts a private escape into books, which in the end become 'wearisome and unintelligible; for the mind will not work to any purpose when it is quite alone' (p. 275). She is only saved by yet another *deus ex machina* opportunity which allows the novel a neat if unsatisfying conclusion.

In the fifth and final part of the book, Dorothy's relationship with the narrator approaches a single voice once more. Yet it is achieved through the opposite end of the telescope used in Part One. Whereas the confusion of the earlier section arose from not being able to distinguish between character and narrator, here we are confident that the voice is Dorothy's alone. The narrator does occasionally interject with ironies or with brief comments, but on the whole the narration presents Dorothy's mind. She is forced into a complete reassessment of herself and, as hinted in the preceding chapters, she opts for a return to her old life. The difference between this and her earlier desire for return is that this is a chosen course, not an unthinkingly accepted one. She is also given the chance to escape into marriage. The marriage proposal is made in a pastoral scene of golden sunlight and isolation, a railway carriage enclosed and entire to itself. But she resists the 'spell', the temptation it offers, as she resists futility itself. The final pages of the book ostensibly present her assessing mind reaching its compromise. Yet while the reader has learned the necessity for compromise, we have also learned the need for continual reassessment. The result is a highly unsatisfactory ending. Dorothy proceeds from the realization that 'Faith vanishes, but the need for faith remains' (p. 312) to the statement that 'It is all or nothing. Either life on earth is a preparation for something greater and more lasting, or it is meaningless, dark and dreadful' (p. 313). But she concludes that this is exaggeration and self-pity, the solution as the narrator comments for her, lies in 'customary, useful and acceptable' actions.

However, starting from the same premise that 'Faith vanishes, but need for faith remains' (p. 312), there is no necessity to reach her next statement. The alternatives the character envisages are those of someone who knows no other religion than a restricted form of Christianity. She is not aware of any potential life on earth which is positive yet not in preparation for something greater and more lasting. As Orwell was to suggest much later in life, one main problem with Western humanism was the need 'to restore the religious attitude while accepting death as final' (*CEJL* III 244). Similarly, there is a double edge to the narrator's comments on solving the problem. While her simple actions may get rid of the problem by ignoring its existence, they do not help resolve it. To invert his comments might lead to a clearer solution: that the reasons and bases of a job should always be considered, that the 'customary, useful and acceptable' are limiting and stupefying if not examined and understood, and that 'comfort' has no place in the difficulty of the problem. If it had not been for the careful and extensive education that the reader is put through in this novel, one could simply take Dorothy's compromise as it stands[10] and view the ending of this novel merely thematically, judging it weak and ineffective. But the entire development of Dorothy's learning process contradicts her conclusions.

The most consistent criticism of *A Clergyman's Daughter* concerns its apparent confusion of the novel and the documentary,[11] its conflict between the desire to express experience of unusual vividness and to create a work of imaginative literature.[12] But Orwell is doing neither. He is shifting away from the autonomy of both. While the character of Dorothy may be interpreted as superficially passive, readings that focus on the interaction between narrator and character rather than on the character as a 'real' person, are clearly directed to this activity of choice. The narrator does leave this ambivalent, yet it would be more precise to criticize the writer for having failed to find an adequate form of writing than for not having tried at all.

Orwell was always worried about dominating his readers, but before he discovered techniques adequate to his writing, his conclusions simply failed, even though they were challenged by the juxtaposition of differing choices. With *A Clergyman's Daughter* it is also necessary to consider Orwell's own particular ambivalence on the question of religion. Orwell felt that religion satisfied a definite need in people, 'man does *not* live by bread alone' (*CEJL* II 18), yet he suggested that faith or loyalty by 'A very slight increase of consciousness . . . could be transferred to humanity' (*CEJL* II 17) away from the Church. The problem deepened when he began to recognize that while the Church imposes orthodoxy and acceptance, it has also been the prime bulwark against 'the modern cult of power worship' (*CEJL* II 18). On the one hand power worship 'is bound up with the modern man's feeling that life here and now is the only life there is' (*CEJL* III 103). Despite their practical despotism, religious systems have 'usually worked against perfectionism and the notion of human infallibility' (*CEJL* IV 66). However, the 'easy way out is that of the religious believer, who regards his life merely as a preparation for the next' (*CEJL* III 243). He does, however, advocate constant attention to the assessment of the problem. It is possibly redundant to note that just such a conclusion would probably be reached by the religious believer in an exactly similar attention to this faith and its relationship with the world.

Keep the Aspidistra Flying : Identification

In each novel the narrator becomes less and less dominating as the works proceed and the individual nature of the situation is increasingly indicated; and at the same time the reader is more actively included. In a clear extension of the concern with language in the earlier books, the narrator of *Keep the Aspidistra Flying* (1936) relates the novel closely to the topics of literature, literary clichés, and the way one goes about writing. Here the narratorial ethos is a corollary for the literary ethos of the writer and more explicitly for the façades through which the individual relates to the public in private life. *Keep the Aspidistra Flying* makes explicit the process of a mind that continually attempts escape by giving the prose over to the character at the beginning. The clarity is possible since Gordon Comstock is more aware, more able to form ideas, and more conscious about language than any of the preceding characters. The narrator no longer has to body forth most of the character's way of seeing: he takes on a separate, responsible, narration from the start of the novel rather than evolving into it.

The opening chapter of the novel plunges the reader almost directly into Gordon's mind, with the exception of a quick interjection from a different humorous voice which notes that he is 'rather moth-eaten already'. Gordon is trying to convince himself not to smoke one of his last remaining cigarettes, and the prose moves into a tension of colloquialisms and rationalization. A little further on an interior monologue takes over completely, characterized by slang, exclamation marks and colloquial elisions. Within the monologue, Gordon progresses to a technique he is often to fall back on, the use of a generalizing 'you' within a fictional situation, which he sets up to explain why he has behaved in various ways. Gordon's mind insatiably seeks connection and explanation even if he has to construct them himself. The first chapter presents him shifting from topic to topic within his personal world, and connecting them all into a unified mesh.

The process by which he makes connections is indicated on the most primary level of image-making when he first views the books in the bookshop where he works. He sees them as 'many-coloured bricks', then as 'Pudding, suet pudding' and finally as 'a vault of puddingstone' (p. 8). The process is additive and associative, with little strict attention to the result. The laxness in construction is no great criticism, most minds appear to work in this fashion. Yet when he proceeds from a consideration of the weather, to a string of similes describing the street scene and thence into the first two lines of a poem, the need for more care is indicated. Gordon views external events as clustered with gratuitous associations. For example, the line 'A tram, like a raucous swan of steel, glided groaning over the cobbles' is filled with weak alliteration, superfluous assonance, lazy connections. If the reader had not already been alerted to Gordon's facility for putting phrases together, he might be tempted to think that this was an external narrator clumsily intent on creating 'atmosphere'. As it is, the character is responsible. For a few moments he moves into a workman-like, conscious assessment of his language, and the difference between this and his everyday thinking is clearly laid out; but 'He couldn't cope with rhymes and adjectives' (p. 11). Finally, as if to justify his carelessness, he moves out to a generalizing 'you' to include everyone else in his inability to cope. His generalizations and rhetorical questions, like the negative irony in *Burmese Days*, depend upon the unthinking acceptance of conventional assumptions. The standards of Gordon's generalizations are drawn from what he desires rather than from a clear logic that can test itself. Just as Gordon constructs fictions around incidents to explain his behaviour, so he does with other people, and with each classification Gordon assumes a different façade from 'the homey, family-doctor geniality reserved for library-subscribers' (p. 14) to the 'gentlemanly-servile mien reserved for new customers' (p. 17). He speaks to others in clichés of gesture and vocabulary, acting up to their expectations of him, and thereby reinforcing their assumptions and his disgust.

Throughout the first chapter Gordon's mind ranges over a series of issues: books, advertisements, the state of civilization and money. To Gordon money makes possible both literature and advertisement. Given life by a money ethic, they both reflect back a meaninglessness that leaves his modern world empty and ripe for destruction. Ironically, Gordon's mind works the way the ads do; they, as he, create types, present clichés and invent desirable fictions. They and he manipulate the logic to create a world in which people can evade responsibility. Gordon argues that he cannot write because he has no money and because of the state of modern literature. He, like Flory, is trapped in a personal world of escape, and can only passively hope for the destruction of the world outside himself, rather than taking any positive action.

The narrator comes into his own during the third chapter when the history of Gordon's family is spelt out. His measured pace, full explanations and qualified judgements, interject a humorous ironic perspective that differentiates his voice sharply from Gordon's. Furthermore, the narrator is completely aware that his account cannot be absolute; it must be 'as the biographers say' (p. 58) fictionalized history. The effect of the chapter is to provide the background to Gordon's escapist mind. Significantly, as a child he could never understand his parents' problems. He asks 'Why couldn't they be like other boys' parents. They *preferred* being poor, it seemed to him. That is how a child's mind works' (p. 57). That is also how Gordon's mind continues to work. He insists that people fit in with the concepts of his personal world, and is shown developing his talent for classification while working for an advertising firm. The reader is shown that the denial of other people's humanity is partly because of his upbringing, his history, social class and education. Basically, the narrator suggests that Gordon is allowing himself to be defined by these external forces; he is constructing his life on an impractical war of hate against them that only reinforces their presence, rather than on positive alternatives or a positive compromise with them.

The close relationship between narrator and character points to a difference in perspective rather than a difference in intelligence, and this is underlined by their different modes of expression when treating the same topics. Gordon is conscious of the escapes that he is setting up; and while he expends his energy on blocking this consciousness out, that he is residually aware of it points to the presence of the narrator as another side of his mind rather than as a distinct and separate consciousness. While Gordon ignores the fact that his attempt to evade compromise is in itself a compromise, the narrator's voice is that of someone aware of the compromise. The relationship between character and narrator is built on Gordon's growing awareness of the need for active self-assessment, that draws the two closer together. And by the end of the book, when Gordon's awareness becomes complete, he takes up aspects of the narrator's voice, specifically his precision, care and his ironic humour, all of which are evidenced when he examines the books on foetuses in the library. The ability to laugh at himself is the detail that indicates Gordon's removal from his earlier escape. The care of his new observations points to his attempts to reassess, and his irony illustrates his conscious acceptance of implicitly understood assumptions that connect him with the rest of the world, of a necessary compromise.

The issues

It is to the question of compromise that the external issues of money, civilization, literature and advertisement, as well as religion and sex are relevant. Money is the overriding compromise of Gordon's life. He wants to escape it, yet he thinks he can only escape it fully through having it. The history he is provided with hints at Gordon's background in Victorian materialism, and the possible reasons for his obsession; but whatever the cause, he wants to escape the money-world, reject the belief that 'Money is what God used to be. Good and evil have no meaning any longer except failure and success' (p. 58). But the naïvety of Gordon's hope is demonstrated not only by his relationship with his rich friend Ravelston which he allows to be dominated completely by money, but also by Ravelston's own unconscious compromise between the theoretical attitudes of the socialist newspaper he runs and the fact that 'life was pretty good fun' (p. 110). Gordon also sees his relationship with Rosemary as being determined by money, but Rosemary's hidden compromises are with sexuality. The point in the end is that it is not the money, not the compromise but the attitude toward it that matters. One has no choice over accepting or rejecting it, but in how one uses it. Money does not degrade civilization, but certain attitudes toward it do.

The literary compromise between poetry and advertising is directly parallel to the economic one. Gordon, while working on advertisements, was able to produce a book of poetry. The poetry was made possible by that compromise. But having done so he leaves. The key point is that he does not especially want to write, but thinks that it will get him 'out of the money-world' (p. 66). In the bookshop he initially thinks that he has escaped money and advertising. But he comes to realize that he is selling himself as effectively in the shop as he was in his advertising job.

The literary compromise is also concerned with 'taste'. Taste is often socially condoned selection, satisfied by similarly self-enclosed worlds. Gordon and Rosemary discuss the weakness of 'Burne-Jones maidens', 'Dickens heroines', 'Rackham illustrations' and James Barrie's fantasies. These artists can stupefy the mind, prettify and make acceptable the world they present as much as the romances and adventures that satisfy the library-goers. Later, just as both Flory and Dorothy escaped into books, Gordon also tries to find solace in the magazines, comics and twopenny newspapers of the sordid little library he is reduced to managing. They are '"escape literature" . . . Nothing has ever been devised that puts less strain on the intelligence; even a film . . . demands a certain effort' (p. 264). The narrator notes that in this state Gordon thinks he is in the 'safe soft womb of earth' (p. 262), 'failure and success have no meaning' (p. 217), and he lies beyond responsibility. Again tied up in the ambiguities is the importance not of compromise, but of one's attitude toward it. In the same way, advertisements, which are initially held up against literature, are here directly compared to the effect of the Burne-Jones maidens and Dickens heroines. They both also have their skilful and involving aspect, something that Gordon only understands at the end of his attempted escape, and which makes possible his return to advertising.

The compromise in literary terms is not between good and bad taste, but between an involving or a mindlessly accepting attitude to writing. The writer may see some need for compromise, but if he goes ahead and produces an active and involving work this is of little practical importance. Similarly there is a responsibility on the reader not to read as if all his assumptions were being reinforced, but actively to assess. Gordon comes to read the trashy novelettes with the ironic emphasis of 'romances' (p. 288) rather than as mindless escape. Immediately one has an indication of his change of attitude. Indeed, he has just been told that Rosemary is pregnant, and he has found a responsibility that he wants to take up. It is interesting that it is Rosemary's loss of her own escape into eternal youth and sexlessness, clearly connected to the list of artistic fantasies Gordon discusses with her, that initiates Gordon's own coming to terms with compromise. Both of them have to discard private worlds before they can break the vicious circle that unconscious compromise imposes on people. Unconscious compromise is utterly selfish. It is entirely private and makes impossible public communication, genuine interaction with, and expression of the external world.

The final topic is that of love for man, not of desire for the external issues

of money, civilization, literature and sex. The parody of 'Corinthians'
throughout the novel, states the writer's dissatisfaction with the traditions
of religion which may insist on human weakness but also tend to provide a
false support, an incantation for dismissing things one should actively
come to terms with. The irony lies in the force of the juxtaposition between
the parody and the original. If the original biblical text were not as resonant
and as well-constructed as it is, the repeated parody would lose its force.
But it does not. The tension of this resistance to parody indicates Orwell's
own need for a religious sense in man, although not tied to a God or an
ideology: one that could reinstitute the 'sense of absolute right and wrong'
(*CEJL* III 100) without the promise of reward in immortality or whatever
else, that reduces morality to success. Much later, in an essay 'Reflections
on Gandhi', Orwell is to discuss this problem specifically. He says:

> The essence of being human is that one does not seek perfection, that one *is*
> sometimes willing to commit sins for the sake of loyalty . . . that one is
> prepared in the end to be defeated and broken up by life, which is the
> inevitable price of fastening one's love upon other human individuals . . .
> (*CEJL* IV 466–8)

Gandhi made no compromises, but for the ordinary human being this is
impossible. Orwell suggests that traditional religious belief implies both
that it is possible and that it is desirable. But the danger of attempting
perfection and denying compromise, is that the isolation of the private may
become complete and human beings may cease to communicate and
interact with the external world.

The mutually exclusive voices of narrator and character also have to
interact and communicate before Gordon can be fully aware of his
compromises. Irony indicates discrepancies, and the narrator's irony points
to the character's evasiveness and denial of discrepancy. Failure to note the
differences as well as the clear similarity between the two voices has led to
many readings which miss the point entirely.[13] When Gordon takes up the
ironic voice at the end of the book, the irony lies in the presence of irony
itself for here its conscious use by the character indicates not Gordon's
evasiveness, as did the irony of the narrator, but his awareness of
compromise. But having reached this conclusion, there are no guarantees
for the reader. Gordon may deflate into the escape of domesticity, and the
irony become negative. Again, it is not the compromise that matters but
one's attitude toward it. Orwell is not providing answers, but a stance
toward activity. He is interested here in neither the extreme of individual
futility nor that of despotism, but in continual reassessment of the
compromise necessary if the private and the public divisions are retained.

The Writer and Reader: Imposition and Involvement

These experiments in stance have been laying out in specific and detailed terms the acceptable and unacceptable methods of persuasion. *Down and Out* presents a basic example of the rhetoric of convention and assumption. The narrator/character's use of melodrama, magazine literature and fantasy recognizes that these modes depend on preconceived expectations, they do not actively assess situations; they encourage prejudice and foster delusion. His immediate alternative is to move to a naïve presentation of personal experience that claims that if 'I' see and then speak of what 'I' have seen, the words are 'true'. However, all the time he is presenting a series of fictions with differing stances and degrees of validity. Hence, there is a split between the basic progression from convention to personal experience here, and the stories which whether fictional or factual, divide into comforts and assessments. The problem with the novel is that too much comfort is involved, because there is not enough assessment of the narrator's strategy. Despite the undercutting of factual strategy by the anecdotal conclusions to both parts of the book, the reader is taken away from magazine conventions but not alerted strongly enough to the conventions of observation.

Burmese Days, although projected before the first book, indicates a greater awareness of the problems of narratorial stance. The character is limited. He learns how to move from the melodramatic to the interactive in language, but the point is that this is rare and difficult and usually fails. Flory's stance is negative; his private language is left in opposition to the official jargon with no discussion between the two and, just like the public despotism he is reacting against, he tries to enforce his private world on others, and when they don't accept it he escapes into its security and comfort by himself. No matter how laudable the sentiments, the activity and discussion necessary for a positive stance in either private or public worlds, is not there.

But a valid stance can be found among the narrator's voices. His initial ironic voice is questionable because it imposes standards on the reader. The voices of experience and observation hover over the border of acceptability as they shift between activity and imposition. But the commenting voice which draws the reader into discussion does attain a validity. The public and private are examined primarily in terms of the political and linguistic issues, and the topics are here in close correspondence: in both cases the two aspects are entirely separate. Private individual worlds oppose the public despotisms, and no interaction occurs. Similarly, private language opposes official jargon preventing any involving discussion between the two. Most people are asked to make some kind of a compromise, and to accept some basis for discussion. But because Flory cannot recognize the negative enclosure of his own world he refuses compromise and kills himself. The problem with *Burmese Days* is that the reader does not have enough perspective on the narrator. Here the narrator withdraws most of the comfortable solutions, but leaves the alternatives up to the reader. The writer appears to have become aware of far greater subtleties in persuasion but comes to a dead end with it.

Such futility is counteracted in *A Clergyman's Daughter* by Dorothy's religion, yet while some solution is reached, it is inconclusive. Rhetorical stance is examined in considerable detail throughout that novel, and again primarily through the kind of language that the character uses. The reader watches once more the movement from the comforts of cliché and jargon, into the difficulty and intensity of expression that occurs when these conventions are stripped away. A different rhetorical strategy of subversion and decadence, with its own anarchic comforts, is presented in the language of survival used by the social outcasts during Dorothy's experience in Trafalgar Square. Dorothy's return to the public world is indicated by her return to a world of caricatures and types, and the character's teaching experience is an astute summary of primary rhetorical strategies. She begins with a positive stance which is active and participatory in the open physical involvement of the students in her projects. It devolves into the negative rhetorical enslavement of rote-learning, numbing repetition and finally into force, the ultimate imposition of control. The methods she uses are specific to her history, her time, her position and job, but the strategies realized in the two stances are common to all periods and to all persuasions.

Questions of language and sex are presented as ambiguously balanced between the stances. In each case Dorothy is given the opportunity of interacting, of combining the public and the private into a positive activity in the same way that the narrator illustrates the stances as he learns to interact with the character in the positive commenting voice. At first the voice of the narrator is general and ironic, but it then develops into a more factual and statistical detached voice, then into the overtly fictional and finally into the satiric and commenting voice. In the end, the narrator is left with no one specific voice, but with the process of learning that has taken place. But while the differing narratorial voices indicate the stance of self-assessment, Dorothy herself never attains the external perspective of the commenting voice. She allows herself to accept without further question the restrictive compromises of her religion, language and sex. She learns, but then rejects her education. The solution reached is confusing because it is ambivalently different for the character and the narrator. The narrator here is explicitly different from those of the preceding works, and in the differing modes of address the writer shows himself far more concerned with his audience. The strategy is to set up a narrator who knows about the escapes and ignorances of the character and can indicate them by contrast with his own perspectives, as did the narrator in the first novel-documentary. But here there is not just an implicit evasion of certain areas of ignorance: here the character consciously chooses to cease learning. The main problem is that although comfort and escape have been withdrawn from the reader, the alternatives are ambivalent and diffuse because the narrator is cut out of consideration. There is no way for us to assess the basis of his perception and criticism.

The fourth novel, *Keep the Aspidistra Flying*, presents a character completing the learning process and actually changing his private fantasy world, and the process of doing so actively involves the reader. Narratorial stance begins with an identification with character that separates into an individual, humorous, positively ironic and commenting voice of the narrator and a self-pitying, spiteful, underconfident and sentimental voice of the character. The latter is defined by its use of cliché and type to characterize and dismiss other people, its rationalistic and narrowing logic, and its associative and careless imagery. With these are a barrage of related techniques, but the factors they have in common rest on their control of their surroundings and their insistence on their own private world, in other words, the strategies of a negative rhetoric. The former, narratorial voice is defined by his detailed observations, concrete examples and qualified even-handed statements that propose opinion rather than judgement, and for the most part invite the reader to participate. The two different languages not only sketch out the different nature of imposing and discussing rhetorical stances that present the relationship between narrator and character, but they establish relationships with the reader that illuminate the whole topic of language and literature.

The reader is involved in the text in a more fundamental way than in *A Clergyman's Daughter* because the separation and interaction of the two voices needs to be recognized if the process of learning that takes place in the novel is to be appreciated. That involvement makes clear that the character knows he is evading actuality, and that the narrator speaks directly for that part of the character which is not evading. When Gordon, the main character, moves into egotism the narrator provides the perspective by becoming negative and ironic, ironic at the expense of the character in order to downgrade the evasion. Once again, he fades out in the end; but this time the character, having a more conscious and intellectual mind than Dorothy's, recognizes clearly the commenting voice which discusses the balance between the public and private compromise. Gordon's final movement into domesticity is shown to be a choice of conscious compromise not a solution. And, whereas Dorothy moved back to traditional religion away from nihilism, Gordon progresses from a limited religion to love for humanity. Yet Gordon's positive response is often lost and misinterpreted because the narratorial voice is so close to the character. The narrator does surface in a final line that could be read as an exposure. His final remark indicates his own potential ignorance because it points to a certain interpretation of the Comstock family that may be called into question. But the implication which might help to provide a perspective on the stance of the narrator himself is light and left undeveloped.[14]

The stance for evaluating in each novel is determined in terms of the character's attitude to knowledge, fact and experience. The narrator's function is primarily to indicate the self-centred nature of all the characters and to present their varied ability to learn. The problem is that while he tries to control the exposing of their ignorance, he never fully reveals his own, and since the writer still allows the narrator to make the final criticisms the result is too dominating and authorial. In *Down and Out* the writer appears to realize that in using a first person narrator in the manner that he has, he is implying that the final knowledge is complete. So he moved on to a split between character and narrator in *Burmese Days*. But this is too divided; the knowledge and ignorance are so far apart that it implies that in actual terms learning is impossible. The character/narrator split is definite but much closer in *A Clergyman's Daughter*, but the possibility for real learning is left ambivalent. In *Keep the Aspidistra Flying*, the narrator assumes the other half of the character's voice, distinguishing himself by prose techniques, attitudes to fact and history and the manner of conducting an argument. Here there are some very slight indications of an external perspective on the entire narration, but the perspective is not clear enough to be fully effective and involving.

CHAPTER TWO

Communication and Culture:
The Road to Wigan Pier

The early novels indicate that Orwell quickly learned most of the fundamental lessons of contemporary rhetorical stance. He discovered that there are rhetorics that control by imposition and rhetorics that discuss. Those that impose count on assumption and convention; they create isolated worlds both public and private, that provide escape and are maintained by an evasion of reality. These stances may also devolve all too easily into the imposition of ideas, and ultimately the use of force. He comes to recognize that alternative stances cannot define specific answers because these too often become aspects of dominating control. This does not imply that a solution should not be put forward but that one should not do so with the implication that it is the only solution. Alternative rhetorics need to involve, suggest and discuss.

Orwell also begins to understand that it is not entirely a question of the speaker or writer, but that audiences too have their own rhetorics which either impose upon the text or interact with it. And it is this extension into audience, into the relationship between writer and reader, that fundamentally changes the nature of his writing. This has been noted by a number of critics but their attitude is ambivalent. There is considerable disagreement over whether the writer is trying to dominate his audience or is dominated by it. The split underlies the critical figure of a 'paradoxical' Orwell who is both victim and victimizer: a theory that Raymond Williams puts forward in his interesting study of Orwell in 1973, and which has influenced the majority of commentators ever since. Again, I would argue that to keep the critical discussion caught between these poles is to restrict involvement with the text. The activity of rhetorical stance is not a matter

45

of the reader or writer identifying with the topical field, but of informing that field with an interaction that provides it with a valuable context.

The writer also discovers that although specific tactics may differ in terms of literary or social issues, the strategies remain similar. At this early stage, all the novels portray some interest in religion, history, sex, politics and language, but concentrate most on the issue of language. Indeed the other topics are primarily expressed in terms of strategies within language and literature. Throughout these works analogies are developing between attitudes to language and literature, and the other topics. Personal fantasies, slang, swearing, private stories and language, parallel the accepted conventions of melodrama, magazine writing, the literature of certain kinds of poetry and advertisement, as well as briefly the techniques of fact and statistic in more scientific literature. All come to be analogous to official language, political or religious jargon, in their ability to create isolated worlds which control and define other people. In the early novels alternatives are posed in Bozo's self-defining language, and for a short time in both Dorothy's and Gordon Comstock's attempts at active choice, but while the writer suggests that one cannot allow the man-made conventions of language to control one and that one has a responsibility to define oneself, there is not the same sense of that need to interact with the materiality of language which infuses his later writing.

Orwell also becomes aware that the narrator's stance itself has to be clarified if the audience is to interact. A first person narrator of 'documentary' literature provides expectations of 'truth' and reliability that discourage assessment and active involvement by the audience. As a result the initial narrator is quickly left behind because a certain distance is necessary to separate the writer from the narrator and provide perspective. But the first person narrator also allowed the writer to present a 'type', an ordinary magazine reader with whom his audience could identify and, with that identification, trust and learn. So although one gains perspective by moving to a third person narrator, it also becomes far easier for the reader to find loopholes for escape from the implications of the text by denying identification with either narrator or character and by dismissing any topical discussion as 'fictional' and therefore false.

When Orwell moves on to *The Road to Wigan Pier* he returns to documentary narrative and to a first person narrator, but with a changed outlook on the relationship between writer and audience as well as between narrator and character. One important aspect he has learned to make obvious is that the differences between fiction and documentary, whatever else, are not primarily those between truth and falsity. The lesson makes his approach to documentary singularly interesting for his era. At the same time, the emphasis shifts from language and literature as the primary analogy for the activity of the other topics, to language and politics. The shift occurs partly because politics provides a more immediately practical context for the questions of stance being explored and hence throws them into relief, but also because, as Orwell was later to observe, political topics were impossible to avoid.

From the earlier literary development within the stances of the novels, it is not surprising to find the narrator of the *Road to Wigan Pier* treating himself as a character in Part One and moving out to an external perspective on the narrator and character combination itself in Part Two. There are two main problems arising from this strategy. The first is structural and the second historical. Structurally, because the narrator is part of the character, an identification with the one implicitly involves identification with the other. Further, since the narrator later goes to the opposite extreme and sets up the character as a type, almost as a caricature not as an individual, the solution reached becomes generally applicable. As with *Down and Out* general solutions tend to be resisted because they demand too inclusive an identification from the reader, especially when the option of allying oneself with the voice of either the character or the narrator is cut away by their superimposition. Historically, this resistance to the general solution proffered is compounded by the writer's audience. Writing for Victor Gollancz as he was, it would have been fairly clear that he would be speaking to socialists.[1] Hence, setting the narrator/character as a socialist makes it even more difficult for the expected reader to resist identification, even though he wants to do so. The strategy of insisting on identification with their socialism is wise because the writer is challenging, not simply spoon-feeding his audience. But the strategy of insisting on full identification with a general solution is a problem and a major flaw in the book.

This said, *The Road to Wigan Pier* is otherwise structurally exciting. What the book is about is not what the writer saw, but how he saw it. It is a discussion of assumptions and prejudices, how they govern our attitudes, our approaches and the way we see things. Underlying the study is one specific proposition that the author states clearly and attempts to prove: that class differences are not simply economic, but cultural. Orwell at this time appears to have little understanding of the possible economic bases for culture. What is implied here by 'economic' is simply crude finances or money; for example, he refers to the restricted idea of giving the working class more money to get rid of class distinctions, as economic, whereas it is rather a superficial exchange of money. However, he is certainly aware of the more radical issues with which socialist economics claimed to be concerned. For the writer, class war is a deep-rooted matter that will take years to work through and the immediate financial needs of the working class should be considered separately in order to stop the advance of fascism that preys upon their poverty. Class war is a matter of prejudice not simply of money, and what is more important than questions of finance, culture or economy, is the matter of stance. He is asking for real change not just readjustment, and for the loss of or denial of self necessary to any such change. Concurrent with these concerns is an examination of why prejudices occur and how they are maintained. It is suggested that they are escapes from reality that allow us to pretend that things are all right, that we do not have to change. Ultimately, the narrator suggests that all prejudice indicates a totalitarian way of thought, and here one is brought to the most controversial aspect of the book: its comparison of fascism with socialism. Socialism, as Orwell sees it, asks people to radically change, yet at the same time it forces them into types. It generates a tension between the individual who actively re-positions his or her ideas, but is then pushed into group interpretations. On the other hand fascism makes people into types by not asking them to change, by simply bolstering their existing prejudices. Both maintain prejudices through a propagandic rhetoric of imposition that aids the *status quo*, promotes sentimental acceptance of values and escape into a world of adequacy. Examples of such negative persuasion may be found in jargon, clichés, or the use of weighted statistics. Their alternative is a positive propaganda that makes re-examination of one's grounds essential. Orwell here extends the function of the tramps' stories, of the manner in which Flory's inability to communicate tied him to imperialism or in which Dorothy's loss of language and subsequent regaining of it tied her to memory and personal history, and finally, of the way Gordon viewed literature and advertising as keys to his own history. Positive and negative strategies of language are at the core of what the writer is doing in this work. They define how he sees what he sees: the extent of his prejudices and the possibility of lifting them. To understand the full complexity of his study of assumptions and their effects, it is necessary to explore first the way he sees things and how that process defines them.

Part One: Narrator as Persona

At the start, the narrator is concerned with creating a persona that can present valid observations. Yet this persona knows very little about his surroundings, so he is faced with the problem of simultaneously learning and reporting. The result is a detached conjecturing narrator, who finds much of what he sees alien, and deals with it by placing it in a humorous perspective. From the beginning, the narrator plunges directly into observation, only gradually reflecting on his situation as the first chapter progresses. Also, from the beginning he emphasizes the conjectural state of his mind, prefacing a comment on factory whistles with 'I suppose . . .' This indication of his external personal stance is then generalized as he includes himself with the other lodgers in the house. The technique not only allies him with the scene, giving him a certain authority to discuss it, but also acts by including the reader, asking him to follow along with the narratorial persona. Since the writer is addressing a middle-class audience interested in socialist issues, he can fairly expect them to find acceptable the simultaneous detachment from, and inclusion in, observation of the working-class scene.

The pattern of observation and conjecture interspersed with generalizations, continues for much of the chapter. Each scene is carefully presented in terms of detail, measurement and precision focusing initially around a particular object: the bed in the bedroom and the table in the kitchen work in this way. Having been carefully described they then provide the basis for a personal opinion or conjecture, 'I believe . . .' in the first case and 'I suspect . . .' in the second. From this point the narrator moves into generalizations, here, about the smell of the bedroom and the dirt on the kitchen table, sometimes conveyed with a generalizing 'you', for example: 'You did not notice it when you got up, but if you . . .' (p. 6), or introduced by 'Generally the crumbs . . .' (p. 7). These generalizations , which are often humorous, yield the conclusions on the scene itself that eventually make up the background being described. The procedure is followed throughout the first half of the chapter, and incorporates not only the physical scene, but the characters who people it as well. The effect is of a narratorial persona who can be trusted to record precisely, who places his opinions in the perspective of conjecture, and who can be at once familiar with the scene and humorously detached from it. The process of familiarizing and detaching himself extends to many further techniques. Exaggeration is used only to be undercut. Horrific observations such as one on the injury of the Scotch miner (p. 6), are placed in brackets as if they were simply additional information. Or he describes an appalling disease with the throw-away line 'cancer, I believe' (p. 9). He downplays the implications of the scene with comments such as 'curiously enough' or 'strange to say', but above all presents himself as someone not to be caught out. He has 'heard dreadful stories' about the tripe shop, but follows them with balanced deductions; and he casts doubt on statements with 'It was said . . .' The end result is overtly of a scene which is unpleasant, alienating and disgusting, and further, of a group of people who are dirty and unthinking. Yet the attempted mitigation of this effect by all the judicious comments and well-balanced opinion, leaves one appraising the narrator as valid while retaining the horror of the scene. One incident points to external verification for our reaction: the narratorial persona meets a lodger who 'suddenly divined that I was a fellow Southerner. "The filthy bloody bastards!" he said feelingly' (p. 16). The narrator is ineradicably alien to the situation, and so is his expected reader.

Gradually, the narratorial persona is added to by an older, more reflective voice which clarifies the tension in the stance. Commenting on the fact that the lodgers were never served tripe, the narrator says ironically, 'I have since thought that it was merely because we knew too much about it' (p. 8). At another point, dryly presenting Mr Brooker as a cadger, he notes 'in some way I did not understand, Mr Brooker was dodging the Means Test and drawing an allowance from the P.A.C.' (p. 13). Later, he generalizes more widely, saying 'The most dreadful thing about people like the Brookers is the way they say the same things over and over again' (p. 17). The tone of this reflective narrator is ironic. He is counting on certain cultural assumptions held in common with his readers that will ally them to the implicit condemnation of these statements. Yet the condemnation is based on ignorance, on failure to discuss the real problems of the situation. When reflecting, the narratorial persona shows himself to be passive in the acceptance of the norms he is faced with. Although he appears to be detailed, accurate and precise, about his surroundings, he is reducing them and their occupants to 'types' that are recognizable objects of prejudice: the 'spongers'.

Oddly enough, the process subtly establishes the narratorial persona as a type as well. He has the kind of mind that thinks in generalities, makes opinionated comments, cannot see human beings except in obvious terms. The concluding section of chapter 1 shifts away from this to the narrator's observations on himself which are significantly different. The tension in the prose which has been alternating between long precisely observing sentences and short sharp conclusions, relaxes into more descriptive constructions that include apparently superficial detail. His mind is presented not in terms of what he does, where he works, and how much he earns, but by way of three distinct images.

The first image is of a woman unplugging a drain, the second of D. H. Lawrence's vision of the country, and the third, of two mating rooks. The narrator almost catches the eyes of the woman, but his reaction to her is that she is the 'usual' working-class woman. He has sympathy for her, but does not understand her predicament. Similarly, the narrator comments on D. H. Lawrence's image of the country as 'like muscle', saying 'It was not the simile that would have occurred to me. To my eye the snow and the black walls were more like a white dress with black piping running across it' (p. 19). The contrast of this impersonal and pretty image with Lawrence's underlines the narrator's alienation and lack of understanding. The final image of the rooks mating incongruously returns the reader to the narrator's observations on the Brookers. He has never seen the situation before; it is 'curious', and he reports it in exactly the same precise and detailed manner that he did the lodging-house.

All three images arise while he is travelling by train away from the town. The narrator is warm, safe, enclosed from the cold outside; the train is an escape bearing him away from the disgust of his earlier experience. Rather than thinking about his past experiences, the narrator is slowly putting them out of his mind and moving into the clean countryside. He has come to the conclusion that 'it is no use saying that people like the Brookers are just disgusting and trying to put them out of mind. For they exist in tens and hundreds of thousands . . . You cannot disregard them if you accept the civilization that produced them' (p. 17). But this is exactly what he is doing. The ease with which he evades the implications of his reporting and can forget, becomes an important factor in the later discussion of ways in which we see and respond to systems different from our own. This ambivalence and evasion has been noted by a number of readers, but because of the tendency to fuse 'Orwell' with the narrator many commentaries fail to perceive that it is a device of stance that should alert the reader. It is an underestimation that has led to several restricted readings.[2]

The second chapter is a great contrast. The pattern of observation is similar in its movement from a particular situation out to the generalization, but the internal strategy is quite different. The narratorial 'you' is no longer generalizing about types, but is a vicariously experiencing 'you', who familiarizes himself with the situation by active experience, and who familiarizes the reader by involving him in response to the recreation of experience. The ironic narratorial persona of chapter 1 has disppeared, and the humour of this chapter is mainly directed against himself. A different kind of detachment is also established. Rather than being alien, the narrator here is serious and almost formal. Indications of this are given in the opening vocabulary with its references to 'metabolism' and the simile likening the miner to a 'grimy caryatid' (p. 21). The detachment is emphasized by the rare use of 'I', except on small points of detail, or on matters specifically to do with the narrator himself such as his height. And while the prose is relaxed, it is not colloquial. Odd clichés that do get used are filled out such as the statement that the mines are 'like hell, or at any rate like my own mental picture of hell. Most of the things one imagines in hell are here' (p. 21), or the description of the miners looking as though they are 'made of iron. They really do look like iron-hammered iron statues' (p. 23).

The primary voice of the chapter is a narratorial 'you' that addresses and involves the reader directly. It takes you through the process of going down a mine step by step, providing precise detail and consistently explaining if an unfamiliar point comes up. He is not presenting a generally accepted view of a mine since first hand experience of one was rare. Hence, he cannot rest on ideas shared with his audience. He asserts that he is not exaggerating, and he has to deal with objections from his readers almost before they arise. The largest concern is how to make familiar a situation that lies outside the lives of most of his readers without imposing a private and dominating interpretation on it. This he achieves primarily through juxtaposition. Statements of fact are made to stand starkly alone and alert the reader before he comes to the explanations which follow. Those images which are usually applied to reinforce ideas, are here used for purposes of difference, to point up new ideas and connections. The reverse device of using familiar images not in different ways but in the same way applied to different things, also involves the reader in the activity of the experience. A good example of this last device is the progression the narrator makes from an image of the miner being buried under a mountain, to being 'at the bottom of the Piccadilly tube' (p. 25). The first is an acceptable, normally expected, image that makes the second even more odd than it might have been. Other familiarizing techniques include the humour against himself, as well as an introduction of the specialized vocabulary of the miners, which generates an illusion of being educated in their language.

Despite the alienation from the situation, the reader can accept identification with the narratorial 'you' through his serious detachment, his willingness to point to his own weaknesses and to explain the unfamiliar, and lastly through the juxtaposed ideas and images that involve us directly in an assessment of the experience. By restraining his involvement as a narratorial persona, a far more definite sense of a speaking subject is defined. When he says, in conclusion to the experience, that 'the work would kill me in a few weeks' (p. 33), it is not a melodramatic claim from some 'type' persona who overreacts, but an individual and personal statement that we can evaluate and probably agree with. Similarly, the final discussion of the relationship that an average person makes between coal and mining, is a personal one arrived at by a narrator we trust because we know him as an individual voice, not because we recognize his type. Whereas the narrator unthinkingly demonstrated the passive escape of his type in the conclusion of Chapter 1, here he consciously points it out. He notes that 'only very rarely, when I make a definite mental effort' (p. 33) does he connect coal with mines and labour. From the personal he progresses to the general, saying 'most of the time, of course, we should forget that they were doing it' (p. 34), and this too is acceptable. Rather more difficult to accept is our identification with the 'Nancy poets and the Archibishop of Canterbury and Comrade X, author of *Marxism for Infants*' (p. 35), but it is made easier by the recognition that these are 'types'; we and the narrator are not. The effect of this is to reinforce our agreement with him, aligning ourselves as knowledgeable in comparison with them.

Having created an experience of the mine, the narrator now moves on to a different kind of knowledge based on facts and statistics. The third chapter moves from one aspect of mining life to another, continually building on preceding facts or interpretations. The movement of the detail about washing, to shifts, wages, stoppages, health and compensation, builds an intricate and complex picture of the economic structure. The examination of many of these specific details is also a process of stating a commonly held assumption, and going on to demonstrate that it is unfounded; in this way it is implied that understanding of this complex situation is low. The narratorial stance is one of necessarily personal interpretation. Everyone has facts and figures, yet each man interprets for himself. To validate his own process he points to his personal ignorance or limitation, saying 'I cannot get hold of exact figures' (p. 37) or 'I shared the wide-spread illusion' (p. 40). He often perzonalises quoted figures by relating them to specific people, and is heavily dependent on examples as if the figures mean little without them. Yet at the same time, he is exact, detailed, uses few images. He notes the lack of precision in other works and gives references for his own information.

The process may be exemplified by the section on wages and stoppages. The narrator carefully constructs this beginning with the 'loosely stated' reported wage of a miner. He moves logically on through all the unseen aspects affecting this reported wage, in terms of seasonal work or piece-work, and other aspects, to a revised wage. He then shifts to five specific wages slips he has 'before me', making concrete the discussion. These actual wages are averaged out and then the accepted number of stoppages is put in, with the codicil that the accepted number is agreed to be far more in actual experience. From here the narrator relentlessly pursues this rational logic into the imposed deductions for insurance and equipment, and the personal deductions such as fares to get to work, and, finally, to an optimistic 'real wage' which is far different from the initial reported wage. The process of augmentation is applied to other details such as the description of mine accidents. The result is first to create an impression of inevitability and depression, second to emphasize the points he wishes to make by reaching conclusions that he then goes beyond; and third, to alert us to the need for personal assessment by making what seem to be important comments, only to move on to demonstrate that they are essentially trivial or preliminary. Significantly, each area examined starts off with a prevalent assumption, as, for example, the 'reported wage' of a miner, and proceeds to break it down. But in no case is the assumption crudely denied. The amplification and step by step logic pursue each concept to a clear weakness, and provide a concrete alternative.

By the end of the third chapter the narrator is confident enough to address the reader again, and make a humorous dig at his own situation to remind the reader of his position. The conclusion to the chapter moves off into the issue of class assumptions. Where the previous concluding notes have concerned the forgetful nature of the middle class, here the writer examines the passive role of the working class. In doing so, contrary to the the previous assumptions that he made, he appears to endorse it. From his own experience he has found that working-class man 'does not act, he is acted upon. He feels himself the slave of a mysterious authority'(p. 49). The writer refers to the omnipotent as 'they', with a sceptical 'evidently' (p. 49), and goes no further; but the whole tone of this passage asks for a denial of this assumption by the reader, for he should have learnt by now the assessment that is expected of him.

That the reader is expected to have learned how to assess the situations presented, lies at the root of the ensuing strategy. Chapter 4 is an active attack on the reader, in which the narrator undermines his own position at the same time as defamiliarizing assumptions the reader may hold. The narrator initially moves away from facts and figures into personal observation of the situation and ends his first paragraph with the blunt statement that 'at the time when these houses were built no one imagined that miners wanted baths' (p. 51). Despite the open-ended nature of this statement, the reader can reasonably be expected to have learned enough from the preceding chapter to make his own evaluation of such an attitude. When the observations then progress to the housing shortage which 'means very little to anyone with an income of more than £10 a week' (p. 52), the reader is clearly being encouraged to distinguish himself from this common ignorance and learn from what follows. Yet the narrator proceeds by transcribing 'a few extracts from my notebook' (p. 53), for which he promises explanations later on. At first, the notes appear to validate the narrator. They contain measurements, precise descriptions, accounts of rent paid and added details. Yet, having gone on to explain some of the terms, the narrator concludes:

> But mere notes like these are only valuable as reminders to myself. To me as I read them they bring back what I have seen, but they cannot in themselves give much idea of what conditions are like . . . Words are such feeble things. What is the use of a brief phrase like 'roof leaks' . . . ? It is the kind of thing your eye slides over registering nothing. And yet what a wealth of misery it can cover! (p. 57)

After this the writer lets himself go in a string of examples and expansions on examples, creating interminable lists and using repetition, exclamations and various other devices in an attempt to describe the misery he has seen. In effect, it conveys little to the reader except the impossibility of comprehending the situation.

Throughout, the narrator notes his own inaccuracy, the impossibility of asking certain questions, for example, about deaths, and his ignorance of key issues. At the same time, he is breaking down conventional ideas that his reader may have about the lives he describes. Again, he dwells on the sanitary arrangements to remind his reader of the practical, physical aspects of such a life that he might prefer to disregard; and he concludes his description of the misery of these people with the image of a woman who 'felt as I should feel if I were coated all over with dung' (p. 63). While the comparisons are distasteful, the narrator controls them firmly by making them a report rather than a sensory experience and by interjecting detached comments. The reader is left with many of his ideas about the life of the working class disrupted, and with no explicit statements from the narrator about re-interpretation.

However, by this stage the narrator has made clear what he is doing to arrive at his own conclusions. He begins with assumptions, looks at the facts, qualifies them, moves on to correct the assumptions by way of images and comparisons, ties in concrete examples, and examines the specific situation of people. An example is found in his study of the financing of corporation houses, which the narrator makes his own choice but still leaves it open because he wants the reader to participate. As he says concerning life in the caravans, 'No doubt there are still middle-class people who think that the Lower Orders don't mind that kind of thing . . . I never argue nowadays with that kind of person' (p. 64). If the reader is responding to what he is being told, and reassessing his prejudices, neither will he ally himself with 'that kind of person'; but even if he were not responding, the second half of the statement demands that the reader make a choice, align himself or stop reading. Later, the narrator is even more explicit about the ignorant assumption that the working class are simply moaners, saying that 'It is not that slum-dwellers want dirt and congestion for their own sakes, as the fat-bellied bourgeoisie love to believe' (p. 70). Such a statement does not leave much room for a reader who refuses to learn. The narrator is not only showing the reader how to learn, but saying that if we want to identify with the narrator and his experiences we have to be willing to effect real change in ourselves.

Chapter 4 builds from the earlier contention that the middle class are 'leaders'. If the working class are passive, the middle class have a responsibility to find the causes for ills, and to attempt practical solutions, not those of 'Bishops, politicians, philanthropists' (p. 65). Most of the assumptions about dirt, crowding, passivity and smell were part of the judgement made by the initial persona as a 'type' of middle-class observer who failed to truly examine situations. And now the reader begins to recognize the role of that initial 'type' persona with whom he was invited to identify. As the narrator has corrected the illusions of that persona, so he expects any reader who identified with it to correct his own view, not by being told what to think, but by learning how to evaluate a situation from several different perspectives. By the end of the chapter, the writer states clearly his findings concerning the patience and kindness of the working class remarking on 'the extraordinary courtesy and good nature with which I was received' (p. 73). He puts his attitude on the line in the most personal way possible by referring us specifically to a review of his own work, of 'Mr. Orwell's' writing, which appeared in the *Manchester Guardian*, and which, on the basis of these first four chapters, the reader can evaluate as incorrect. Just as the quoted review is wrong about him, so his notes are inadequate to describe Wigan. The narrator ends with reference to Wigan Pier, a joke based on the knowledge that it does not exist. The joke provides an analogy for all the assumptions that he has broken down. They, too, were founded on no substantial reason, and when understood are themselves a joke.[3]

These four chapters are a discrete exercise in education by example. At their conclusion the reader will either have identified with the narrator and the process he puts forward, or else, have dissociated himself from it. The remaining three chapters in Part One move on to examining methods of assessing ideas and examining one's prejudices. They consolidate the suggestions that have been previously put forward. Having either persuaded or alienated his reader, or established a relationship that the reader has chosen and not had imposed upon him, the narrator can now afford to be friendly. But it is also a strategy to include the willing reader in self-criticism.

The main drift of the fifth chapter is an examination of the problem of unemployment. It is approached in the now familiar manner of stating an assumption, roundly claiming that it is an illusion, and proceeding to demolish it by careful references to facts, statistics, concrete examples and actual effects on personal lives. The narrator employs a stance of being mistaken, ignorant and inaccurate, and counteracts this by explicit personal experience, footnotes, numbers, and references to earlier conclusions, that create an illusion of solidity. But in this study he also moves into an element of fiction as he attempts to construct the experience of being out of work. The implication is that experience and factual knowledge are still not adequate, and that one has to make an effort to interact with the personal responses that such conditions create.

The conclusion on unemployment is in terms of its effect on the attitudes of the working and middle classes. The narrator insinuates the presence of a revolutionary movement, something feared by the middle class, when he says that 'The attitude of the submerged working class is profoundly different from what it was seven or eight years ago' (p. 85). The expectation of revolution is then reversed by his conclusion that on the contrary working people are more passive. It is worthwhile noting that the writer here makes clear that he does not think of the working class as inherently passive but as having become so due to the recent depression.[4] The device neatly presents both the attitudes he wishes to discuss. First, the current passivity of the working class and, second, the fears of the middle class. It is suggested that working-class passivity results from the undermining of traditions of work and the fear of debt brought by unemployment. Instead of fighting back, they cope by 'lowering their standards' (p. 88). They escape into cheap luxuries − a hire purchase system, clothes, movies or gambling. Having been plundered of 'all they really need [they] are being compensated, in part, by cheap luxuries which mitigate the surface of life' (p. 90). The middle-class fear of revolution or insurrection has effectively been quashed by the development of this passive attitude, but the narrator implies that they still mistakenly retain the fear. As the reader shall find, this becomes the basis for later criticism: that the middle classes are concerned about the working class only for their own sake. They fail to examine the causes of the problem because they are not truly concerned with the working class itself.

The narrator examines the escape pattern of the working class in terms of food and fuel. As he does so his stance becomes increasingly personal. Chapters 3 and 4 contained references to himself as an individual with an actual past, but it is important to note that the references are not autobiographical. He is using personal incidents fictionalized to provide points of contact for his experiences. That he has mentioned the name 'George Orwell' points to this explicit fictionality. The name was one the writer had been using for only four years, and always in the context of his writing. In 1935 most of his friends still knew him as Eric Blair. The writer is not here writing an autobiography, but a fictional documentary in which he adjusts his façade to the strategies called for. In adopting a more personal stance, the writer is building on the identification tentatively established in the previous chapter between himself and his reader.

The tone of this study in chapter 5 is more humorous, less didactic and more openly strategic. He employs positive irony, ambiguity and satire, all devices needing active interpretation by his reader, and by this point the reader should be aware of the different methods he can use for evaluation. If there is any doubt in his mind, the narrator spells the strategy out, saying with reference to working-class diet: 'The results of all this are visible in a physical degeneracy which you can study directly, by using your eyes, or inferentially, by having a look at the vital statistics' (p. 90). Although these devices explain why the situation exists, they do not explain how it has arisen. To uncover reasons for the more fundamental problems the narrator turns in chapter 6 to a story. He examines the paradoxical contradiction of wastage and want which are both elements of escape in the working class. On the one hand, the people go for cheap luxuries and unnecessary food that actually wastes what money they have in order to create an illusion of comfort. On the other hand, want drives them to doing illegal things such as stealing coal, in order to survive. The point here is that the middle class should drop their easy assumptions about the 'thieving' nature of the working class, based on an illusion that they have all they need. The narrator uses the word 'thieving' and then qualifies the word, noting that it is not as straightforward as it looks. In order to get to the root of these assumptions, the narrator proceeds to a re-creation of the event of 'thieving', a story in which we are asked to participate. When he concludes, using the words 'stolen' and 'robbing', the reader has a vicarious experience from which he can reject their implicit judgement, and only then does the narrator give his reasons for why it is not stealing.

Chapter 6 concludes with a 'picture' of Lancashire. There is neither direct address nor attack: simply the picture of the coal mounds and an implicit comment on the uselessness of Social Credit. But the reader does not need a conclusion; he has been taught how to read. Immediately following are the actual photographs of mining life, the first being of the scene that has just been described. The juxtaposition of the photograph with the written portrait is a strategy that alerts the reader to the necessity of evaluating the pictures, and actively looking at them. The bracketed comments in the sub-titles also point to the active interaction being required of the reader. The transition from the mining photographs to the slums of London extends the implications of the comments on the working class away from mining and the north, into a more general problem. The movement also provides a bridge into the final, seventh chapter of Part One.

The initial narratorial persona made a specific distinction between northern and southern habits, and the earlier chapters reiterated this 'Southerner' stance of the narrator. By chapter 7, the assumptions implicit in this stance are taken to task and used as the basis for criticizing all attempts at 'typing', all unexamined assessments: it is an aspect which, if dismissed, leaves the reader with the superficial impression that the writer is making a genuine evaluative distinction between the north and the south.[5] The narrator begins by taking us back to the train journey at the end of chapter 1. The resonances of 'villa-civilization' and the 'real ugliness of industrialism' (p. 37) with the former description tie the two explicitly together. Yet, whereas there, he was escaping into the green spaces, avoiding the implications of his recent experience, here he renders in detail the cities and the underlying class tensions. This time standing in the country yields a classic pastoral perspective on urban life, generating questions out of the differences involved, rather than providing an escape.

From this vantage, he suggests that the fundamental differences between north and south have their roots in 'tradition, are not affected by visible facts' (p. 142). The old spectre of the strong, powerful and industrial north, which began the fanciful separation, is 'cant . . . nowadays a pure anachronism . . . But traditions are not killed by facts' (p. 145). They are at one with the same absurd logic that maintains nationalism. He concludes that:

> All nationalistic distinctions – all claims to be better than somebody else because you have a different-shaped skull or speak a different dialect – are entirely spurious, but they are important so long as people believe in them. (p. 143)

He himself had such prejudices when he went north, but he found that they could not be maintained in the face of personal experience.

Class differences too are based on the unexamined traditions of both middle and working classes. But here the narrator pauses. He has brought the reader with him to this point, brought him to the edge of saying yes, yes we will discard our prejudices, and he stops. He says here that it is not 'possible to be really intimate with the working-class' (p. 147), that the important fact is that 'your middle-class ideals and prejudices are tested by contact with others which are not necessarily better, but are certainly different' (p. 147). All 'typing' of people is destructive, and results from your acceptance of the concepts that make you yourself a 'type'. While re-examination of your own standards is essential, they need not necessarily be discarded. The writer hints here at the development in Part Two of the impossibility of getting rid of one's own class standards. The involvement of the reader with 'we' and 'us' is arrested as the narrator makes his personal opinion clear, and he concludes with a highly emotive picture of 'working-class' interiors. For the reader who has not picked up the evaluating processes that have been described, this is a cosy comfortable ending to reinforce a desire for no real change.

Indeed this picture is a key point in criticism of *The Road to Wigan Pier*. There are those who read it and the book, as a sentimental portrait of cosy working-class values. There are those who go a little further noting its position of balance at the end of Part One, with the Brookers' house at the beginning, and who read it as a naïve presentation of someone 'understanding' and appreciating the working class. Interestingly, these readings have both praising and condemning adherents. However, for the reader who has learnt, this is first of all a recognizably limited picture that indicates by juxtaposition with actuality the effort needed to maintain such a standard of life, and points ironically to the growth of passivity in the 30s that will ensure its eventual destruction. But further than this, because the picture is a story that we have been shown how to read, it may move out of its chronological time and the reader can come to question the desirability of the very standards it indicates.[6]

The narrator has begun by establishing a persona representative of a group of middle-class assumptions, and has shown the limited extent of his observations of the working class and his attempt to escape the implications of what he has seen. The following chapters first exposed the persona as limited and restricted, demonstrating that his prejudices were unfounded, at the same time as he presented methods for reassessing standards in terms of experience, factual information and observation. After an attack on the reader's assumptions, which concludes either with identification with or alienation from the narrator, he proceeds by reiterating the different approaches to reassessment, underlining the result that facts, figures and even personal experience are not the whole story. The reader has to be able to understand and interact with the minds and responses of the working-class. To do so, one needs the ability to enter a fictional world that will allow one to participate and learn for oneself: a world where the connections are not static, not defined and fixed and known. Fiction and assessment become corollary activities in a positive rhetorical strategy. But the narrator is also indicating that there are different types of fiction. There is the conventional image of working-class life found in the fantasized picture of the family gathered around a cosy fire; but this is mere wishful thinking and delusion. But there is also participatory fiction based on the kind of activity found in the analogical juxtaposition of the story of the coal mines with the photographs at the end of chapter 6. This story asks for the reader's involvement in an assessment of working-class 'thieving'. This kind of fiction is also the basis of the two working-class interiors that the narrator provides. If the reader enters people's lives through participating in fiction, then he is able to see them, not as types, but as people. The narrator concludes that this cannot be achieved without first accepting that 'typing' of all kinds is, like nationalism, based on setting up one's own assumptions as a spurious standard of superiority.

Part Two : Narrator as Bourgeois Type

The progress has been one of a middle-class narrator looking at the working-class 'type' his assumptions have led him to expect, and gradually breaking down those prejudices to arrive at a more understanding view of the working class. But, as the narrator hints in the conclusion of the final chapter, such activity occurs because the middle-class persona is a type himself. Fundamentally what the persona should be examining is not some philanthropic intent to aid the working classes, but his own tradition, why he thinks the way he does. This approach to stance is probably the reason that Orwell does not incorporate nearly as much about the working class in *The Road to Wigan Pier* as there is in his diary.[7] The writer can never adequately deal with who or what the working class is – it would be pure arrogance to think that he could – but he can discuss the role of his own class and examine how that class fits into and adds to the problem. The second part of the book proceeds to do just this.

It is essential that the narrator be able to present the middle class both as a type and as an actual person. The only basis on which this can be effectively carried out, in what is ostensibly a documentary, is for the narrator himself to place his own character under surveillance. From the start there are two aspects to this character. The book begins by presenting the narrator as a fixed 'persona' with a number of easily identifiable prejudices. But in the second chapter there is an abrupt switch into the narrator as a learning character becoming aware of these prejudices. The second narrator develops a strong individual voice as Part One progresses, while the persona only surfaces momentarily, and it is important to note that when it does so it is accorded all the 'autobiographical' references of 'George Orwell', his youth and experience in 'Burma'. The public details of the author's life are firmly attached to the persona of a middle-class 'type' not to the learning narrator and the effect is twofold. First, a very specific type is being generated so that any criticism will not appear to attack the reader directly. Second, the reader is being told quite firmly that he can never 'know' or fully understand the writer. This may be 'autobiographical', but the nature of autobiography is to be selective and curtailed. Writing attains to no objectivity or 'truth' simply by being allied to an individual's name. And doubly so here since it is an autobiography of the narrator as George Orwell not as Eric Blair.

In Part Two the narrator splits more decisively. There is another more external and personal voice retaining the characteristic tone of the aware and learning narrator. And there is a younger persona who takes on the overt elements of 'Orwell's' life and is presented in much the same way as the initial 'type' narrator of Part One. The narrator suggests that it is this type of person, financially at the same level as the working class, who is most responsible for class differences because of the assumptions he breeds. The only way he can separate himself from the working classes is by maintaining certain traditions that will identify him as different. It is suggested that these barriers were initially due to the fear of overt aggression from the working class, but with its growing passivity, they become simply habit. Basically, the maintenance of these habits is a fear of becoming working-class, and that fear resides in the very assumptions that the middle class creates for its own protection. The effect of the strategy of developing the younger persona, is to detach the reader from the topic being presented so that he can view and assess this specific case from the outside.

The fears the older narrator discusses in Chapter 8 are different in each case, but centre on that of the persona: that 'The lower classes smell' (p. 159). The study of the prejudice is a strategy designed to involve the reader. The build-up to the statement is quite considerable in its exaggerated emphasis and series of short sentences. When it comes, it is ludicrously forthright. The immediate reaction is that 'people shouldn't say so' and the following discussion points out that that is exactly the reaction that causes the most harm. The narrator provides the further example of his class attitude in his childhood aversion to drinking from a bottle that had been passed around several people, and how personal experience of doing so with tramps 'cured' him of it. Similarly, there is the middle-class socialist who invariably finds lower-class eating habits repulsive. Here the narrator is not suggesting, in contrast to general critical opinion, that working-class eating habits are better or worse, but that even if they do not take up those manners, middle-class socialists should recognize the barrier not evade it.[8] Just as he has learnt from his attitude to communal drinking, they should realize that the eating habits are a genuine issue of difference that separates them by tradition from other classes.

In this eighth chapter at the start of Part Two, the narrator reverses his strategy of direct identification because he has to at once criticize and alert the middle-class reader without antagonizing him. The main strategy is an unspoken identification of grounds and assumptions between the older narrator and the reader. That it is unspoken allows the reader to detach himself where necessary from the implicit condemnation of the middle class; and at the same time it encourages him to make that condemnation because he does not have to face the fact that it also applies to him. However, the separation of narrator from the persona is a model for such self-criticism, and the reader's identification with the narrator by corollary, turns his own criticism of the persona into self-criticism. If the reader is to understand the point about class assumptions being generated from a kind of rhetorical evasion that denies class differences, like the reaction to eating habits or smell, he has to understand that this operates within himself as well: that he too has to self-criticize. But, while the direction of criticism is not strong and the reader may avoid its implication of himself, the narrator has, so to speak, his foot in the door.

The younger persona is developed more fully in the following chapter, chapter 9. This persona provides a series of concrete examples for the theory of doublethink, the rhetoric of evasion and living on two levels, and the reflective older self harshly condemns his youthful development into 'both a snob and a revolutionary' and the 'pure prejudice' of his behaviour in Burma. The persona's melodramatic and naïve statement that: 'I was still half afraid of the working class. I wanted to get in touch with them, I even wanted to become one of them, but I still thought of them as alien and dangerous . . .' (p. 183), along with his comment 'I had read the unemployment figures but I had no notion of what they implied' (p. 181), alerts the reader to the position of the narratorial 'type' at the start of this book. In doing so it involves him more explicitly in the drama of the situation, the self-criticism that is going on, by presenting from a different perspective a character whom he already knows. Because this persona and the earlier narrator coincide they reinforce each other, and the reader's earlier involvement in criticism of the initial narrator is transferred to the young persona, and vice versa. The detached, humorous, and slightly ironic stance of the older narrator to the younger also allies the reader in the criticism by again counting on shared knowledge of the situation.

The essential point at each stage of the younger persona's development is the reflection on personal experience that leads him to reassess his prejudices. The narrator cannot explain rationally how to lose prejudices, so he presents the persona as an example from which the reader learns. Just as facts, figures and observations are of essential but limited use to an understanding of the working class, here too one must go a step further through the fictional persona of the narrator/character into the experience and attitude of mind of a middle-class person to comprehend his situation. At this point the alert reader should realize that the process is no solution. A method yes, but it will not provide any fail-safe answers. The unwary reader, for whom the writer is always on the look-out, will however be brought up short by the introduction to the next chapter which warns him explicitly of the limitations of the approach. One may indeed learn by example but in the end nothing will do but constant self-vigilance.

The narrator here performs the most difficult and most questionable strategy of the book. Gradually, the younger persona has been chronologically coming closer to the period of the older narratorial voice. At the end of chapters 8 to 10 a new persona emerges: that of the fully-fledged 'bourgeois socialist', and the narrator withdraws from the older detached voice to fuse with this 'type'. But what has in effect happened is that the narrator has asked the reader to transfer his identification from the personal to the type. This generalizing leaves little room for evading the conclusions, and the reader may quite reasonably be taken aback by the request. It is, however, an identification that the narrator wishes to insist on if the reader is to come to terms with his own prejudices.

At the same time it is important that the reader be aware of the difference between the two voices: between the stance of a 'type' and the stance of a learning individual voice. If he has not been alert to this, in the first place, and many critics of Part One illustrate that they are not,[9] then the conflation gives him no choice but to fully identify with or reject the 'type'. It is at this point in the reading that many people reject the narrator completely and blame him for being too 'subjective'. Thus they miss the point of the following discussion as well as the entire education in self-criticism that the book presents.

To present himself as a 'bourgeois socialist' the narrator returns to the example of his life with the tramps. Here he was accepted as one of them, 'on the bum' with the rest. But significantly, the tramp world is artificial, it is a 'world within-a-world where everyone is equal' (p. 187). It provides an escape for everyone who inhabits it. Any attempt to join the actual working class is impossible: 'It is not a question of dislike or distaste, only of *difference*' (p. 188). It is always difficult to admit to personal snobbishness, to difference, and middle-class socialists simply evade the fact and pretend that no difference exists. The result of evasion, of escape into self-delusion, is that one cannot cope with the reality. Here the narrator turns to Galsworthy, a writer who initially claimed that he wanted class differences overthrown. But when having to face the reality of this he backs off, and reverses his opinion. The conclusion is that the evasion brings 'the inevitable fate of a sentimentalist. All his opinions change into their opposites at the first brush of reality' (p. 190).

The narrator then states that underlying these escapes, as it also underlies much revolutionary socialist thought, is the belief that things will not radically change. Both the maintenance of and attack on the *status quo* imply a faith in it or in something that will satisfactorily replace it. Real change involves 'abolishing a part of yourself'. The narrator has presented the theory, through the example of his own persona, and as he did in the characters of his novels, that individuals are historically and socially determined. Given this, real change involves the enormous sacrifice of recognizing that change means cutting away part of yourself. This is quite emphatically what the characters of Orwell's early novels were unable to do. Here the narrator ends with the ambiguous statement that 'whether I say Yes or No probably depends upon the extent to which I grasp what is demanded of me' (p. 194). He is not claiming here that real change is desirable or necessary, only that in the first instance people should recognize its extraordinary difficulty.

These conclusions are followed by a discussion of middle-class socialist types and working-class types who both evade the extent of the problems that lie between them. Each is initially presented as a caricature and then reassessed from an individual point of view. The strategy here indicates first that it is primarily modes of expression which reduce these people to types, and second that because of their expression, despite all personal effort to the contrary, they will be viewed as types by people from other classes who are not aware of the shared grounds underlying their behaviour. Once more the author is concerned to study just how far language, the primary medium for human interaction, both controls and is controlled by the people who use it. The expression that types them is founded on jargon or 'cant', the private code that each class maintains for talking to its own members. The narrator indicates it through use of clichés, bracketed phrases, quotation marks and exclamation marks: all clues to a superficial unexamined vocabulary. It prevents people from seeing others as individuals, and it encourages individuals to hide in their self-enclosed worlds. The end result is again that of the sentimentalist. A brush with reality suddenly alerts the type to real danger which he has not prepared himself to come to terms with. His reaction is to about-face, and retreat into fascism.

The narrator cleverly uses D. H. Lawrence as a working-class type, to demonstrate a problem that he implies resides in both classes. The middle-class reader can go along with the criticism of Lawrence, and if he is actually learning from the narrator's process, will be able to take the next step and apply the criticism to himself. But it is still true to say that a reader caught soundly within his own world will not notice the subtleties of the argument, and will be likely to interpret many of these examples as something he is not connected with at all. It is this reader who objects most strongly to the strategy of chapter 11.

The chapter starts by stating that the intention of the first half of the book was to present working-class conditions. It continues by spelling out the study of an 'anachronistic class-system' that occurred in chapters 8 to 10, and indicating that chapter 12 will deal with the 'underlying assumptions' that alienate people from socialism. In this chapter he is 'merely dealing with . . .' the bourgeois socialist type. The intention of such explicit instructions from the narrator must be to ensure that the reader does not misread the section. It downplays the importance of the devil's advocate position he is taking up, in order to avoid antagonism. Further, it makes such an approach formal and artificial, hence more acceptable as criticism. Again this should come as news only to the reader who has missed the extensive and detailed lead-up to this strategy. And this does prove to be a problem for readers such as Victor Gollancz, who chose to interpret the devil's advocate strategy as an evasion or trick. When these misreadings occur, they undermine the stance of the remaining three chapters. In these final chapters, the writer shifts from the rather orderly narration explaining the prejudices of the younger persona. Although the attack is sharper and the images more distasteful, the writer often undercuts his logic, uses understatement and points to his personal opinion and unique experience. The effect is to force evaluation on the reader himself.

Picking up the earlier repeated resonance of 'Bishops, politicians, philanthropists' the narrator shifts here from a comparison of socialism with politics and imperialism to one with Catholicism. Several analogies between the two are set up, but not fully developed, so that the reader is forced to sort out and assess his own assumptions about Catholicism before he can understand working-class assumptions about socialism. But the explicit comparison is made with reference to Bernard Shaw, who sees the working class as a group of types whose problems are 'to be abolished *from above*, by violence if necessary' (p. 211). From here it is a short step to a comparison of communism and fascism which equally order other people's lives as if on a chessboard. The strategy is not intended merely to convince of similarities, but to raise differences; and the narrator underlines that the two are alike only 'from the point of view of an outsider'. It is '*the form in which it* [socialism] *is now presented*' (p. 214, Orwell's italics) that is important. He is not trying to denigrate socialism, but to alert socialists to the impression they give other people.

The socialist type and socialist propaganda hinder any real communication of aims because they are indissolubly tied to the working-class idea of a middle-class type conveyed by their mode of expression. Just as the middle class has been shown to have illusions about the working-class, the reverse also occurs. The assumptions of one are based on and breed the assumptions of the other. No real change can occur without a radical shake-up. What is interesting is the ambiguous status in which the writer leaves his own work. He states that socialism does not draw great writers to it because a writer's 'political opinions are more directly and obviously connected with his work' (p. 215), and socialist propaganda, which appears to insist on following 'imposed' reforms, hinders creativity. The reader is forced either to condemn the writer as a non-socialist, or to recognize the injustice and limitation of such imposition. Again the reader either aligns himself against the narrator or with him, but the narrator's ambiguity makes it the reader's decision. Significantly, to align oneself at this stage against the narrator, who has been set up as a socialist, implies a thoroughgoing reworking of a defence for socialism; and even if it is despite all, simply a shuffling of assumptions, this is better than submissive acceptance or rejection. It may also account for the passionate nature of the attacks on the book.[10] The writer compels active response whether the reader likes it or not.

The analysis of the socialist type is followed by a close examination of the party line of socialism itself, and its assumptions as they appear to most people. Strategically the narrator has established the bourgeois socialist as a type with whom he and his reader may identify, and he now withdraws from it to underline the necessity for self-examination. If the reader has not been alert to the two voices throughout, he may feel at this stage that the narrator has left him high and dry – identified with a type that the narrator now abandons without recognizing that this is simply part of the whole process of self-criticism that the narrator is advocating.

The first assumption is the connection between the socialism and machinery, and the second is the negative influence of mechanization. The narrator states clearly that 'my job here is to supply the logical steps that are usually left out' (p. 223). Machinery, as presented by the socialist line, is to make life 'soft and safe'. But is this really desirable? It will end by destroying the current attitudes to both work and play. The following discussion of machinery becomes an interesting analogy for the process of acquiring traditional assumptions. Man begins with an inventive faculty that he wishes to use in order to lighten the workload of other people. Initially, this can be most helpful. But the range of personally executed activity contracts and taste is corrupted. Not that taste is made 'poor', but that people cease to exercise the faculty of choice because their options are increasingly defined for them. Yet the problem lies deeper than this, for machines function automatically. Hence, one is not aware that one has ceased to choose; machines maintain the *status quo* for one. They are in the end drug-like and habit-forming.

Based on the previous discussion the reader can see the implications: in just this way class assumptions become easy ways out, escapes from reality. The interesting juxtaposition of machine-culture with socialism only underlines the process that occurs both overtly in the alliance of the two, and implicitly in the imposition of ideology that a socialist party line carries out. The discussion opened with a description of the Marxist reaction to a 'bourgeois sentimentality' that rejects vulgar materialism. The narrator says:

> Marxists as a rule are not very good at reading the minds of their adversaries. . . Possessing a technique which seems to explain everything,

they do not often bother to discover what is going on inside other people's heads. (p. 219)

While Orwell's view of middle-class Marxism was restricted to a small group of pro-Stalinist intellectuals, the point he makes had wide application. This kind of Marxist, because his assumptions are so total, can be just as sentimental as a bourgeois capitalist: both hide within the illusion of completeness. The narrator goes on to give a specific example of how much Marxist literature is created upon a jargon that maintains assumptions, and that fails to recognize important issues that lie outside.

The interesting aspect of the particular example used is its exposure of the Marxist neglect of a spiritual attitude. In Orwell's view, concentrating on finance, Marxists of his time failed to come to terms with the issues of belief, doubt, faith, loyalty, individuality, and so on that lie beyond, and as Orwell elsewhere notes, that Marx himself found very important. The narrator takes this up in the conclusion to his study by noting that while fascism has a similar interest in machines as socialism, it does not assume that man is without a soul. However, the writer is not condoning fascism: what he is suggesting is that it is far more attractive to the average man because it appears to deal with this aspect. It is also far more dangerous because the manner in which it does so may close the ring of totalitarian control irrevocably tight. The writer suggests that socialism is not only unpopular because it fails to deal with the soul, but that it has a duty to fight totalitarianism by reinstituting the possibility that there are other bases for the evaluation of justice and liberty than an imposed totalitarian control or an unsatisfactory materialist 'fact'. They must first get rid of the materialist domination found in the association of machines with socialism, and, secondly, get rid of the assumption of imposed efficiency, order and reform associated with socialists. In other words, they must destroy the 'types' that apparently define, limit and alienate them from the rest of the populace.

The final chapter begins with a reiteration of the form of the book, the first part describing 'the mess' the country is in, and the second examining why 'decent' people reject the only apparent solution: socialism. The narrator now returns fully to his personal stance and recapitulates the drift of his conclusion to the latter problem, confidently including the reader and often juxtaposing 'we' against 'they', or 'we' against a general 'you'. Assessing his role in writing the book, he concludes that he was able to communicate the poverty and financial crisis of the poor while remaining culturally and socially different. This leads him to suggest that the class issue is being mixed up in and complicates the more immediate problems of poverty and deprivation, that while cultural differences are important and deep-rooted, they should not be allowed to impede pressing financial needs. Cultural and class differences are central and very difficult to solve, but should be separate from financial issues over which the classes could co-operate. If this does not happen the writer suggests that fascism will take over. Whereas socialism will eventually have to face the issues and could tackle them step by step, given willing members of both classes, fascism aims at closing off any assessment of class, and at maintaining the *status quo*.

The only manner in which the writer can conceive of the separation between class and financial problems occurring is through recognition that the classes are different in tradition, that there is not only money but a gap of communication and culture between them. As he has demonstrated, socialism and socialists appear to deny any difference apart from the financial. He repeats that this blindness is strengthened by their propaganda. A vicious circle develops in which propaganda becomes responsible for 'types', people who do not reassess; and they in turn produce more unthinking propaganda to back themselves up. The elements of jargon and cant, the private isolating languages of the propaganda, fundamentally rest on a belief that one has all the answers. For the socialist it often comes down to whether Marx said something or not. If he did, then no further thought, discussion or argument appears necessary. What is being criticized here is not Marxism itself but first, the unthinking turning toward some 'authority' and, second, the blind faith in the absolute nature of language and communication as able to convey unquestioned 'truth'. What is needed instead is 'intelligent propaganda' (p. 262), based on the strategies of self-assessment and discussion that this book has proposed as essential, and that puts forward two main concepts: that 'the interests of all exploited people are the same' and that 'Socialism is compatible with common decency' (pp. 262–3). The 'ists' and the 'isms' should be discarded for a communication between actual people.

Alienation
The strategy of this book, which demonstrates first the breaking down of prejudices about the working class on the part of a middle-class person, and, second, the re-examination by that person of his own middle-class assumptions that could impede socialism coming to the aid of the working class, is so clear and so well-directed that the foreword that the publisher, Victor Gollancz, wrote to the book, appears to indicate a reading of considerable limitation. But this is easy to say only in hindsight. It is reasonable to suggest that most left-wing intellectuals were not aware of the Stalinist atrocities that were occurring, and Gollancz was reading *The Road to Wigan Pier* during the highly emotive time in politics of the early stages of the Spanish Civil War. What is interesting is that most people on both left and right have tended to continue to read the book in this manner, and particularly those on the left have used the reading as the basis for their charges that Orwell undermined the Labour movement in Britain.[11] Gollancz denies that socialists of 'his acquaintance' are jargon-filled: he insists that the writer is not merely a devil's advocate but speaking in his

own person. And most important, he states that the writer simply envisages an 'elemental appeal of "liberty" and "justice" ' (p. xiv), hence disregarding the structure and the ethos of the entire first section with its method for self-assessment and evaluation, and its application to socialism in the second section.

I can reach only three conclusions about such a reading having been arrived at by so many people. The first is that the criticism hit home and they are attempting to evade its implications, and second that Orwell had a reputation for clear straightforward factual documentary that encouraged people to concentrate on the surface of his text; both are inadequate to explain the reaction. I would suggest that the root of the problem lies with the third issue, that in constructing a narratorial ethos out of a generalized character he was asking for too much identification from the reader. A different and possibly more effective strategy might have been to set up two different representatives of the bourgeois socialist, one positive and the other negative, thereby allowing all socialists the possibility of saying, yes it's terrible that that other type does exist but I'm not one of them. However, this would probably have been far too easy an escape route. It is, for example, the strategy behind his early novels. If the reader does not identify with the character, he can with the narrator; and just as there, where a final choice is ambiguous, here, too, reassessment would have been unlikely. The key to this limitation is that the narrator himself superficially appears infallible. In *The Road to Wigan Pier* the personal narrator seems to offer a general stance that he has already achieved, whereas in effect all he has achieved is the strategy.

CHAPTER THREE

Language and Tradition, Criticism and Compromise: *Homage to Catalonia* and *Coming Up for Air*

Homage to Catalonia : Language and Tradition

Another alternative for Orwell could have been to discard types and personae altogether, simply presenting the individual case from different historical perspectives and leaving narratorial fallibility open and overt. The solutions provided would be individual and specific and the reader could choose to identify with them or not. Orwell's next work *Homage to Catalonia*, which restates the concern with communication and culture as the 'gulf of language and tradition'; does exactly this. And the change of strategy is probably at the root of a clearer stance. In contrast to *The Road to Wigan Pier*, *Homage to Catalonia* normally receives acclaim and praise,[1] yet the writer is criticizing many of the same activities as before. It is possible that the overwhelming tide of reassessment concerning the background to and events of the Spanish Civil War, has made it easier to accept the criticism in *Homage to Catalonia*, just as it is possible that the continued antagonism to *The Road to Wigan Pier* reflects the continuing relevance of its criticisms.

The initial chapter is concerned once more with presenting a past and a present narrator, but here neither are 'types'. Few generalizations are made and the characters are created either from description, if directly experienced, or from the gradual build-up of observations. But first, the reader is plunged into an anecdote, a complete analogy for the situation in which the narrator finds himself. The book begins: 'In the Lenin Barracks in Barcelona, the day before I joined the militia, I saw an Italian militia-man standing in front of the officer's table' (p. 1).It is an abrupt start to the book. There is no introductory prelude for the 'I' who writes. The reader is thrust into a situation which he is supposed, in some way, to recognize: the detail is so concrete it assumes our familiarity with it. Further, the relaxed movement of the sentence from balanced phrase to balanced phrase to lengthy clause, indicates the conversational pace of a narrator confident of our attention. The scene has been established through both immediacy of detail and a careful relaxed detachment from it. Such internal tension will define all that follows.

Slowly the narrator builds a series of descriptive statements about the Italian soldier that indicate an elusiveness about the situation, an inability to explain the precise connection between the experience and his response. The indefinable but charged reaction culminates with 'Queer, the affection you can feel for a stranger!' (p. 2), which reaches out to include the reader.

The moment is summarized in the comment about 'bridging the gulf between language and tradition', and moves on to distance the narrator by way of an explanation of his final response, ending with the detached general statement, 'One was always making contacts of that kind in Spain' (p. 2). Then, as if making the progression from a past to a present voice, the narrator specifically states that he has begun with this anecdote because the man has stuck in his memory; he 'typifies' the time and is bound in with the memories of red flags, trains going to the front, war-stricken front line towns and muddy trenches. It is the strategic difference between the type who statically 'stands for' certain standards and attitudes and this type which comes to present and indicate an activity, that will inform the development of the text in *Homage to Catalonia*. The reader is left with the experience of that odd tension between immediacy and detachment, to wonder why this particular anecdote should tie together all the other memories of the front; and the elusiveness of the experience, the questions that it raises, is a fundamental activity of the stance in this writing.

The main strategy that the writer uses to generate a stance is based on two differing narratorial voices that are carefully established in the first five chapters. Initially, the narrator anchors the story firmly in the past, saying that it occurred 'less than seven months ago as I write', but having done so a past narratorial voice is allowed to proceed. In the interruptions he says that he 'did not understand, in some ways I did not even like it' (p. 4), or more precisely 'Also I believed that things were as they appeared' (p. 4). The movement from optimistic fervour to criticism alerts the reader to a duality of naïve commitment yet clear detachment in the narrative. The duality is primarily one of chronological difference. There are two narrative voices: the earlier, immediately experiencing voice of the past, and the older, more reflective voice of the present. Yet the past narrator also observes. He builds scenes with a straightforward sentence construction, internal repetition of words and few connectives, that creates a stasis, a picture, not a process. Important to this technique are the adjectives of red, and red-and-black – the colours of the Communist and anarchist flags and scarves – once mentioned, they clarify each street situation without going into political explanations, and follow up the implication of political difference contained in the description of the Italian soldier as looking like 'an anarchist, though as likely as not he was a Communist' (p. 1).

In contrast, the older, more experienced present narrator is explanatory and cautious, but he realizes that he alone cannot fully present the past without our losing a sense of the experience. So the past narrator exists in tension with him, generating ambiguities and paradoxes. The reader is led to trust the past voice, which carries the burden of the narration because of his detailed description and his fervour. There is an air of innocence surrounding him, yet he is undoubtedly ignorant. The lack of knowledge, combined with innocence, paradoxically creates for the reader an elusiveness similar to the response to the Italian soldier and points to the past narrator's inability to define the situation. Neither the reader nor the past narrator can understand the situation properly. Yet the more experienced present narrator knows that he cannot explain it without involving the reader in the experiential process that the past narrator underwent.

While the dual perspective is being established the text moves into a pattern of background description, generalizing comment, and concrete experience on the part of the past narrator. He moves through topics of the physical situation, the army conditions, the state of discipline, and finally, the atmosphere of humanity. Each concrete situation defines another area of concern, and posits a basis for the reader's identification. Yet he also talks about the friends he makes, the fact that frustrations with individual attitudes are more than compensated for by the humour and enthusiasm of the men and women he meets. The topics are presented, not defined or explained. The reader is not to know their future significance. Similarly, the final scene of excitement as the men pack into a train leaving for the front is interwoven with the images of red and black flags, focusing ambiguously on the 'political commissar standing beneath a huge rolling red banner and making us a speech in Catalan' (p.16), and fellow militia-man Williams's wife who gives them wine and sausage just as they leave. The implications of contradiction and conflict attached to the vagueness of the commissar, the fact that he cannot be understood but appears impressive, in contrast to the concrete nature of Williams's wife bringing that sausage 'which tastes of soup and give [sic] you diarrhoea' (p. 16), are hinted at in a comment from the older present narrator: 'How natural it all seemed then; how remote and improbable now!' But his stance of refusing to explain without providing the experience, leaves the picture as ambiguous for a first time reader as for an initially experiencing past narrator.

The images of flags, trains going to the front, front-line towns and muddy trenches which the encounter with the Italian soldier coalesced in the mind of the more experienced narrator, appear general and arbitrary. Only gradually does the reader become aware that each image provides a focus for each of the first three chapters. Similarly, the topics of terrain, army life, equipment and romance, are to establish the pattern for story development in each of these chapters. It is as if the narrator is creating a series of 'takes' on a group of interrelated positions at four different historical moments. The changes, shifts and discrepancies between them are part of the learning process of the past narrator; and just as he cannot encompass them until he assumes the reflective voice of the older, present narrator, neither does the reader appreciate their pattern until much later on in the work.

The second chapter is a complete contrast to the first as it moves into the description of the war-struck towns of the front. The past narrator takes up the stance of an observing 'I', whose position is continually undercut by reversals in his expectation or by ambiguities in judgement that occasionally proceed from the older, present narrator. He mentions the fascists in the ambiguous statement that 'all the best matadors were Fascists', implying at first a cruelty of manner but second, an intrinsic connection and importance to Spain as a country. When he finally shoots at a Fascist soldier in the conclusion of the chapter, the man is not an enemy but 'a human being' (p. 26). The detachment of the younger narrator's vision is continually jeopardized by similar realizations of ignorance, and the uneasy balance of past tense verbs reporting situations 'now' reflects his confusion. The tension is presented as an individual response to the war, but it is also connected to wider external issues through the various topics described: for example, the arbitrary decision that assigns weapons and houses to people, whatever their ability to use them. Each topic contains an implicit criticism but with an indecisiveness of judgement arising from lack of knowledge. The reader is left outside simply watching the play between detachment and involvement.

The final scene in chapter 2 which presents the narrator on active duty, is narrated in a melodramatic overdone manner reminiscent of previous untrustworthy, unknowing narrators. This too concludes ambiguously, when shots are fired over the outpost, with the past narrator crying 'Alas! I ducked' (p. 26), and the present narrator then reflecting that 'the movement appears to be instinctive, and almost everybody does it at least once'. The reader is left to sit back in judgement on the past narrator because the perspective from which we should be viewing him is not indicated. Just as with the first chapter, the reader is placed in the position of this past narrator, with restricted knowledge and little guidance about how he should respond to the situation.

In the third chapter, the past narrator moves out of the confused ambiguity of his initial position and into a more confident reported past. He is actively experiencing the war and from this perspective his voice is perceived as valid. Most of all he is provided with a sense of humour about the situation. Humour indicates a self-possession in detachment from events, a separation in which the speaker can place himself in perspective. The result is an impression of balance and while the past narrator continues to present life in the trenches he can use the validity of this voice to involve his audience by familiarization. Yet when he moves from description to reflections on the meaning of the military issues, the tone becomes once more melodramatic as he gazes 'passionately' or marvels at the 'futility of it all'.

It is the definition of these military elements by the topic of human relations which reintroduces the narrator's ambiguity. The comparison between the Popular Army and the militia is probably the most telling example. The Popular Army functions as does the British Army on the basis of a hierarchy, but the militia has a 'social equality between officers and men' (p. 32). The result in the militia is confusion. The narrator says that 'at first sight the state of affairs at the front horrified me' (p. 33). The past, experiencing narrator summarizes much of the confusion of these early chapters repeating that 'the apparent chaos, the general lack of training, the fact that you often had to argue for five minutes before you could get an order obeyed, appalled and infuriated me' (p. 35). However, the present narrator continues with a more detached assessment of the situation. Against the claim that discussion 'just won't work', he places the statement that it is 'in the long run' (p. 34) the more effective discipline: ' "Revolutionary" discipline depends on political consciousness – on an understanding of *why* orders must be obeyed' (pp. 34–5), and this takes time. Conventional military training into automatic obedience also takes time, and its army is based on fear of punishment for desertion rather than on the loyalty of the revolutionary army. Hence, the latter is more likely to remain firm, as the militia did while the Popular Army was preparing itself.

The past narrator comes to the situation with the assumptions of the British Army. As a result he is at first confused by apparent disorder. But the present narrator implies that such humanity, although frustrating, is more rewarding even in practical terms than the efficiency of a conscript system. The barrier between the past narrator and his army comrades is at first presented as one of nationality, an incomprehension between the English and the Spanish. In the long run it can be surmounted only by discussion, not by the fear generated by a hierarchy. The final barrier, by implication, is the military war between themselves and their enemies, which can only be resolved by such discussion. The ambiguity of the similarity between the fascists and socialists is shown to lie in the military nature of their confrontation, which precludes any discussion.

The past narrator can speak with confidence of the military aspects because they are to hand and clear. But when he considers the reasons that the democratic militia system functions so well in the end, he becomes confused and frustrated, and the present narrator takes over and explains. His ignorance is that of 'political consciousness' which requires understanding, not orders; and in terms of the specific politics of the war itself the past narrator is shown to be just as ignorant. The more experienced narrator comments that 'the stagnation on the Aragon front had political causes of which I knew nothing at the time' (p. 40). In the end his earlier political ignorance makes his military knowledge questionable.

The following chapter makes more obvious the transition from the military to the political war, by examining the day to day military routine in contrast with the propaganda efforts being made by both sides. It is left to the past narrator to recount much of the routine. At this stage he is barely distinguishable from the present narrator, and when the subject of the propaganda war arises the present narrator moves in almost imperceptibly with a comment placing the topic in hindsight. He comments on the ineffectiveness of the military war and the important role of propaganda, summarizing the suspicions of the previous chapter and underlining the susceptibility of a conscript army to overt persuasion. Interestingly, he bases his condoning of the propaganda technique on the fact that it is a recognized and accepted tactic for deception in war. Recognition should alert each individual to the tactic and it is up to him to judge for himself whether the enemy's accounts of hot 'buttered toast', being given over a propaganda megaphone, are to be trusted or not.

The last recounted event in which the fascists celebrate the fall of Malaga with an undisciplined shooting at the narrator's outpost, fuses the physical activity of the war with the propaganda issues, and indicates the uncertain meeting of the two in newspaper reports of manoeuvres. In the papers this brief fascist celebration becomes an all-out attack. But whereas the soldiers involved are aware of the probability of deception, the implication is that propaganda going beyond the front lines to civilians, is playing on people's ignorance and is ethically unsound. The brief fusion of voices then separates as the reader learns of the first doubts to enter the past narrator's mind concerning 'the rights and wrongs [about the war which] had seemed so beautifully simple' (p. 57). We are reminded that the present narrator has recently left Spain possibly not to return, and the implication is that he has done so because of these doubts germinating in the mind of his past self. However, neither self is portrayed negatively. The tension between an experienced and fully detached present narrator and an ambiguously involved yet observing past narrator, is not a battle between the two, but a tension in the reader as he tries to come to terms with which point of view to accept, and the way in which the one finally becomes the other. The writer's strategy has been to encourage identification with the experienced, present narrator, with the result that the reader becomes anxious to discover what the past voice learned to make him change his mind. But the writer also knows that simply stating the information gained would not help toward an understanding of the process. The reader also has to learn from experience, not only from the narrator, but also from his own experience within the text. Taken as a whole, this interaction between writer and reader, generated by the strategy based on the two narrators, describes the new stance Orwell is developing.

Chapter 5 provides a transitional movement away from the initial description, toward the events that transform the past narrator into the present narrator. The stances of each narrator now become important in themselves, as do the strategies that maintain or change them. And it is the reader's involvement in and understanding of the narratorial rhetorics that provides an analogy for the writer's new stance. In this light the choice the reader is then presented with, to 'skip' the political parts of the following narrative, involves not only a decision about whether we are willing to learn or not, but also whether we are willing to interact with the writing, make our own assessments. The present narrator explicitly states that: 'If you are not interested in the horrors of party politics, please skip ; I am trying to keep the political parts of this narrative in separate chapters for precisely that purpose' (p. 58). Yet he is discussing them because it is impossible to speak about the war 'from a purely military angle' (p. 59). This said, it is difficult for any reader having picked up the off-hand criticism in the previous chapter about the obvious and finally ineffectual nature of the military war, to dismiss the study that ensues. Chapter 3 stated the political and chapter 4 the propagandic nature of the war. Effectively, if the reader chooses not to read chapter 5, he remains with the initially limited past narrator and with the physical events of the military war, which describe but do not attempt to understand or resolve the conflict. On the other hand if we choose to read this chapter, then the emerging change from past to present narrator can be seen in its educational process.

In a chapter primarily dealing with propaganda, the present narrator has to be most attentive to the manner in which he is presenting his material and the reader has consciously to be aware of the possibility of being persuaded against his will. The narrator carefully interpolates the entire structure of the story and his relationship to it in a brief commentary on the three stages of his experience: active duty, riots in Barcelona, and his escape from Spain pursued by the police. In doing so he defines his stance in an unmistakable and pointed fashion. In terms of presentation he becomes detached, highly detailed, factual and closely rationally logical. At all times the reader is encouraged to follow the logic. One example is the statement that 'the Communist parties of all countries can be taken as carrying out Russian policy' (p. 69). This is led into by a brief historical analysis which is set up in opposition to a prevailing opinion. Having made his personal statement the narrator immediately backs it up with three solid reasons, and refers out to other comments in the text and to footnotes which verify it. The process of rational proof stands clear to be evaluated by the reader himself, and indeed he may reject it. The essence of the strategy in this chapter is to underline the fact that the past narrator would not have agreed with much of what the more experienced, present narrator says. Since the reader's identification is mainly with the experience of the past narrator, he is torn between going along with that earlier judgement, and an awareness that the present narrator has learned something that invalidates the judgement. Indeed, as if recognizing the difficulty of agreement without practical experience, the narrator refers continually to future experience which will bear out the rational logic. The effect is to leave the reader partially enlightened; in effect to place him once more in the position of the past narrator at this time.

The main reason proffered for the past narrator's ignorance, is his failure to examine the political situation personally, and his dependence on the newspaper interpretations of the war. Coming so soon after the examples of newspaper distortion in chapter 4, the reader is prepared for the critique of journalism in chapter 5. Yet it is surprisingly strong in such a cool account, indicating the force of emotion that the present narrator feels. Here, almost uniquely, he lapses into an inclusive 'we' and personal 'I' as he castigates the misrepresentation of both the Communist and capitalist English language presses. It is left without doubt, however, that the past narrator was at fault, that he was personally responsible for assessment: he 'accepted' their version, and 'had made no attempt to understand' (p. 59) the reality.

The present narrator then illustrates the first recognition by his past self of the political situation. The litter of initials surrounding the different factions at first appears meaningless to the reader; gradually he separates them out and places them in an historical, political and finally propagandic context. In an attempt to clarify why he opted for communism the present narrator proceeds with an analysis of the political and propaganda division his past self was faced with. The Communist Party defines its policies in terms of a party 'line' to which it expects clear adherence. The POUM and the anarchists by contrast have little or no 'line' and function by discussion of separate and individual issues, which tends to divide them and slow down decision-making. That the Communists were more organized, efficient and seemed to be getting on with the war was enough to convince the past narrator that theirs was a better policy, indeed the speaker notes that 'it was easy to see why' he preferred it.

The comparison is then extended out to the respective newspapers of each party. Against the earlier criticism of newspapers, the narrator's accusation that the Communist Party papers were as dishonest as the capitalist press, carries immense weight. It is explained that to enforce a party 'line' such dishonesty is necessary since a completely open paper would allow contradictory opinions not dealt with by the 'line' and the point is reinforced by comparing Communist with imperialist propaganda. The narrator begins with the statement that the alternative POUM and anarchist papers were 'almost blameless'. Lest this appear too favouring he adds the codicil that after all they had 'much smaller opportunities' to exploit; and finally this too is carefully undercut by recounting the Communist suppression of anarchist papers. The method of continual undercutting of statements ends by creating an impression of fair-minded judgement, despite the heavy weighting in favour of the anarchists.

Nevertheless, at the time the narrator took neither political viewpoint very seriously; the phrases 'I grasped . . . I did not grasp' (p. 86) indicate his position of ambivalence. It is of note that he says he remained ignorant because of his very isolation in the POUM, which never insisted on the acceptance of a certain 'line'. Among the anarchists, it is the individual's responsibility to educate himself; he must not wait to be told what to think. The present narrator goes further in his explanation by noting that perhaps the Communist policy was not suitable for winning the war. Not only is there the questionable use of hierarchy in military matters which has been shown to alienate the average person, but also the Communist 'line' of a 'war for democracy' is so definite and narrow that the propaganda will be difficult to change as the war progresses.

The choices that the present narrator sees in hindsight are divided between a conservative, Communist, hierarchical party based on party 'lines', a party elite, and an enforcing of both military participation and adherence to opinion; and a revolutionary anarchist, populist party based on discussion, popular support and individual responsibility in terms of active duty and opinion. The manner in which I have laid out the options is crude for the sake of clarity. The present narrator is immensely skilful in undercutting any notions of far-fetched idealism surrounding the anarchist party. Not only are his suggestions as to the anarchists' effect on the war considered and practical, there is continually present the knowledge that the earlier narrator favoured the Communist line, therefore appealing to Communist readers and undercutting the argument that he did not consider it.[2] To take a more distanced perspective on the activity of the present narrator in this chapter, the reader may infer from the ease with which the past narrator first accepted the newspaper's version and then the Communist line that we as readers are being warned against simply accepting the anarchist line presented here. To a great extent the more experienced narrator indicates his stance, his personal position and opinion, and does so overtly without insisting on agreement. The process is strengthened by his avoidance of any condemnation of the past narrator, and a sympathetic presentation that encourages the reader's continued identification with the younger, past narrator rather than the present narrator. Of course this is not entirely altruistic, it is necessary if we are to continue to experience the educative process of that earlier self.

The following three chapters, 6 to 8, plunge back into the military war as the narrative creates a strategy for connecting the earlier ignorant narrator with the later politically knowledgeable voice, and one is returned to the now familiar pattern of the topics. Yet although the discussion in chapter 5, is never referred to openly and the present narrator entirely excludes himself from the narrative, one is aware of a change in stance on the part of the past narrator that is indicated by the changes in the techniques of his response. He is far more personal in his comments, mentioning his wife for the first time; he is more reflective and finally more evaluative. He does not simply accept explanations or remain detached from apparent chaos; he actively assesses on the basis of his own experience. Whereas in the past the discussion of the human factor was invariably taken over by the present narrator, here the past narrator takes it on himself. It is interesting that this time he focuses on the plight of the Andalusian peasants in the war, and the changes that the anarchists had brought to the farming system. The section is a physical illustration of problems brought about by the lack of an efficient 'line' or policy, yet overriding the problems is the invariable 'friendliness' of these people: again underlining the implication that despite their apparent short-term failure, the anarchists were creating long-term success and good will. But the past narrator does not in this case logically progress to this conclusion; he simply observes the actual events.

By failing to explicitly point the analogy between actual events and previous theory, the past narrator shifts some of the involvement in the narrative onto the reader. In this chapter the reader is far more caught up with the experience than on previous occasions. At this stage there should be little need to explain to the reader, so the narrator may present a visual or audial image and leave the note of its relevance open for us to complete. And increasingly there is a strange juxtaposition of images as if the narrator is intent on making us connect the two: churchyards, human excrement and rats conflate together; batteries bring to mind the 'picture of a fat man hitting a golf-ball' (p. 111), torpedoes are pub darts, machine guns are 'like the fluttering of wings' (p. 112) and concrete barricades are reinforced with old iron bedsteads. These images serve the double purpose of shocking at the same time as asking for a response of understanding. They bring home the violence, while at the same time they request a perspective on it.

The static tension of chapter 6 is broken immediately by the opening to chapter 7. For the first time at the front, the expectation that nothing will happen is subverted. Here there really is action. Once again, although the political issues of chapter 5 are not overtly mentioned, the essential strategy for this narrative is to portray all the chaotic elements in the militia actually

functioning in war, and to present the POUM as a respectable armed force
with conventional attitudes to loyalty and courage, and with effective
discipline despite their unconventional approach to hierarchies in the
ranks.[3] What he is also doing is clarifying the role of experience in the
learning process. In observing the past narrator, one can see that the more
he becomes involved in action the less time he gives to reflection and
assessment. Action and experience have been important themes
throughout the early novels and in *The Road to Wigan Pier*, yet have never
proved entirely satisfactory; and here one finds a possible key to their
limitation. There must be a balance between action and reflection; personal
experience on its own is not enough, neither is the hypothetical logic of
ideology. Just as the middle-class narrator in *Wigan Pier* experienced
poverty but then had to go away and put that experience in perspective, so
here the reader sees dramatized both the necessity for and the imbalance
caused by action alone. It is an interesting point to note because Orwell is
often accused of being anti-intellectual, too pragmatic. Rather, he is
practical, and afraid of an imbalance in intellectualism which can easily
move away from the actual, cease to assess, and become fixed into rigid
standards.

In military action, the past narrator is in his element. The observer in him
is gradually subordinated to the participator; and the detailed explanation
gives way to reporting, transcribing of sounds and immediate images as he
attempts to make more immediate the experience. The narrator introduces
the military action of the storming of a Fascist parapet, with the naïve
imagery of flashing bayonets, indicating the purity and curious sterility of
the military. Suspense begins to speed the narration, and it finally develops
into a clear relentless sequential logic as he reports the tactics and events of
the manoeuvre. The actions eventually take over altogether until the
parapet is taken. Afterwards, a gradual lessening into reflective prose takes
place, and fluctuates with action more and more frequently toward the
conclusion of the chapter. As it does so, the present narrator momentarily
surfaces with the reflective prose, reintroducing not only the tension
between knowledge and ignorance, but also one between remembering
acts and experiencing them.

In order to recognize this contrast the reader is forced into an actively
ironic assessment of the military expertise of the past narrator. Such an
ironic stand is further required by an earlier comment on the political
ignorance of the Andalusian peasant farmers (p. 104). Against the previous
political background the reader recognizes the irony of their ignorance,
since they are the people to be most fundamentally affected by the changes
brought about by the war; yet the past narrator is identified with them in
their ignorance, and the reader by corollary moves into an ironic
assessment of him that underlines both the futility and reward of the
experience. In chapter 6, the past narrator simply observed the physical

effects of Anarchism on the farmers; next he presented with overt comment the anarchist militia in action; here in chapter 7, he explicitly lives out the anarchist ideal of equality, covering the theoretical discussion with personal experience that subtly alters it, lifts it from a potentially rigid approach into a valid means of establishing stance. Each of the three incidents in these two chapters is one of the future experiences referred to in chapter 5 as the concrete basis for present knowledge. The reader also has to experience them in order to understand that knowledge and appreciate the basis for hope in the situation. The past and present narrators approach each other through this tension of memory but remain separated by their differing experience of war: the futility of the past and the hope of the present.

During chapter 8 the reader is encouraged to actively identify and experience, by the present narrator's construction of further analogies that we have to complete. And it is the series of analogies (pp. 141–3), which are based on the four topics of surroundings, militia, supplies, and humanity, that forms the memory link between past and present and establishes once more the identification with the past narrator. Each analogy increases in its resistance to interpretation. The first is simply a series of pictures reported in the present. Their significance is never stated. One can only infer a quality of human aspiration from the isolated image of the narrator picking rosemary with bullets whistling overhead. The second paragraph presents an incident in itself, once more presented without explicit point as the head of the narrator's unit thumbs his nose at a Fascist bugle-call. Again one can only infer its qualities of courage and humour. The longer incident that follows concerning a bomb attack on the unit's cook-house, contains greater story interest yet points to no clear meaning further than the comic ambivalence involved in a tension between fear of hunger and of death. Yet each of these does indicate possible significance for an active reader. By contrast, the final paragraph re-presents a concrete memory of sentries from opposing fronts singing at dawn (p. 143). The elusiveness of this final incident points the underlying theme of similarity between fascist and socialist/anarchist, which generates at the same time a sense both of the military futility and of human hope.

Throughout, the quality of humanity and individual freedom has been associated with POUM and anarchist policy. While the similarity of these two human beings at the front betokens a futility in the war itself, without this particular war freedom would be available to neither. Seeing the war simply in terms of 'killing a Fascist', as the past narrator has stated his position to be, does generate futility. But seeing it as a human endeavour for community, brotherhood and individual rights makes it generate some kind of hope. Similarly, futility is at the centre of the Communist attempts to make the war one against fascism rather than a revolutionary war for liberty and equality. The limiting rigidity of this 'line' connects the

Communists with the Fascists, and the futility that results eventually aids their enemies. To assess, understand and agree with the position presented by this analogy, the reader is actively involving himself in the theoretical position stated by the narrator in chapter 5. And it is particularly important to note that this has been effected not primarily by the strategies of information or rational logic, but by analogies, small stories in which the reader could participate, interact with the writing and come to personal evaluations and assessments. The past narrator's experience becomes our own, and both are at the base of future knowledge. The chapter has moved the reader from an intellectual identification with the present narrator to a recognition of the past experiences behind it, and from an experiential identification with the past narrator to an understanding of the basis for present knowledge.

The chapter concludes with the irony of 'And after that the trouble began' (p. 143): after the military war the real issues arise, and chapter 9 carefully reintroduces the politics and the propaganda that are the primary concern. Significantly, it opens with the apparently irrelevant image of a train journey from Mandalay. Just as with all the writer's previous train journeys, the carriage allows one to preserve one's initial 'atmosphere intact' until one arrives. Here it maintains the cocoon of military knowledge that encloses the past narrator, right into Barcelona where it is abruptly shattered. While the reader may now perceive a connection, the past and present narrators are still divided: that final image of the two sentries was still a futile one to the past narrator however hopeful to the present. But the past narrator is now also the learning narrator of chapters 5 to 8, rather than the initial naïve voice. He refers back to incidents that have occurred within the narrative, reflects on them and assesses. In doing so he encourages the reader to identify with him, and the reintroduction to Barcelona underlines the strategy.

The past narrator records his second experience of Barcelona in an objective, factual and far less impressionistic manner than did his original voice. However, it is still left to the present narrator to posit explanation, and so the reader has to realize once more the continued fallibility of the past voice. That we here receive another report of Barcelona and that it is so different not only in detail but in narratorial voice, indicates by analogy the discrepancy between the actual and the real situation that the past narrator is unaware of. Increasingly the present narrator indicates how easily the implications of the actual are missed. Almost as if by chance he notes that if he had not been in Barcelona at that particular moment 'I might have accepted the official version of it as truthful' (p. 156). Here he refers to the 'street fighting', and allusions to this incident crop up enigmatically three times during the chapter but are not pursued. In doing so, they create a suspense and a feeling of bewilderment that parallels the distraction and vagueness of the past narrator's judgement. Not only he, but we, are still unaware of the full picture. Even if we know the historical background of the street fighting, which probably means that we are also aware of its contentious interpretations, we are here left completely uncertain about the narrator's attitude toward it.

From this moment the present narrator returns to pick up the political argument where he left off in chapter 5. He examines once again the political lines and their control by party propaganda, but here the focus is on the difficulty of uncovering the truth even when one is actually on the scene. The control of propaganda by the press leads to uncertainty and vagueness concerning events, and in re-presenting the political background, the present narrator tries hard to achieve an even-handedness. But the strategy is to provide a prolegomenon to the following chapters in which the past narrator discovers far more about the real situation, and begins to realize that one has an active individual responsibility to search the implications out for oneself.

To begin with, the past narrator extensively reconstructs his experience of the factional street fighting in Barcelona. The tension between detailed observation of physical events and an inability to assess them is set forth in the juxtaposition of a clear reporting style and a personal confusion and vagueness. However, implicit in the description is commentary from the present narrator, which is only recognizable if the reader actively picks out images and concerns that that narrator has previously employed. An example of such assessment is found in the description of the red and red-and-black flags. Taken simply as observation on the part of the past narrator it merely provides a resonance with the first chapter that underlines the changes in Barcelona. But set against the extensive political discussion about the differences between anarchist and Communist, it is a clear, analogical, guide to potential friction between the two.

The reader is here left to take up a responsibility to learning entirely on his own, and it is a learning based not upon fact or observation, but upon the analogical activity of reading, prefigured in the ironic conflation of the Andalusians with the naïve narrator, and in the series of incomplete images that defined the military war. A further analogy is set up around Kopp, the leader of his POUM militia unit, as the narrator uses his description of Kopp's actions to indicate the POUM role in the entire situation. Here the reader has few resonances to work with, and is thrust into a more immediate and testing activity of reading. There follows an extensive study of the role of propaganda in the street-fighting events. What is important here is that it is the past not the present narrator who is involved in the discussion, and he suggests that ignorance of the true events was encouraged by biased newspaper reports attempting to control the external and internal reaction to the situation. Gradually he becomes aware of the minor ways in which the POUM militia is being suppressed, and at the same time becomes conscious not only of the ignorance created by the newspapers, but also of their active distortion. The reader is referred back to the contrast between a justified war propaganda which is openly employed and of which every soldier is aware, and newspaper propaganda which purports to be objective and truthful and which is therefore morally unsound when it distorts. In the one case conscious coercion to choice is employed, and in the other an unconscious deprivation of choice aims to define each situation for the individual. Unawareness of propaganda leaves one open to manipulation, and also open to being overwhelmed by physical detail. One is the result of allowing someone to provide one's standards for one, and the other a result of forgetting how to create standards for oneself. The end is a world in which one feels ineffectual and lost, which carries on in disregard of the individual, subjecting him to a fear and terror which leaves him powerless.

At the same time, the narrator has to be extraordinarily careful about his stance of presentation and throughout the awakening of consciousness he restrains himself from overt comments on the situation. Reports of the effects of newspaper rumour substituting for truth are immediately followed by concrete incidents (p. 183); similarly statements about his own ignorance are not evaluated but simply illustrated with examples (p. 175). For the reader there are no conclusions or explanations. We may approach an assessment by actively recognizing implicit references to the attitudes of the present narrator, but for the most part, we reach the point of the past narrator's education through an account of his experiences.

Finally, it is the censorship of the anarchist newspaper as 'Fascist', but not of the Communist press, that clinches the past narrator's awareness of the political situation. The detachment that awareness of newspaper propaganda makes possible allows him to become more politically aware. Further, as he earlier notes, 'I realized – though owing to my political ignorance, not so clearly as I ought to have done . . .' (p. 190), there is a responsibility involved. He has blundered on knowledge by chance and circumstance, but the enormity of the implications of ignorance forces a need for the active pursuit of truth onto him.

Having realized his ignorance and also its dependence on an uncritical acceptance of propaganda, the past narrator who came to Spain simply to observe and with no more political consciousness than a desire to kill fascists, becomes one with the present narrator recognizing that such a stance is not good enough. One has an individual responsibility to counteract the 'horrible atmosphere produced by fear, suspicion, hatred, censored newspapers . . .' (p. 197), by aligning oneself with a party on a basis of active consideration, not happenstance, and by contradicting 'many of the lies' (p. 200) despite personal limitations. In other words, 'helplessness' and 'ineffectualness' are evasions and escapes. One has to attempt to participate even if it is only in a limited way. The presentation of the experience has been private; the past narrator has merely illustrated his chance encounter with the actual situation. To conclude, he tests the reader again, telling us that we may skip the following chapter if we are not interested in politics, but that 'it is necessary to establish the truth, so far as it is possible' (p. 200). We too are included in the assumption of this responsibility, and unlike the earlier invitation to 'skip' the politics it is far more difficult to evade the implications of doing so.

Truth and Evaluation : convention, discussion and allegory

Chapters 6 to 10 have concentrated on exploring the strategies that restricted the stance of the past narrator, but once the narrators fuse into the present stance the writing shifts its emphasis onto the strategies that maintain the positive activity of that stance. At the same time it throws forward the elements of the writer's stance as a whole, and focuses on broader questions of politics and literature. Fittingly, chapter 11 turns from the private to the public as the narrator pursues his responsibility to truth. The chapter examines how people may approach not objectivity but personal accuracy, and why it is essential for them to attempt to do so. Yet it begins with a statement from the now combined voices of past and present narrators, that:

> It will never be possible to get a completely accurate and unbiased account of the Barcelona fighting because the necessary records do not exist. Future historians will have nothing to go upon except a mass of accusations and party propaganda. (p. 201)

From the beginning the narrator says that his report will be extremely limited, but he also feels it his responsibility to contradict those lies that he can. His personal stance throughout is a combination of first person comment and third person reporting. It parallels, but from a single perspective, the duality of the voices of past and present narrators. The third person reporter is consistently detached, non-evaluative, and detailed. He provides the now familiar techniques of verification in using direct quotations, footnotes, concrete examples, rational logic, historical background and reports from external sources.

By contrast, the first person voice always stresses the impossibility of telling the absolute truth. It uses qualifiers such as 'as far as I know', or 'roughly speaking'; it downplays its factual position noting 'I must inevitably have made mistakes of fact, not only here, but in other parts of this narrative' (p. 214). The voice always points to private intervention, sometimes merely prefacing a remark with 'My own opinion is . . .' (p. 205), and at others overtly stating: 'I warn everyone against my bias, and I warn everyone against my mistakes. Still, I have done my best to be honest' (p. 215). The end result is not an undercutting of validity, but rather the opposite. In admitting his limitation and stressing the impossibility of achieving absolute truth, he strengthens our trust in his aspiration to that truth.⁴ In the end this aspiration is what he is trying to emphasize as the basis for any attempt at description; and further, it provides the background for evaluation. Unlike the past narrator alone this voice does not state its judgements within the context of private definition. It underlines the fact that absolute judgement is not possible, but personal assessment is essential in approaching any valid consensus of opinion.

Appendix II The background material that is being discussed concerns the propaganda campaign against the anarchists by the international and Communist press. As the press attitude to the POUM role in the fighting is studied, the narrator sets up implications that he then reverses; he introduces doubts that are shown to be unfounded. For example, he suggests that the Communists may have planned the street fighting themselves, a suggestion that the reader easily accepts at this stage, but then goes on to say 'I do not believe it was . . .' (p. 210). Sometimes, as in the case of the newspaper accusations that the POUM was a trotskyist organization, we are initially left to infer the effects; but when the narrator then goes through them himself, and exposes the extent of the faulty logic, the reader may be taken aback at the amount he has missed. In all cases we are encouraged to actively assess by a narrator who sets up difficulties in significance that keep us alert to the extent and maintenance of our concentration. The corollary is that the narrator himself takes on an aura of immense awareness. The reader comes to trust the depth of his understanding for it always appears to be one step ahead of him, yet is never dictatorial or authoritative. Some critics, however, read this as a trick.⁵

Having established his own credibility, the narrator then moves on to criticize the international and Communist press. He notes that an English reporter left early when he should have still been making 'serious inquiries'. Like the earlier past narrator he uncritically 'accepted the official version . . . without sufficient verification' (p. 229), is 'simply repeating what he has been told and, since it fits in with the official version, is not questioning it' (p. 229). Just as the narrator had been ignorant and at the mercy of manipulation by the Ministry of Propaganda, so this journalist is ignorant of the realities of the situation. The key criticism comes with the narrator's condemnation of the Communist manipulation of the charge of 'Trotskyism' for their own reasons. The essence of his criticism is that Communist propaganda functions from an 'air of authority' that never bases itself in actual evidence, only in 'unsupported statements in the Communist press' (p. 235) which were the 'efforts of somebody's imagination', but the Communist Party can successfully use this tactic because it requires adherence to the party line. As a result it controls the contents of newspaper reports which are the main conveyors of information, and it denies any contradictory examination of its opinions. In other words it attempts to construct and promulgate absolute unquestionable versions of a situation, which versions come to stand for truth. The narrator does not simply make this accusation, but indicates the negative effects of such a strategy. He points to similar instances of this 'authoritative air' which have proved detrimental to the war.

One must admit that absolute truth is not achievable, only approachable, and that approach to it can only be made through a consensus of responsible individuals actively attempting the clearest form of accuracy, description and reasonable evaluation they can achieve. And the analogy for his conclusion lies in the narrator's personal experience. He has attempted objectivity yet failed. But his version has been rejected by the Communist and international press not for its failure but for its attempt to question. Failure to achieve truth and the process of questioning are linked: ignorance encourages acceptance of other people's truths which in turn encourages self-satisfaction and further ignorance. But the paradox of the introductory parable to the book is that unless you admit your fallibility you cannot even approach truth. In the attempt and failure to present truth, one achieves the only truth of which one is capable.

The two approaches are studies in positive and negative rhetorical stance. The Communist Party line is based on unquestioning acceptance, adherence and obedience. It defines the listener's world for him, not allowing personal evaluation beyond the boundaries of that world. Further, it combines the opposites of a negative rhetorical stance by being both totally controlling, yet also totally arbitrary and able to shift the 'line' at any time. On the other hand, the narrator is suggesting that positive rhetorical stance depends on 'exhaustive discussion', individual responsibility to choose and evaluate. Such discussion is often untidy and ineffective in the short term, but ultimately creates the necessary foundation for human interaction based on trust. In the light of these conclusions, it is extraordinary that Orwell's ability to challenge uncomfortably has led to unjustified accusations that he was 'cold' and to be held lacking in the necessary understanding of humanity.[6]

At this point the writer has made his political point, not just in an overt commentary on the Spanish war but in the illustrated interaction of the individual with the party that makes up the basis for a positive long-term stance in politics. He is now ready to attack openly the issue that he treated ambivalently in *The Road to Wigan Pier* : the situation of the writer in a political event. This issue is implicit in the book from the start because the narrator is also a writer, and his situation is one of having to learn, to commit himself personally to discussion. Not surprisingly the stance is positive, as is his political view. But the strategies are different. Structurally, he separated his narratorial presentation in order to present both the public and personal aspects of the events. But he opens out the political event most positively through the analogies that involve the reader.

The three concluding chapters specifically present examples of differing narratorial strategies in order to alert the reader to the stance that they help provide. In chapter 12 the reader is taken back to the narrator's experience of being shot. The strategy involved in re-expressing the incident is particularly interesting because it points the difficulty of presenting accurately even experience in which you yourself provide the focus for the action. The initial stages of the expression indicate this difficulty. At first a present narrator notes, most impersonally, 'The whole experience of being hit by a bullet is very interesting, and I think it is worth describing in detail' (p. 249). Then, carefully, he tries to detach his past self from his speaking voice, but even from this distanced vantage point he cannot continue, 'it is very hard to describe what I felt, though I remember it with the utmost vividness' (p. 250). The narration proceeds with a jumbled mixture of an 'I' voice stating in a staccato rhythm the physical sensation, and a 'you' voice generalizing from each sensation to include the reader. The shift in and out of these two voices has the added effect of creating a pulsing rhythm which deprives the reader of a single focus and insists on a process or activity.

Following the immediate reaction to the shot, the narrative develops tension between narrator as the focus of experience and a relatively detached and reporting narrator who records actions and provides direct speech by way of other characters. The pattern of private reaction, followed by report, analysis, and descriptive personal conclusion, is repeated on a larger scale as the chapter progresses. The narrator uses himself as a topic through which to examine the whole situation of wounds, hospitals and conditions of treatment. Constantly he moves from himself, to the surrounding factors, to a clear analysis and conclusion. The downplaying and undercutting of the event only make it the more horrible in detail, as do the oddly juxtaposed images such as the 'red jelly of a half-healed wound' beneath 'a net of butter-muslin'. Yet this narration culminates not in personal conclusion but in a carefully constructed allegory of soldiers going to the front. The image is a hard kernel that tells the reader more about the experience of the Spanish war than any information. Far more densely than the analogies constructed at the conclusion of the narrator's first stint on the front of the Spanish war, which embodied an elusive disquiet with the events because of his ignorance, this image becomes for him 'an allegorical picture of war'. It combines once more all the elements surrounding the initial image of the Italian soldier. These soldiers too are Italian, filled with an unmistakable grace of action. The potential sentimentality is carefully undercut with an off-hand comment about their death 'a few weeks later'. The red flags of the anarchists, the trains and the front all combine, but in this case not because of the original naïvety of the narrator but in spite of his knowledge. They transcend his doubts and revive 'that pernicious feeling, so difficult to get rid of, that war *is* glorious after all' (p. 260).

The image functions allegorically because it does not re-create an experience, but re-presents a series of resonances that have little significance in themselves. They attain significance only in reading and, if the reader has been alert, he will recognize the density of the construction which is achieved by its difference from the original. Between the two lies the one salient experience of personal fallibility, and that this later analogy is so positive indicates that somewhere in the 'picture' the narrator finds a factor that lies beyond that individual fallibility. The reader is guided by the note of the specifically anarchist flags to the fourth topic of the original past narrator: the fraternity and human contact that was always able to override the negative features of the other three. The reader's ability to read this depends largely on his aptitude for recognizing key phrases and resonances in the current narrative that indicate previous experience and throughout the chapter he is called on to do so. It is not necessary in terms of information, but it is essential for evaluation. The doctors who cheerfully state that the narrator will never regain his voice, speak with that 'air of authority' (p. 262) that we have been taught to distrust. And sure enough they are wrong.

The intensely personal stance of chapter 12 is important in reinforcing the process of the narrator's writing of experience. He has learned to leave it neither with subjective impression, nor with objective and detached reporting and analysis, but with an attempt at a balanced, descriptive but overtly personal conclusion. If he wishes to move further than opinion he must turn to analogy and an allegorical stance. The process both clearly presents a point of view and asks for comment on it. As if to underline the importance of analogy to a positive stance expressing morally valid opinion, chapter 13 turns to the difficulties involved in other strategies. These are explored in coarser detail as the narrator returns to the problem of balancing the primacy of experience with reflection, so that one is not left open to manipulation by external propaganda. The reader is asked to involve himself fully with this problem in his response to the differing techniques of retrospective reporting and direct conversation.

The retrospective stance is primarily concerned with revealing fallibility. The narrator recapitulates the intangible horror that is brought about by lack of personal values and susceptibility to propaganda. He returns to the voice of the inexperienced narrator back in Barcelona, yet this time he has the ability to assess and evaluate. Significantly, he summarizes the features of negative rhetoric, saying that the uneasiness was caused 'by rumours that were always changing, by censored newspapers and the constant presence of armed men' (p. 267), spelling out both the arbitrariness and the control, and the common feature of negative political rhetoric: forcible oppression. The concern with fallibility indicates the paradox that a passively submissive ignorance is a denial of fallibility. Ignorance makes possible effective negative rhetoric, but attempts to rectify it, although they will never fully succeed, make that manipulation difficult. He proceeds by a process of familiarization from English soldiers, to an English atmosphere, to English patients, encouraging the reader to make the analogy between England and Spain, to discuss the statement that such confusion could not happen in England because 'political intolerance is not yet taken for granted' (p. 267). Yet he does not conclude. The matter is left open to our own judgement.

From the ignorance that allows experience alone to dominate it, the narrator moves to reporting and impartiality. Having been discharged from the Army he now feels that he can sit back as a completely detached and uninvolved observer. He reintroduces the techniques of detail, observation and omission of evaluation that characterize this stance, and the reader is again implicitly asked to criticize. As if in recognition of the limitations of this strategy, the third section swiftly takes over and a completely new technique is employed. Here the narrator simply presents reported dialogue, in all its fluidity. More than any other technique this dramatizes the loss of bearings in pure action with no reflection; there are no guidelines as to how to read this section, yet oddly it presents the narrator for the first time as if through an impersonal filter. He is shown to be analytical and with common sense, but also to be tense, edgy, sulky and impatient. The contrast is important for we not only become aware of his ordinary imperfect human nature, but also the presence of imperfection lends weight to the qualities of reliability that are also present. The negative qualities are again portrayed as a direct result of allowing action to dominate reflection, as he notes 'That was about as far as my thoughts went. I did not make any of the correct political reflections. I never do when things are happening' (p. 288). At the same time as the strategy underlines his imperfection, it also involves his wife much more so than before. The entire tactic operates by removing the narrator from a simply journalistic role to one of much broader human implications. In doing so it also subtly involves the reader in an identification that will be much more difficult to shake off than that of a conscientious report of the Spanish war. We are being involved in an extension of the process of thought out to all facets of everyday living.

Underlying the three narrative strategies in chapter 13 is the narrator's final return to Barcelona, his discharge, and the discussion of the arrest of Kopp by the Civil Guards. The fugue-like structural variation upon a theme reveals significance through differences in repetition. Such contrasts are not spelt out, but they exist in the narrative for the reader to respond to, just as many other differences in resonant images exist. From the first description of the anarchist posters in their now incongruous state and the torn down red flags, the reader is encouraged to make comparisons with the two previous accounts of Barcelona, and to draw his own conclusions on its present situation. Similarly, the narrator's attempt to retrieve Kopp's credentials from the police, is in direct resonance with earlier analogies between the POUM unit leader and the values and standards of the anarchists. At the end of the incident the official who brings the credentials back suddenly 'stepped across and shook hands with me' (p. 301). The moment is of great significance to the narrator, for despite the official's duty to arrest POUM members, despite the general suspicion of fascist spies, a bond has been created in his recognition of the narrator's individual courage and loyalty. And the action resonates strongly with the handshake of the Italian soldier in the introduction to the book.

Curiously, the consistent acts of courage that the narrator performs in his attempts to help Kopp never appear self-righteous or self-applauding. Granted the narrator carefully downplays his role, but more than this, it is as if he has become with Kopp neither a naturalistic character nor a standardized 'type', but an analogy for a certain kind of thinking. Just as the Italian soldier 'typified' the war, the narrator's actions are not personally laudable, but indicate the general individual activity of people of the anarchist persuasion. The suggestion is even more acceptable because the narrator's comments on the totalitarian aspects are tempered and not extreme: part of the contrast being established functions by pointing out the near impossibility for totalitarianism to work effectively in Spain. When the police search his rooms 'in the recognized Ogpu or Gestapo style' (p. 303) they fail to search under the bedclothes because his wife is in bed. The references to the Spanish humour and generosity that often provided the substance for the fourth topic of the earlier discussions are here explicitly transformed into the statement that 'Few Spaniards possess the damnable efficiency and consistency that a modern totalitarian state needs' (p. 303). And the reader should of course note the casual conflation of Russian communism and German fascism into a single totalitarianism with the reference to Ogpu and Gestapo. Further, the narrator is not entirely naïve about the desirability of such inefficiency. The final incident of his attempts to escape gains its suspense from the inability of trains to leave on time: the train he wanted to catch went early, leaving him behind.

Technically, the chapter presents an even mixture of narratorial voice in which the past and present narrators are virtually identical. As a whole it is curiously thick with indiscriminate detail and shifting perspective, as though the narrator has not had the opportunity to distance himself, condense and select the salient points. It is another more immediate manner of seeing and recounting which again asks the reader to involve his evaluative faculties in an assessment of the account. The contrast that lies between all that Kopp maintains and all that the police carry out would be missed if the reader did not pick up on the resonant images and assess the difference they now sustain from earlier references. The difference in situation is also extended out from Barcelona to Paris, as the narrator weighs up the changes between the Paris of the early 1930s and that of 1937 after his escape. And then to England where, significantly, the differences are hard to discern. Once more the narrator is safely in a railway carriage watching the 'deep, deep sleep of England' (p. 314). But this in itself is a difference. Other places have changed. England does not appear to have done so. Although not explored, for the whole concept of using analogy is to encourage the reader by using juxtaposition and difference to examine for himself, the implications are that perhaps England is changing but that here it is more difficult to perceive and one must be even more alert to the details necessary for assessment.

The use of analogy, of difference, is of importance to a narrator asserting a rhetorical technique of discussion as against that of 'party line'. Rather than metaphor, which moves to construct coherent symbols that generate specific experience, analogy functions by providing a series of alternative parallels and separations that allow allegorical readings. For example, if the narrator had wanted to create a coherent personal response to the Spanish war he could have built the metaphor of red and red-and-black flags up into increasingly accordant resonances, one generating a positive concept of honour and loyalty and the other a restrictive and negative repression. Instead, the repetition of the image of the red flag rarely connects fully with the preceding reference. The first use of red flags points to a response of naïve fervour; but the use of red flags on the hospital train is both an ironic comment on the reality of that fervour and an implication of other qualities of courage and loyalty. The disappearance of the flags in the final chapters has little to do with the original fervour, rather it indicates the existence of suppression. This does not mean that it is completely divorced from the earlier implications, but that they are no longer the focal point of the image. Rather than growing in depth and intensity, analogies grow in breadth and density. And in contrast to the movement of a single response, however complex or profoundly moving, allegories move to alternative ends often subverting previous responses. Both metaphor and analogy when used constructively ask for the reader's active involvement; they do not want him simply to accept the symbolic resonances or allegorical juxtapositions. However, allegory is more conducive to alerting the reader to his responsibility to read, because its inherent difference must be bridged. The allegorical stance is presented as a positive rhetorical stance, and Orwell, as his literary criticism of the 1940s indicates, is developing the term 'allegory' as a rhetorical term that lies outwith genre. And it is significant for current studies of allegory that Orwell avoids the confusions that limit the term to generic strategy by treating it as a description of a positive rhetorical stance.

The narrator concludes *Homage to Catalonia* by again disclaiming his ability to 'convey more than a little of what those months in Spain mean to me' (p. 312). He says:

> I believe that on such an issue as this no one is or can be completely truthful.
> It is difficult to be certain about anything except what you have seen with

your own eyes, and consciously or unconsciously every one writer is a partisan. In case I have not said this somewhere earlier in the book I will say it now: beware of my partisanship, my mistakes of fact and the distortion inevitably caused by my having seen only one corner of events. And beware of exactly the same things when you read any other book on this period of the Spanish war. (p. 313)

He can not impose a single interpretation of events. This is not simply because he does not want to, but because the whole point about his political education is that he has begun to think for himself, to assess and evaluate. He cannot expect the reader to receive the same political education without the same choices. The final three chapters have been object lessons to the reader in writing about experience, and in reading that writing. Having demonstrated his ignorance and fallibility as a past narrator, he has to go on to demonstrate it as a continuing problem. One can never find a plan or an answer that will fully suffice. There is a continual individual responsibility to establish personal standards of evaluation.

The narrator tries to stimulate the reader into such activity primarily through the strategies of difference, either imagistic, structural or narratorial. But he is not claiming that it makes for what is accepted as poetic writing. He notes in 'Why I Write' that the political sections, now seen as essential to the exposure of ignorance, spoil the work as literature: 'I did try very hard in it to tell the whole truth without violating my literary instincts . . .' (*CEJL* I 6), but that the 'long chapter, full of newspaper quotations . . . must ruin the book'. Similarly, in his advocation of individual responsibility to combat totalitarianism he admits that these examples of human brotherhood necessitate frustration and inefficiency as well as participation, action and involvement. Just as he suggests that such a political stance is more effective in the long run, so the present reader can say that the literary stance as well is more effective in the long run. Contrary to the writer's fears, *Homage to Catalonia* gains and does not lose by those 'intrusions' of political discussion. The further one moves from the historical events, the more important does their structure become. There is less interest in the elusive 'facts' of the history, than in the perception of them and the experience they generated. Similarly, the book gains and does not lose by the author's attentive qualification of perspective. He does not insist on identification since he resolutely keeps to the individual. But he moves from the sense of private conclusion only possible within a subjective world, to personal assessment and evaluation. He is not providing a complete story as potential answer, but inviting the reader to a discussion, at first the personal discussion he makes with himself, but, more importantly, the public discussion he wishes to have with his reader through the analogical resonances of the text.

Discussion

The concern with the verifiability of character develops in the documentary fictions to the verifiability of the narrator as a first person voice. Because it is personal in *Homage to Catalonia*, the narrator can expose his ignorance and indicate the learning process without putting the reader in quite such an uncomfortable position as he held in *The Road to Wigan Pier*. *Homage to Catalonia* extends the discussion of the issues of language and tradition in terms of a need continually to reassess which is made possible by the support of a human community. And the process of learning is not extended out to the readers through an including type, but through analogy. Analogy not only underlines the differences between the narrator and the reader, hence placing him in a more acceptable position for response and asking for an active individual assessment of stance, but also indicates the very process of that learning which functions by difference, by the resistance to a simple typing of oneself or others.

Yet even in *Homage to Catalonia*, the strategy is antagonistic simply because it challenges.[7] It has to challenge to make its point, but challenge by its very nature is painful: identity is questioned and in this case the implication is that there are aspects of identity which need to be discarded in the necessary process of learning. Here the issues are taken beyond a class war of money and status to a broader political war of values, beliefs, questions of life and death. The narrator indicates that it is necessary to commit oneself, but also to know what one is committing oneself to through an individual evaluation. The one extreme of no commitment is as negative as that of complete party adherence. In effect, he comes to recognize that the one implies the other. Adherence to a party line is a commitment to a word which has no referent, no meaning. This is not because there is no inherent meaning, but because there is no assessed meaning, simply superficial significance.[8] You accept the surface connection and neglect to examine the implications.

In *The Road to Wigan Pier* it was the propaganda, the habitual use of alienating and typing jargon that kept the classes apart and made an active assessment impossible. Here again it is propaganda which creates party lines, but the stress is on the conscious promulgation of that line, its manipulation, and its effect of allying Communist with Fascist aims and alienating the average worker. *The Road to Wigan Pier* portrayed jargon as clumsy and ignorant, possibly generated at first by a fear of the opposite class which now no longer exists. In *Homage to Catalonia* political jargon is an active tool for domination, again probably generated by fear, but here it is a genuine fear that a true incorporation of the working class would destroy the Communist Party system as it existed. In the earlier documentary negative propaganda is an outworn defence, in the later it is an active manipulation and aggression.

Both cases depend on a submissive acceptance of propaganda, but the later work indicates that the writer has moved his study one step further up the rhetorical ladder to the origin of the rhetoric, the person who is consciously employing negative rhetoric, not just his mouthpieces. One should remember that from references in *Homage to Catalonia* the writer is aware of, and has probably just read, Hitler's *Mein Kampf*, which spells out the conditions for negative political rhetoric in a manner close to that of the narrator. One of Hitler's main strategies was to set up groups of people who would speak for him, which was an effective media technique to widen the extent of his propaganda. He also perceived that these mouthpieces of official propaganda must believe in the truth and virtue of what they are saying in order to be effective. To make this possible they are distanced from the responsibility of decision-making, and are bound up in a series of strategies that ensure that personal assessment in unnecessary. Hitler's rhetoric insists first on an adherence to party line without examination of grounds, hence laying the arbitrary basis of its absolutist logic. Second, it insists on total control of opinion. And third, it includes, if necessary, forcible oppression. The writer has simply moved from the first restricted effect to the second, recognizing that they imply each other. While he notes the third he realizes as do all other major political rhetoricians that overt forcible repression is a dangerously crude short-term tactic.

Coming Up for Air : Criticism and Compromise

Orwell's last work of the 1930s, *Coming Up for Air*, shifts the narratorial strategy of the documentaries into a novelistic device in order to re-examine the question of definition and self-definition in terms of a public and private compromise. On one level the novel suggests as did the earlier novels that continual reassessment is idealistic and that compromise seems to be the only solution. The suggestion is made by means of a first person narrator, similar to that of the documentaries, examining an earlier self and learning, but finally capitulating to compromise. It is a natural conflation of the novel and documentary strategies. However, *Coming Up for Air* establishes a perspective for the writer himself, a voice beyond that of a narrator, which resides in the choices of techniques, vocabulary and expression that the main narrator/character employs; hence, beyond the overt compromise lies another voice clearly criticizing it. In doing this the author establishes an external perspective on the narrator himself: something not previously achieved. It is an interesting development, but as the author himself appears to realize, limits him to a negative rather than a positive perspective. He can indicate his approval or disapproval of what the narrator/character does, but cannot suggest anything further.

Coming Up for Air is a novel in four parts, the first of which sets out to establish the narratorial tactics that will carry the story and the rhetorical stance. Initially the narrator introduces himself as George Bowling, and as he looks back on his past self his vocabulary is colloquial, the structuring conversational and the story-telling filled with clichés, clumsy parallelisms and repetitions, cheap comparisons that weaken the effect. The entire narration by this character functions through assuming common ground with the reader, pulling him in and asking him to accept the familiar techniques being used. Yet the obvious nature of these techniques indicates a further comment on the narrator himself. Through them the writer captures the tone of an amateur raconteur, continually slipping out of control over his own story. It is an active irony which is missed if the reader is unaware of the parody of story-telling which takes place in the course of the narration, and one which portrays George Bowling as a naïve, humorous and sincere character, yet self-deceiving and evading of reality.

Bowling's own attempts at irony consist of a heavy-handed negative irony which defines an expected response for us, as with his description of his wife, or a series of ambiguous comments on his past self. In itself this difference in irony is revealing. The present narrator is reluctant to devastate his past self, which he portrays experiencing an average domestic morning, in a conventional manner. Yet he does want to criticize that domestic life, and so he vents his bitterness on his wife and children instead. Immediately the reader is aware of an ambiguous evasion of responsibility. In effect, although the present narrator is concerned to portray his past self as different from, and less experienced than he is now, the two are not as separate as at first implied.

It is not only the separation and connection between past and present selves that illustrate ambiguous splits in character. The past character himself feels separate from the 'face [that] looked back at me out of the mirror' (p. 9). He even has two names: ' "Fatty", they mostly call me. Fatty Bowling. George Bowling is my real name'. And the narration of the present character, which reveals splits in his attitude to his past self, also reveals a duality of response to the other topics he discusses. For example, at the end of the first chapter his satiric attack on his children, summarizing their lives in a list of clichés, is suddenly followed by a sentimental comment made solid with biblical reference (p. 15).

The narrator/character progresses to a more concrete presentation of the relationship between his past and present selves. He indicates that looking back on his past self is a means of objectifying who he is, by separating himself from the habitual actions he makes every day. The separation also clarifies the difference between his outwardly public and inwardly private selves. The actual method of his narration, filled with clichés, associative patter, unconnected statistics, indicates the slick public nature of his character. Yet the implied irony against this clichéd aspect of his life points to his more observant, more careful and sensitive private attitudes. The ambiguously ironic relationship between the narrator's past and present character, reflects the complicity of his past self in the public and private compromise of the first chapter.

The nature of the compromise is more fully explored in chapter 2 through a discussion of his appearance. Throughout the description that ensues the vocabulary is far more coarse, often interrupted with crude comments, and more concerned with actual occurrences. The past character is involved in a situation of seeing and counter-seeing with a group of other people who look at and label each other in terms of their newpapers, clothes and physical shape. This question of public appearance leads neatly into a discussion of Bowling's size of which he is very conscious, but which he sees as distinct from his mental slimness. People have expectations of how fat people should behave and George Bowling has allowed himself to develop 'most of the characteristics', yet he sees his private self as something quite separate. Behind this separation within the past character is a criticism of the process of labelling. We allow ourselves to be defined by society because it is easier, we fit in with the public compromise and maintain private identity as separate. Yet in the end this causes problems because personal nature, generated by interaction with the public, is hidden and thwarted.

The discussion of physical appearance takes place in a train carriage, and the use of this significant image indicates the analogy being constructed. Just as the fat public man comfortably fits in, so the carriage induces a feeling of safety and protection from the bomber planes outside. Yet just as the thin man inside the body is the private identity, so the violence, the threat of war is the other side of the situation. It is the compromise between the two sides that hides reality and pretends that all is just as it was.

The discussion of the war parallels the introduction of crudity and violent images in the narration of the present narrator/character and the reader is alerted to a different aspect of his make-up. No longer do we simply have the amateurish conventional story-telling techniques, but a surfacing of deep-rooted bitterness. This is naïvely yet startlingly expressed, for example in 'zoom, whizz, plonk! Houses going up into the air, bloomers soaked with blood, canary singing on above the corpses' (p. 29). Such disruptions of conventional narrative increases substantially toward the conclusion of the first part of the novel.

The final strategy of the writer is to allow the present character to try to explain why the individual compromise exists, at the same time as suggesting reasons as to why the political compromise exists. The experiencing, past character, trying to fill in time before his new false teeth are fitted, goes into a milk bar for a hot-dog. The eating of the hot-dog, one of the most disgusting pieces Orwell ever wrote, is described in conjuction with two other elements: the use of headlines in newspapers and German ersatz commodities. The linking feature is that each of these has a publicly accepted value belied by its actual nature; the hot-dog is made of fish, the demure caption 'Legs' refers to the recent discovery of two severed legs in a brown paper parcel, and the ersatz movement is an attempt to manufacture goods that resemble the real thing. All three are connected to the 'sort of propaganda floating around, mixed up with noise of the radio, to the effect that food doesn't matter, comfort doesn't matter, nothing matters except slickness and shininess and streamlining . . .' (p. 31), which are part of the public compromise that tolerates even the abdication of personal integrity to maintain the *status quo*, the temporary satisfaction of conventional desire. Yet underneath you get 'Bombs of filth bursting inside your mouth' (p. 33). The entire section is narrated in a tone aimed at shocking and disrupting the reader out of complacency. Once Bowling has his false teeth in, however, the mood changes. The teeth provide a new confidence that allows him to discuss the future in all its corruption and fear prophetically, but significantly it is a fictionalized account. He can guess at the results of war, but is unable to analyse the actual steps in its creation that might prevent it.

The scene shifts from the political to the individual as the present character moves off into reminiscence. The focus for Bowling's memory is the church in Lower Binfield where he spent his childhood, and while he attempts to defuse sentimentality, he inevitably falls prey to it. As he forms the historical background to his character, he unwittingly reveals the causes for the contemporary situation, for ironically, the stability and order of his remembered past are also a source for the oncoming war. The strongest indication of his self-delusion about the comfortable safety of past values is that the narrator lapses back into his conventional narrative style.

At this stage the reader may not be as clearly aware of the defining voices as he will be later, but the blind rote learning of the Old Testament on which the narrator's religion was based, illustrates the passive acceptance of the values of that society, 'You never understood it, you didn't try to or want to, it was just a kind of medicine' (p. 40). The mistakes made because one didn't understand the words were negligible because the rhythm and sound of the words took over and dominated meaning. Such loss of consciousness was desirable and enchanting. Bowling clearly illustrates this, saying 'it was a good world to live in' and including the reader in his past. At the same time there is something ambivalent about the nature of his final images; the nostalgia for the past is betrayed by the conscripted 'recruiting-sergeant', drunks 'puking in the yard behind the George', and the absolute stasis of the representatives of the State and Church 'not doing anything exactly, just existing'. For the reader this discussion of the past, following so immediately from that of the present and future, places them in juxtaposition. The labelling of ersatz commodities becomes parallel to the fictions of the past that comfort. Furthermore, just as the past character is sometimes unable to 'counter-see', to look at himself and see the public illusion, while the present self can do so, so the present character is also blind to aspects of his public compromise. The split between the two characters underlines that this ability to see and counter-see is a function of learning and perspective. At the same time, the individual and political compromises are shown to exist because people allow themselves to be uncritically defined by history and language.

The overall strategy of the writer in this first part of the novel is to alert the reader to the extent of the present narrator's awareness and ignorance of his public and private compromise. The second part is an attempt to establish a history for this present narrator. He suggests that it will explain him, indicate why he behaves as he does and what has defined him. Yet the process of creating individual history, linked as it is here to the function of memory, is essentially self-definition. Memory is fluctuating, varied and selective, the final tool in a relative presentation of the past. The first three chapters of the part indicate that the narrator is partially aware of the ambivalent nature of memory, and he tries to establish an acceptable stance in terms of remembering and reporting rather than commenting, and loses much of his earlier satirical and negative tone. These responses are limited and straightforwardly set out in commonplace expressions or in lists unrelated to any interpretation. The reader is thereby encouraged to supply recognition and connection for the detail himself, and when the generalizations of the older narrator arrive they assume our knowledge, invite agreement.

The older narrator specifically appeals to the reader's knowledge of memory as he moves from private detail to generalization. The stance is familiar, conversational and colloquial; we accept it for its apparent normality: an immediate hint as to the unexamined nature of its grounds. Beyond this the writer is providing Bowling with double-edged examples that he takes for granted yet we read rather differently. His offhand condescension to his father's belief in newspapers and his mother's steady, habitual consumption of 'Hilda's Home Companion' point to a naïve desire for such simplicity. To the reader they speak of the ease with which people unaware of propaganda could be manipulated, and of the danger of substituting a fantasy world of vicarious experience for the real thing.

The type of past being created provides a backdrop for more important issues. The following five chapters of the second part, 2 to 6, each pick up and expand on the theme of youthful passion, and portray the narrators in a fluctuating relationship as the present dallies with the implications of the past. Chapter 4 moves to discussing the younger self and fishing; it becomes taut, shocking and emotional. Fishing is set up as representing the anarchy and passion of youth. It is cruel and selfish, yet strangely allied to religious ecstasy and poetry. He notes: 'Killing things – that's about as near to poetry as a boy gets' (p. 91). Yet a few sentences earlier he has disclaimed any poetry in childhood, disclaimed sentimentality. The ambivalence recurs when he finally breaks down and confesses, 'I *am* sentimental about my childhood – not my own particular childhood, but the civilization which I grew up in' (p. 92).

While the joys of fishing are discussed the narrator takes on a younger voice full of exclamations, direct address to the reader and involvement. But gradually the older, negative, satiric voice takes over, converting the experience into nostalgia. This narratorial technique guides the reader into his own assessment. Rather than learning from the earlier memory, Bowling is escaping into it. The ambivalent juxtaposition of fishing with modern life is paralleled by his attitude to reading. It should be noted that in common with all the other potentially active elements, literature may also simply provide an escape. On the one hand this is part of Bowling's ambivalent response, yet on the other it is a warning to the reader about how he should be reading this book.

In chapter 7, modern civilization, a job and the Army are increasingly allied with external, public definition. And during the eighth chapter the writer places them through Bowling's associative mind, in a direct line to the authoritarianism of bureaucracy that 'was like an enormous machine that had got hold of you' (p. 136), thus linking the individual with political acts of self-definition as he did in part one. During this extension of topics central to the novel, the present narrator reveals why he behaves in the manner he now does. The discrepancy between the awkward clumsiness of the present and the literary finesse of the past voice underlines the loss of confidence as he grows older, the clinging to lists and details, the false challenging of the reader only on the narrator's own grounds and from his own assumptions. The reader, partly because he is brought so close to the present narrator through these techniques, watches him becoming satiric, slick and salesmanlike, revealing the lack of confidence that results from the stabilities of the past life having gone. However, our alertness to narratorial change is controlled by the writer, not Bowling himself. He is able to be shockingly casual about a dead baby in a personally oblivious manner that makes the images doubly distressing for the reader. Indeed, by the end of chapter 8, the reader is both more involved in the narration and increasingly able to distance Bowling's character and read further implications into his stance.

The concluding two chapters to the part return us firmly to the present narrator who steps in to defend his modern way of life, his salesman's attitudes and talk by saying that they are means for coping with the modern world. Yet Bowling both satirizes and participates in the social and economic conditions of his world, and his simultaneous acceptance and rejection provides the basis for the writer's criticism. His reality is manipulation and abuse, and his escape is to convert his childhood and the past into nostalgia The ambivalence of the narrator's attitude to the past lies in blindness to the true reason for modern authoritarianism; this has not occurred because past civilization has been rejected but exactly because it never changed. Childhood and youthful anarchy are positive; not in their detail, which generates nostalgia, but in the activity that supports a fresh assessment of the world and of self, a radical self-definition that is essential to a healthy society. By the end, the reader understands Bowling better than he does himself. His solutions of total rejection and destruction of the world or escape into the past are abdications of responsibility generated by his acceptance of the public and private compromise.

The third short part of *Coming Up for Air* portrays George Bowling swinging between these solutions of violence and nostalgia. Gradually he realizes, by applying the analogy of politics to his own life, that he has to work out a further alternative. In terms of narrative technique the presentation remains very much as it has been, with an alternation between lists, details and observations of types occasionally interrupted by violent imagery. But here the reader is allowed to follow the process of reasoning behind Bowling's narration. Much of the initial chapter is given over to Bowling's attendance at a political meeting held by the Left Book Club and his later discussion of the issues with his public school educated friend, Porteous. The concept of labelling which arose in the first part in regard to ersatz commodities is here allied with the narrator's own tendency to 'type' people. The speaker at the Left Book Club meeting is a 'well-known anti-Fascist' a label that is repeated later to emphasize not only Bowling's 'typing' analysis, but the speaker's own acceptance of the slogan.

The description of the speech he hears at the Left Book Club is an illustration of such labelling in action. It is a 'line of talk' that fades into slogans of Democracy and Fascism, conveying little meaning. The audience has arrived with a preconceived idea of what it is all about. Significantly, during the speech, Bowling notes the essential quality of Hitler's negative rhetoric, that the speaker '*means* it', 'Every slogan's gospel truth to him' (p. 180). Pursuing this line of thought, he questions whether the man has a private life at all, suggesting that 'even his dreams are slogans' (p. 180). Here one comes to the crux of the private and public compromise. Total compromise, complete rejection of the private self, implies complete manipulation by the state: Bowling notes that if he ceases listening to the words and places himself in the rhythm of the speaker's delivery, all the speaker is conveying is hate. The speaker is in effect making public a simple desire for violence and killing which is the result of private fear. The need for an authoritarian leader is also a result of private fear. Fear weakens confidence, especially when one has no valid grounds for individual responsibility and evaluation, and generates a totalitarian, violence-dominated vision of the future. Here it is important that the previous disjunctions between the past and the future worlds are seen to be connected. It is the maintenance of submissiveness inherent in a nostalgic past that will encourage authoritarianism, because that is what authoritarianism needs and thrives on.

Moving from political, public violence allied with killing, to the other escape of private nostalgia, the narrator talks of his friend Porteous. Porteous concentrates entirely on the state of culture and the arts instead of assessing modern political progress. Observing this, the narrator comes to realize that an outright denial of the importance of Hitler is as dangerous as an unthinking party line acceptance of his menace; neither examines the origin of the situation. Porteous, he concludes, is dead. He has lost 'the power to take in a new idea'. In a devastating condemnation of all the compromises reached by characters of earlier novels in the name of 'decency', a condemnation not widely recognized in critical readings,[9] Bowling says, 'They're decent, but their minds have stopped' (p. 197). He is forced into decisions during this first chapter of Part Three. He does not allow himself to be persuaded by words, but by the vision he has of the way people live. The mundanity of his wife's life, the hatred in the life of the professional anti-fascist, and the short-sighted complacency of Porteous, all point to a world of authoritarian restriction and loss of liberty. In reply to the blind hatred of the communists listening to the anti-Fascist speaker, who naïvely demand that he go out and 'smash' the enemy, the narrator overtly condemns the war, yet with Porteous realizes that real change is necessary. In doing so he places himself outside the scope of his previous solutions to the death of civilization.

The second chapter of this part portrays the narrator directly confronting his public salesman persona and his private sentimental side. Relapsing at first into a cold-blooded assessment of his own propaganda, the irony of his unique position in understanding totalitarian propaganda is driven home. In its own right, his discussion of sentimentality is redolent with nostalgia and cliché. By contrast his attempts to discuss the beautiful and to avoid sentimentality are hopelessly unsuccessful. The increasing struggle with words indicates the narrator's increasing involvement in a new situation which he cannot control with salesman's clichés nor dismiss with shocking images. The moment that finally makes him decide to visit the scene of his childhood at Lower Binfield, that convinces him the 'Life was worth living', is the rather different visual image, a small fire with glowing red embers which 'gives you more a feeling of life, than any living thing. There's something about it, a kind of intensity, a vibration . . . It lets you know you're alive yourself' (p. 200).

The final chapter of the third part is a brief account of Bowling's journey to Lower Binfield several months later, during which he experiences several temptations to return to the ordinary and to his escapes. But he manages to resist them. The chapter, though short, stresses the immense difficulty of carrying through what has seemed so simple a plan. Strategically, it interposes a necessary, momentary halt and consideration between the decision to go to Lower Binfield that occurred in the preceding chapter, and the realization which makes up the fourth part of the novel.

Essentially the decision is still a form of escape. While the narrator is not moving to complete evasion, he does think that he will gain respite through his journey. Yet from the moment he enters Lower Binfield his memory is in constant clash with actuality. Strategically the narrator undercuts the reader's expectation by explicitly noting that memory is invariably deceptive; this strengthens the force of his actual reaction to these differences. At this point, Bowling addresses the reader directly, saying, 'Oh yes, I know *you* knew what was coming. But *I* didn't' (p. 179). The invitation to greater knowledge that goes out to the reader is an overt confirmation of the external perspective that we have gained on Bowling's life during the novel. Yet until now this has been restricted to the writer's control of the narrative presentation. Emphasis on our position is oddly placed, but necessary for the ensuing development of the section.

The fluctuation between memory and actuality is portrayed through changes in narratorial style, from clichéd reminiscence to down to earth humour, shocking images, or matter of fact observation. The narration becomes increasingly concrete, as the narrator reports the step by step dismantling of his illusions. The attempt to 'come up for air' before the war is a self-deception, for war is here in Lower Binfield: 'It's in the air you breathe' (p. 239). Bowling finally realizes that the decision to visit Lower Binfield was definitely a mistake. The present narrator comments: 'there's no escape' (p. 274), he says, no escape into the internal privacies or external public selves that generate the compromise.

The point here is that this is Bowling's conclusion after he has realized what the reader has realized all along: his self-delusion. If the reader accepts the distanced perspective of this knowledge, he also accepts the responsibility of its conclusions: that there are no fixed solutions. But further than this, the reader can see the weaknesses in Bowling that even he doesn't recognize, and from these is expected to take on even greater responsibility. At the same time as Bowling realizes his self-deception, he constructs a further form of escape around an SOS message that the radio broadcasts about his wife being seriously ill. He knows that she is not, and that this is just a dodge to get him to return home. But while at first he is angry, the reader observes him becoming amused, deciding that the ploy is ingenious and building a new illusion around her: that she is imaginative and resourceful.

In the discussion of the war which follows in chapter 6, it is made clear why this strategy of distanced knowledge is being employed. The war, as Bowling observes it, is the violent alternative to nostalgic escape. His description of it places it parallel to his earlier study of memory, and it yields an ominous, unfulfilled parallelism that Bowling doesn't comment upon. He simply notes that 'The blood was beginning to get mixed up with the marmalade' (p. 272). The conclusion on the one hand that 'Fat men of forty-five can't go fishing', has an implied parallel on the other that people cannot ignore the war. Bowling fatalistically notes that the war is 'just something that's got to happen' (p. 228); and while he knows why – because people never truly change, never take on an individual responsibility for their lives thus allowing authoritarianism to happen – he doesn't know what to do about it. The answer again lies in the realization that one must continually reassess one's life, try to avoid the easy escapes from responsibility. Bowling cannot take the step that extends this out, but the reader can. The strategy is fundamentally different from the technique of correction by example in the documentary novels; it challenges the reader to take responsibility on himself. But while he is likely to do so in terms of the recognition of the delusions that Bowling goes through, he may not be so ready to take that further step based on his distanced knowledge provided by the writer's perspective.

The final chapter portrays the narrator going home, succumbing to habit and custom in 'the line of least resistance'. He reassumes his clichéd conversation, reintroduces his idiomatic form of expression, and with each dialogue interchange with his wife, is beaten back closer to his original self. If the reader has moved only with the narrator, he will remain unsatisfied by the conclusion of the book. Of the alternatives left to Bowling concerning his wife's discovery of his trip to Lower Binfield, two are habitual and one active. But considering that Bowling has retreated so far to his original self, the implication is that he will continue to delude his wife, to allow her to go on thinking what she always has, and to take the line of least resistance. In doing so he finally evades responsibility for her, for the habitual life that she represents in him, and for his social role. The reader who goes further than Bowling on the guidance of the writer knows that this is not good enough, that one has a responsibility to work out problems, a responsibility inevitably more difficult and strenuous than ignoring the issues or destroying them. The public and private compromise does not have to exist if the individual puts aside mere adjustment and attempts real change. Defining oneself completely in private terms is just as much an escape as allowing oneself to be completely defined in public terms. The two should contribute to each other in personal realization. The fat man that Bowling tries to take as a façade covering his actual self, cannot simply be used to to perform a social role as a 'type', but is a reality. To pretend otherwise is delusion.

Summary : interaction

The apparent implication of *Coming Up for Air* is that despite the need to recognize the relative nature of society's rules and to change, one cannot live idealistically. There has to be some public and private compromise because it is impossible to re-examine one's life continually. But beyond this the writer places the narrator/character into a different perspective. He indicates that this is a second-best conclusion that is not sufficient. As with the two documentary novels, constant attention to evaluation itself and to the bases for it, is the key here to both private and public definition.

Although the implication of the structure and techniques in *The Road to Wigan Pier* was that it is necessary to apply the process continually, it was not actually stated. There is no need to explicitly state the process in *Homage to Catalonia*, where the topic under discussion is parallel to the structure and technique. The work is a rhetorical examination of rhetorical stance; it evaluates the process of evaluation.

In *Coming Up for Air* the author has placed the process of learning in a perspective that clarifies the ease with which new learning becomes rigidified. The main problem however, as I suggested earlier, is that the perspective is negative, not positive. The central character may be identified with up to a point but no further, and the further identification with the writer is not clear enough to be rhetorically effective, as shown by the number of readers who read the novel as immediate subjective experience.[10] The final criticism of Bowling's attitude is not positively set out. As Orwell was later to note in a diary entry, novels written in the first person are always restrictive, because they limit the writer's comments on the character's actions; they restrict the view of his opinion necessary to assess the basis of the criticism being made. The reader is not actually involved in that criticism because he cannot see its foundation; and is hence unable to apply it to himself. Although it is interesting that in the search for generic definition critics of the book begin to look further afield and read it as a parable, a pastiche and, more revealingly, as a prose dramatic monologue. In all these is an element of the distance and difference that Orwell was seeking.[11]

Orwell appears to have thought that by using the split first person narration of the documentaries and providing a novelistic setting to give an external perspective on it, he would avoid the problem. But here he has only created different problems. The character, narrator, writer or author may each be fallible, but until the reader also admits this and enters a rhetorical pattern which uses it positively, as in *Homage to Catalonia*, there can be no possibility of finding an alternative to the authoritarian. In effect, that possibility is itself a contradiction in terms. Having reached one position of interaction which has the defect of possible antagonism, the author now goes searching for another. But it is not until he learns to use the lack of a basis for opinion as a positive rhetorical strategy, as he does in *Nineteen Eighty-Four*, that it can prove successful.

II   Essays, Letters, Broadcasts

CHAPTER FOUR

The Writer's Stance

By 1940 Orwell's fictions state and evidence an undeniable dislike of authoritarianism, at first in social and then in political terms. The early question of a public and private compromise is now phrased as a tension between the individual and his society, and the only solution seems to be a complete separation between the two. The social tension is paralleled by an artistic one, based on a realization that art is inevitably also propaganda, an involvement the writer finds problematic and worrying. The essays, criticism and letters written up until 1940 explicitly set forth an exclusion between the two that the writer also suggested in his early novels. As a result, he finds the individual powerless in social and political terms, and the artist impotent. But he comes to the conclusion that there need not be this separation, that developing the self contributes to and develops the society. Similarly since all art is propagandic it may be responsibly and personally so. Expression of one's own understanding of issues is a social and political role the individual should actively take up.

During the early period of his critical writing, 1929–39, the essayist's concept of expressed 'meaning' is of something quantifiable. It is related to his intellectual understanding of the concepts of language, truth and history as things exact, definable and absolute. However he comes to recognize two complicating factors: the first is that an impression of exactitude and accuracy is a matter of a specific 'line' of interpretation being imposed on events; and the second, the corollary of such control by imposition, that it is at most arbitrary. These factors are seen as complicating rather than reversing the direction of his topics. Orwell's recognition of the flexibility of interpretation and the arbitrary nature of definition arises from the practical experience of his own fallibility, the knowledge that as an observer he can never be absolutely exact. He has a personal responsibility to indicate the extent of his control over his expression, and to involve his audience in an active participation. These factors also lead him to a definition of the function of party politics, and then to totalitarianism and its use of propaganda to sustain itself.

In the novels, knowledge of narratorial fallibility and the corollary factors of private interpretation as both too definite and too arbitrary, are included in some form or another from the start. The necessary reassessment by individuals in society and by both writer and readers participating in literature, is searched out in the various kinds of interaction that he explores through his narrators and characters, who are simultaneously defined by and yet defining aspects of history, sex, religion and language. There is a balanced, distanced perspective in the novels which does not exist in the early essays. In the critical writings the sense of distance from himself grows only after he has written his documentary works since they bring to the fore problems of stance and private interference. The novels and the later essays present an obsessive concern with the danger of non-involving stances, perspectives that attempt to evade the responsibility of personal choice. I would suggest that it is because the writer feels that their particular danger is very close to himself. For example, the lesson against 'typing' spelt out in *The Road to Wigan Pier* is not simply an artificial one invented to make an artistic or social point. Orwell himself notes his own tendency to 'type'. In a letter to Stephen Spender after an attacking review of the latter's work he apologizes for some of his comments, making the excuse that 'not having met you I could regard you as a type and also an abstraction' (*CEJL* I 363).[1] As the fictions make clear, for Orwell typing is a result of assuming that one can personally define other people in an absolute manner.

The ambivalence of the essayist's conscious response to stance is manifested clearly in three major essays of 1940: 'Charles Dickens', 'Boys' Weeklies' and 'Inside the Whale'. These summarize the ideas of previous work, and are focused specifically in 'Inside the Whale'. This ambivalence has led to much conflicting criticism of Orwell himself since it is a point of admittedly limited perception from which he moves away during the following years. The essay 'Charles Dickens' criticizes Dickens both positively and negatively in that 'his criticism of society is almost exclusively moral'. But he concludes that Dickens is sincere; he hates tyranny; and his moral approach is just as revolutionary as a social approach. Yet problems arising from the division that Dickens constructs between the social and the moral, are indicated only by occasional notes on the essayist's part. 'Charles Dickens' is interesting in tone because all the criticism of limitation or restriction is only implied. The result is that the essay appears far more positive than it in fact is. The 'generous anger' of a nineteenth-century liberal appears to be approved, but set in the context of Orwell's other work, it is being criticized for its separation from real things, from society and from interaction with group needs.

This essay is probably best known for Orwell's statement that 'All art is propaganda . . . [but] not all propaganda is art' (*CEJL* I 448), which raises the question of what it is that is added to or taken away from propaganda to make it art as well. The question need not inevitably be phrased in this manner, but Orwell's early ideas on the topic lead him to do so. He speaks of the aesthetic preference as 'either something inexplicable or it is so corrupted by non-aesthetic motives as to make one wonder whether the whole of literary criticism is not a huge network of humbug' (*CEJL* I 448). The idea is a development from earlier comments on the purity and potential meaninglessness of art. A review written in 1930, on a book about Melville, states that interpreting a poem is to reduce it 'to an allegory' (*CEJL* I 101), here using a crude one-to-one concept of allegory as emblem that has changed utterly by the time he writes *Homage to Catalonia* seven years later. This also indicates the static and absolutist quality of Orwell's early attitude to meaning and interpretation. The suggestion is that one should 'accept without seeking knowledge' (*CEJL* I 19), look at the form not the 'meaning'. Three years later a letter to Brenda Salkeld restates the suggestion saying that the highest aim of the writer is to produce '*good writing*, which can exist almost as it were in vacuo and independent of subject' (*CEJL* I 126).

However, this total exclusion of aesthetic from meaning changes radically from 1933 to 1936, perhaps because of the writer's tussle with authorial intervention in his fictions. By late 1936, the essayist explicitly states the development of his views. He notes that six years previously 'art for art's sake was going strong' (*CEJL* I 257) and that although now discredited, critics still have a temptation to revert to it 'according as it suits them'. Books are actually judged on ideological bias but theoretically 'on purely aesthetic grounds. Few people have the guts to say outright that art and propaganda are the same thing' (*CEJL* I 257). By the time he writes 'Charles Dickens' he has moved on further than this to an understanding that not all propaganda is art. And the keypoint in Orwell's development is his experience during the Spanish Civil War of more sophisticated forms of persuasion and manipulation. 'Spilling the Spanish Beans', published in July and September 1937, on his return from the war, and as a dry run for *Homage to Catalonia*, concentrates on the use of propaganda, particularly by the Communist Party, to subvert the popular revolution. Whereas before this experience the writer had been anxious to note the excesses of the 'art for art's sake' movement, from now on he concentrates on the negative dominance of propaganda. And all through the letters written during the post-Civil War period, Orwell evidences growing awareness not only of press distortion but also of questionable propaganda used in day to day life.

From Orwell's experiences in the Civil War, came the knowledge that he could not avoid propaganda, could not exclude it from his art. Yet at this stage he is curiously ambivalent about it. A letter to Jack Common (conjectured date, March 1938), notes his concern with 'selling my intellectual virtue' as he is torn, with other writers, between 'i Art for art's saking in an ivory tower; ii political propaganda and iii pulling in the dough' (*CEJL* I 310). Of *Homage to Catalonia* he observes 'I hate writing that kind of stuff and am much more interested in my own experiences, but unfortunately in this bloody period we are living in one's only experiences *are* being mixed up in controversies' (*CEJL* I 311). And in his explanation of why he joined the Independent Labour Party (June 1938), he fuses his concern for private and public interaction with his perception of the interaction of art and propaganda:

> I am a writer. The impulse of every writer is to 'keep out of politics'. What he wants is to be left alone so that he can go on writing his books in peace. But unfortunately it is becoming obvious that this ideal [is not practicable] . . . (*CEJL* I 336)

In 'Charles Dickens' the public and private compromise is taken further to the question of personal and party politics. Given that any age demands a private and public interaction to determine moral stance, this age asks for further interaction between that moral stance and society, in other words, a personal politics. For Dickens the element that made his propaganda into art as well was the fact that he cared. This quality and the quality of sincerity, both of which Orwell called 'talent', anchor propaganda in art. Yet one has to set this against what Dickens does. He cares morally but not socially. While he is against authority he seeks no way of changing it. He is sincere, true to his private isolated standards, but not honest, taking no account of social contingency. Ultimately one cannot escape this responsibility. Art and propaganda lie together where the private and public connect. But unless one is consciously extending this connection into political realities there is always a danger of propaganda without art.

The second major essay of 1940, 'Boys' Weeklies', presents a highly detailed account of the rhetoric used by comic magazines, and examines their stance, structure and audience relationship. It is worthwhile listing here the techniques considered intrinsic to such writing, for they provide the basis for all of Orwell's future criticism of fantasy literature, and lay the foundation for his analysis of totalitarian propaganda. Structural details of the weeklies include: tautology that is not simply for spinning out the story but essential for 'creating the atmosphere' (*CEJL* I 464), repetition of meaningless expressions, slang and nicknames, and more specifically, a constant recurrence of 'stylized cries of pain'. Characterization is simple and clear with a strong moral separation between the good and the bad. More subtly, there is no character 'whom some or other reader does not identify with, except the out-and-out comics'. The key to their technique is indeed an easy identification between reader and narrative that should generate 'a complete fantasy life'. The techniques all aim to ensure the solidity of that life: 'There is a constant, untiring effort to keep the atmosphere intact' so that 'The mental world . . . is safe, solid and unquestionable. Everything will be the same for ever and ever'. The biblical resonances of the final phrase are not casual; they underline a suggestion that religion too constructs a safe evasion from the responsibilities of this world.

The analysis focuses first of all on the *Gem* and the *Magnet* boys' weeklies and summarizes their effects as innocuous. It then moves on to the study of other magazines which are better technically and yield more variety. With apparent praise the essayist notes: 'There is a marked advance in intellectual curiosity and, on the whole, in the demand made on the reader's attention' (*CEJL* I 476). The approval is qualified when he adds that the attention is gained by an appeal to violence and sensationalism, to 'bully-worship' . In this case,

> the reader is left to identify . . . with some simply all-powerful character who dominates everyone about him . . . This character is intended as a superman, and as physical strength is the form of power that boys can best understand, he is usually a sort of human gorilla . . . (*CEJL* I 476)

Read in the context of *Coming up for Air*, these references immediately link this form of literature with totalitarian strategies. In common with the more innocuous weeklies totalitarian strategies use a jargon. Here it is created by a 'pornographic use' of endless brooding on violence that recalls Charlie's first melodramatic story in *Down and Out*. This has the power to shock if its conventions are not understood; but since this literature aims to shock it has to employ rhetorical techniques that hide its conventions. Similarly, the essayist comments that women's magazines have their own jargon that encourages a passive readership and creates a 'pure fantasy-world'.

Underlying the criticism is the recurrent issue of popular demand. These magazines do provide what the public wants to read. While on the one hand such demand appears to justify the existence of such literature, on the other it comes wrapped up in a subtle propaganda: 'the illusions which their future employers think suitable for them' (*CEJL* I 481). Here the essayist notes the explicitly submissive nature of audience response that is required, and the corresponding need to hide the grounds on which the argument is based. Just as the danger of war propaganda lay in not realizing that it was war propaganda, so here the propaganda is 'All the better because it is done indirectly, there is being pumped into them the conviction that the major problems of our time do not exist' (*CEJL* I 482). The boys' weeklies, superman comics and women's magazines proffer no political development, no advance in social outlook and continually present fantasies of being rich and powerful.

After his Spanish Civil War experiences, Orwell came to believe that the modern problem was one of power (*CEJL* I 147). Power and machine guns can be used with impunity because the totalitarian power maniac assumes that he is the purveyor of absolute good: 'Nothing but the good prevails' (*CEJL* I 34). A diary extract concerning a speech by Mosley in 1936, had observed the Fascist Party technique of combining violence with excellent oratorical persuasion. Significantly, the persuasion used will not admit any questions from the audience. One man who 'was only trying to get a question answered' (*CEJL* I 203) was thrown out with unnecessary violence. By 1939 Orwell has recognized that sophisticated propaganda is more effective than machine guns. Mental violence more successful than physical. His review of Bertrand Russell's *Power* notes the 'huge system of organized lying upon which the dictators depend which keeps their followers out of contact with reality' (*CEJL* I 376). Another early article suitably placed in 'G. K.'s Weekly' and undoubtedly influenced by Chesterton's own attacks on totalitarian propaganda, prophesies the day 'when the newspaper will be simply a sheet of advertisement and propaganda, with a little well-censored news' (*CEJL* I 13). Again by 1939 this threat has become more than a prophecy. The 'sinister possibilities of the radio, state-controlled education and so forth' (*CEJL* I 376) make the deception of people by a ruling caste probable, and the writer suggests that such deception already exists. Concealment of fact, construction of false environments, the evasion and hiding of meaning are the ultimate aims of power-oriented totalitarian propaganda. And while they operate on a much smaller, less harmful scale, weekly magazines do the same thing, and the detail of their technique is instructive.

'Boys' Weeklies' is the least ambivalent of the three major essays of 1940. It discusses the techniques of escape clearly, presenting such literature as the basis for propaganda which is not art. The persuasion of fantasy writing is most effective if it is without opposition from both the private individual and society. As Orwell was later to note, a similarly isolated public propaganda is always in danger of becoming totalitarian.

With the third of Orwell's major articles we come to a study of adult fantasy itself. 'Inside the Whale' is one of the most widely interpreted articles ever written or commented upon. Some readers even say that the essay advocates the 'inside' of the whale which condones a passive literary response to politics, abdicating all responsibility, whereas I would argue that Orwell is explicitly attacking this position. It is worth paying attention to the cause of these radically conflicting critical analyses of it.[2] In effect the conflict is probably a result of Orwell's own changing stance at this time. He can see the attractions in the passive attitude, but it is rash for the reader to assume his agreement with it. The essay serves as a gathering point for all his ideas of the period. His ambivalent attitude to Henry Miller's work which runs thematically through many other essays[3] becomes the basis for this discussion and clearly presents the tensions of the public and private compromise in Orwell's mind at the time.

Literature and Politics

'Inside the Whale' discusses the effect of totalitarianism on literature, and the resulting construction of adult fantasies that are either completely private or completely public, The essayist begins with a reiteration of an earlier comparison between James Joyce and Henry Miller. Both authors are masters of a technique that familiarizes, generates 'the peculiar relief that comes not so much from understanding as from *being understood*' (*CEJL* I 495). Without the context of Orwell's earlier remarks on the necessary active involvement of both writer and reader, this does read like an approval. Indeed Orwell would never condemn writing simply because he disagreed with the argument. However, when he moves on to compare Miller to Walt Whitman the criticism is clearly stated. Miller is not protesting 'he *is accepting*', just as Whitman did. But Whitman accepted the world when it was politically easier to do so despite glaring injustices such as the condition of negroes: 'To say "I accept" in an age like our own is to say that you accept concentration camps, rubber truncheons, Hitler, Stalin, bombs, aeroplanes, tinned food . . .' (*CEJL* I 499). The essayist then goes on to reinforce his point, saying: 'To accept civilization *as it is* practically means accepting decay. It has ceased to be a strenuous attitude and becomes a passive attitude – even "decadent", if that word means anything'.

The essay develops from a discussion of Miller into a glance at the literary movements of the 1920s and 1930s; and it is the changing historical climate which causes the essayist to condemn Miller in comparison with his contemporaries. Looking at the residue of the art for art's sake movement in the early twenties which denied purpose or message to art, the writer notes that 'no book is ever truly neutral. Some tendency or other is always discernible, in verse as much as in prose, even if it does no more than determine the form and the choice of imagery' (*CEJL* I 506). The reaction of 1930s writers against purist art turned them toward 'an orthodoxy, a discipline' in order to have something to say, but orthodoxies were also generated by the totalitarian air that surrounded the period.

For a novelist there were two possible paths to not being frightened by that totalitarianism. The first was not to toe a party line, not to follow the political orthodoxy. The second is to withdraw from politics altogether. It is the second path that Henry Miller takes. In his work,

> one gets right away from the 'political animal' and back to a viewpoint not only individualistic but completely passive – the viewpoint of a man who believes the world-process to be outside his control and who in any case hardly wishes to control it. (*CEJL* I 519)

The historical study in this essay is not against 1920s and 1930s criticism, but is an attempted explanation for a response to totalitarianism and its effect on literature. Neither is the essay advocating passive literature, but explaining why it exists. An extensive but important quotation summarizes both the dangers of, and the seduction in, Miller's attitude:

> The whale's belly is simply a womb big enough for an adult. There you are, in the dark, cushioned space that exactly fits you, with yards of blubber between you and reality, able to keep up an attitude of completest indifference, no matter *what* happens . . . short of being dead, it is the final, unsurpassable stage of irresponsibility . . . there is no question that Miller himself is inside the whale . . . he feels no impulse to alter or control the process he is undergoing. He has performed the essential Jonah act of allowing himself to be swallowed, remaining passive, *accepting*. (*CEJL* I 521)

The conclusion to the essay is not an advocacy of irresponsibility in writing but a statement of the need for choice.[4]

But the essayist is once more ambivalent about his own rhetorical stance. Unlike the novels in which a narrator and character enact a stance in the tension between them, or the documentaries which represent the narrator as a character with his own stance, the essays bring the writer as close to his own person as it is possible for a writer to be while maintaining some necessary detachment. The writer is here not willing to 'type' himself even for the education of his readers; he is essaying in the true sense, attempting to find out despite his uncertainties. At the same time, 1940, Orwell had personally come to accept a patriotism that differed from nationalism and called him out in defence of his country. But such a step was a serious one for him, not an evasive about-face, but a chosen reversal of his earlier attitude.[5] Such a man is questioning, testing, not sure of himself. It is also worth remembering that Orwell, for all he wanted to say about the role of the writer in society, for all his book reviews, was not at this time an experienced literary critic. And in each of these essays that is what he is attempting to be. It would be surprising if the personal opinion of such a learning essayist or narrator provided an easily recognized rhetorical stance. Miller can communicate to the ordinary man because his is a 'voice from the crowd', from the recurrent safety of the albeit 'third-class railway carriage, from the ordinary, non-political, non-moral, passive man' (*CEJL* I 501). An ordinary person tends to use language as a collection of clichés, as if afraid to forfeit social contact for communication. But for Orwell words such as 'political' or 'moral' carry resonances which lift this bland statement from its apparently uncritical observation to challenging criticism. In the context of the novels we can recall the earlier occurrences that define the vocabulary of this quotation. Taken alone, the words possibly lack the emphasis necessary to explicit rhetorical stance, but given this context it is important that political and moral attitudes are here combined, for it indicates that the step away from the isolated individual toward the political is being taken.

This said, 'Inside the Whale' does introduce several ambiguities which do not result from ambivalent stance but from the essayist's changing attitude to language, truth and history. The writer contrasts Poe's short stories with the novels of Julian Green and from this contrast the writer arrives at his earlier definition of talent as 'a matter of being able to care, of really *believing* in your beliefs, whether they are true of false', 'for a creative writer possession of the "truth" is less important then emotional sincerity'. Lying behind the definition is an attitude to truth as something absolute that individuals deviate from. What he has not yet come to realize is that belief in such an absolute implies the corollary that deviation from it is completely arbitrary. Individual 'sincerity' becomes indistinguishable from expedient interpretation. It is his ambivalent trust in such 'sincerity' that leaves the essayist partly justifying Miller because he at least is reacting against totalitarian orthodoxy even if it means severing himself from politics completely.

But the essay ends with the flat statement that Miller is not a great author, that while imaginative he is 'completely negative, unconstructive, amoral ...a passive accepter of evil, a sort of Whitman among the corpses'. Both the overt propagandists and the passive accepters are tools of totalitarianism. Without art, propagandists are essentially passive, spouting a party line, not their own ideas. Passive accepters, while being overtly passive in reaction against totalitarianism, in effect provide an audience that makes its propaganda possible for they never argue back.

The ambiguity of this essay does not lie in Orwell's analysis of the situation as symptomatic but in his neglect of spelling out the alternatives. He hints at the novelist who is not frightened and who presents unorthodox opinion but he does not expand on the dangers of this alternative reaction to totalitarianism. He demonstrates the necessity for a public and private interaction to arrive at a personal politics and he illustrates the negativity of party politics alone, but he does not go on to present his own stance toward the two aspects. Attacks on his stance in the essay come from his own failure to make it clear. And this stems from the formal problems posed by the genre of the essay, and from more fundamental changes in his attitude to perception and knowledge.

These three essays of 1940 summarize the essayist's ambivalent attitude to history, truth and language. He is not unaware of the dangers in totalitarianism, but he is unsure of the suitable solution. The problem resides in his hankering after an absolute. Not until he works for the BBC propaganda service during 1942 does he consciously sort out the contradictions, although the fictions have already recorded a shift in focus from the social to the political that the essays are slow to catch up with, as if the writer finds the intellectual statement far more difficult than the practice. And in effect the practical stance of *Homage to Catalonia* has already laid out the only effective solution for him. In the documentary fiction, the writer came to realize a fallibility extending much further than the personal, toward arbitrary, historical interpretation, relative truths and fluctuating language. One has only the actual, the physical and often sexual, experience on which the writer has so consistently insisted. But all communication distorts the actual, especially 'fact' which pretends that it is not doing so. As he comes to recognize both that there is no absolute manner for re-presenting actual experience, and that interaction with the world and other human beings depends upon a consensus or agreement about actual experience, he proposes a stance that does not impose upon the audience but tries to involve it directly. The suggestions in his documentary fiction are that the narrator's stance be made openly accessible to evaluation, and that writing should be structured on techniques that lack authorial completion – techniques such as analogy, juxtaposition and non-parallel repetition, which call for participation by the reader.

Political stance
From the start Orwell recognizes that the politics of his time is based on power and leader-worship. And from the start he also recognizes that it is tied to effective propaganda. The 1939 review of Bertrand Russell's *Power* repeats a form of a catch-phrase first used in *A Clergyman's Daughter* : it is 'an age in which two and two make five when the leader says so' (*CEJL* I 376). The essential aspect of leader-worship is for the leader to deceive others but not himself. The deceit depends on effective propaganda so that a single line of interpretation can be imposed. Further, such imposition can only be carried out if those involved in the leadership are aware of possibly conflicting facts and are then able to simultaneously consider and exclude them. Here lies the genesis of the doublethink process essential to the maintenance of a totalitarian state. *The Road to Wigan Pier* presented bourgeois socialists following an unconscious doublethink, but Orwell now realizes that it is also a technique for conscious self-persuasion into acceptance and passivity. In an article for *Time and Tide* of early 1940 Orwell takes 'leadership', 'progress' and the 'earthly paradise' of socialism to task. It is suggested that politics has attempted to usurp the place of religion and supplant God with a crude materialism (*CEJL* II 16), and that the rigid absolutism involved is destructive. By 1943 he is claiming that it is necessary 'to dissociate socialism from Utopianism' (*CEJL* III 63). Socialism should not claim to make the world perfect but better. Increasingly the essays written after 1940, stress that the absolutist tendencies in all party politics can only be controlled by personal participation and interaction, in other words not a submissive acceptance but an activity. Because it is an activity it involves choice and through choice it introduces morality. Furthermore the writer makes the point with a restrictive religious analogy and says that man 'is not likely to salvage

civilization unless he can evolve a system of good and evil which is independent of heaven and hell' (*CEJL* II 103).

Orwell is firmly against capitalism and its imperialist basis, but much of his writing from 1943, when he had left the BBC, leaves it aside as manifestly limited. Instead, Orwell concentrates on the solutions being offered by the Left. He says that the new system cannot simply be the solution of materialist progress offered by a crude Marxism. He concludes that both capitalism and the partial collectivism of Marxism in Communist states, are negative political systems because they depend on a restriction of the individual's right to choice, and thereby of his moral sense. There is no way out of this unless a planned economy can be somehow combined with the freedom of the intellect, which can only happen if the concept of right and wrong is restored to politics (*CEJL* III 19). This is the liberty of choice that Orwell associates with 'liberalism'. One should note what he has to say on this since he has so often been lumped in with nineteenth-century liberalism, when in fact he criticizes that as the basis for absolutism and modern totalitarianism. For him 'liberal' means liberty-loving, a defence of the freedoms of thought and speech not private property, free enterprise and free trade (*CEJL* IV 159).

Because the Left is not fully collectivist it tries to destroy the individual. As it stands in Soviet communism, it is 'a show covering a new form of class priviledge' (*CEJL* III 320). Political thought on the Left attempts to think for its members. It is a 'sort of masturbation fantasy in which the world of facts hardly matters' (*CEJL* III 295). The problem with thinking for others, with manipulating interpretation and creating a self-enclosed world, is that it will turn on its leaders unless it is totally controlled. Later on Orwell specifically notes that 'the weakness of all left-wing parties is their inability to tell the truth about the immediate future' (*CEJL* III 396) – that socialism will probably be uncomfortable in its early stages. And as one of his last diary entries comments, the problem is that the Left having built 'itself up out of nothing, it had to create a following by telling lies. For a left-wing party in power, its most serious antagonist is always its own past propaganda' (*CEJL* IV 515).

Modern political propaganda of all kinds is 'founded on "realism" and 'machine guns"' (*CEJL* II 18). In effect 'realism', which is the key to the development of political propaganda because of its ability to damage the 'sense of reality' (*CEJL* IV 81), is descriptive of the activity of doublethink. The word stands for the manipulation of truth and history to enforce a single party line, and is a concept essential to power politics. Neither of these aspects of coercion or manipulation is effective in the long term, however, unless interpretation can be completely controlled. The absolutism implied in the rigid religious qualities of modern power politics and the total control that is necessary to maintain it, will similarly destroy what it creates. And it is at this point, in the post-BBC period of 1943–44, that Orwell begins to recognize the extreme dangers of totalitarian politics, because totalitarian 'realism' is complete, its propaganda more thorough and technologically advanced.

Once he has realized this, other political alternatives of anarchism, revolution and pacificism are placed in perspective because while they are not overtly based in power they all end by inducing conformity and acceptance. In considering this range of political alternatives, Orwell initially sees revolution as positive because even though they all fail 'they are not all the same failures' (*CEJL* III 244). He does not agree with Koestler that the revolutionary process is in itself corrupting, but says that all revolutions become corrupt 'because of the impossibility of combining power with righteousness' (*CEJL* III 238). Gradually, however, more suspicion enters and another essay states that 'In the minds of active revolutionaries . . . the longing for a just society has always been fatally mixed up with the intention to secure power for themselves' (*CEJL* IV 18). Revolutionaries work for one particular end that they think of as the best conclusion. All their choices and alternatives are limited to that end, and they become as isolating as the politics they supplant, and he gives the example of State Communism.

Similarly, Orwell sees anarchism and pacificism as only appearing to be free from 'dirty' politics. In effect they too encourage 'this habit of mind' which desires power, for by consciously setting out to seem separate from material gain they bully people into conformity through a show of self-righteousness. He notes that 'The distinction that really matters is not between violence and non-violence, but between having and not having the appetite for power' (*CEJL* IV 301).

Having discarded this range of alternatives, what is Orwell left with? His religious belief in the individual limitation of human beings generates a sense of the necessary community human beings belong to: communism in a refreshing sense of the word. As early as 1940 he says, 'Man is not an individual, he is only a cell in our everlasting body, and he is simply aware of it' (*CEJL* II 17). The non-party communism he desires is a form of humanism, not a humanism created on the concept of the authority of man the private individual, but on the consciousness of the interactive community of human beings. The suggestion for the long term is a humanism that integrates the private individual and the party so that such division is replaced by an interaction that radically alters the idea of the individual and the government. Its insistence on active choice and participation would provide a fundamentally different approach to the conformities of party politics, revolutionary politics, anarchism and pacificism. But in the short term, being of necessity a practical politician, Orwell realizes that this is immediately impossible. The dangers of totalitarianism became for him far too great to allow political idealism to interfere with its eradication.

Language, truth and history

It is with this danger in mind that he turns to a closer examination of how totalitarianism effects its control through propaganda. Totalitarian 'realism' is the complete control of language, history and truth, that is founded on doublethink: the (con)fusion of absolute and arbitrary. After his work for the BBC propaganda team broadcasting to India, he gradually realizes that one must recognize and point out the impossibility of absolute truth if one is to approach any semblance of accuracy, and if one is to maintain freedom of re-interpretation. The poem 'As one non-combatant to another' written in 1943 just after he leaves the BBC says,

> All propaganda's lying, yours or mine
> It's lying even when its facts are true (*CEJL* II 302)

'Facts' can no longer be neutral since they depend upon the most powerful person in a specific field of politics, history or science insisting on his interpretation of events. Once people who actually experienced or observed those events have died or have forgotten the actuality, 'for practical purposes the lie will have become truth' (*CEJL* III 88). Orwell pursues this analysis in a later essay where his growing distrust of 'facts' as simple tools manipulated to prove cases, generates a more explicit discussion of the weaknesses of science. One article observes that while science 'ought to mean acquiring a *method*' in the end it is 'simply piling up a lot of facts' (*CEJL* IV 12). 'Politics vs. Literature' (1946), implies that it is through the dependence on absolute and exact fact that the state will one day turn its powers of control toward physical actuality, and it is a weakness in the dominant rational logic, primarily used by scientists but also underlying most aspects of contemporary humanism, that will make this possible. The essayist gives the example of the earth being round: when one asks how we know that the earth is round the average person goes through a series of suggestions that leave the idea 'rather precarious'. He then comments that in order to prove most other common assumptions 'I should have to fall back on the expert much earlier, and would be less able to test his pronouncements'. He concludes that scientific 'fact' and much else that defines our acceptance of the world 'does not rest on reasoning or on experiment, but on authority ... This *is* a credulous age' (*CEJL* IV 260). The moment any method rests on unquestioned authority it is subject to manipulation. The potential distortion that results is an object lesson to those who think that fact guarantees security. A rational logic restricted to a method for acquiring bits of information is not good enough. One needs a logic that tests its own process of assessing if one is to resist manipulation. Only through discussion can a belief be maintained without being limited. It is carelessness, the easy fall into negative rhetoric through rational logic, that may leave the consideration of any topic vulnerable to totalitarian control.

This manipulation makes the historian's job of 'objective' presentation virtually impossible.[6] The only counteraction is the residue of a 'liberal habit of mind, that thinks of truth as something outside yourself, something to be discovered, and not something you make up as you go along' (*CEJL* III 88–9). This is not a contradiction in terms. The externality of truth does not necessarily make that 'truth' a fixed object. From this perspective truth is no longer viewed as existing within man-made consciousness as an ideal to be obtained or gained, but it lies within the material existence of the world, radically different and outwith human beings. Maps, photographs and statistics begin to be viewed as 'tricky things' (*CEJL* III 92); they are no longer an index of dependable and complete information. The essayist has been suspicious of statistics since the Spanish Civil War because 'one never knows what factors they leave out of account' (*CEJL* I 379); now he recognizes that their hidden relativity will provide the basis for scientists and historians to pervert the materiality of their worlds through negative propaganda.

The complete disillusion the writer experiences during World War II over the presentation of truth, history and fact is only rescued by his belief that one has individual responsibility to recognize ambivalent elements and indicate one's own standards for evaluation.[7] He states: 'I believe that it is possible to be more objective than most of us are, but that it involves moral effort' (*CEJL* III 299). As 'Politics vs. Literature' points out, each individual must fight for the right to report 'as truthfully as is consistent with the ignorance, bias and self deception from which every observer necessarily suffers' (*CEJL* IV 61). On one hand the historical impulse is to see things as they are (*CEJL* I 4), but on the other the historian is in effect faced with a multitude of prejudiced views. Orwell actually comes to question whether a record of 'the true facts, so far as one could discover them' might not be as accurate as making 'the whole thing up' (*CEJL* IV 16). All history functions to:

> impose a pattern on events, or at least to discover a pattern, and for that purpose a sound general theory, or even an instinctive grasp of probability, might be more useful than a mountain of learning. A history constructed imaginatively would never be right about any single event, but it might come nearer to essential truth than a mere compilation of names and dates in which no one statement was demonstrably untrue. (*CEJL* IV 116–17)

In *Writers and Leviathan* (1948), the writer concludes that 'the belief that the truth will prevail . . . [is] distinctly questionable' (*CEJL* IV 409). But this occurs because he alters his attitude to truth. Rather than thinking of it as an absolute that all people will recognize in the same manner, he has come to view it as an external materiality that each person evaluates differently. What can be in common is the activity of evaluation, not the end product, and that activity requires a challenging moral effort which many people shun.

An analogous and more far-reaching development occurs in Orwell's attitude to language. At first language is presented in the essays as inadequate, clumsy and hindering. The writer concentrates on the possibility of increasing communication by increasing the accuracy of language. But, surprisingly in view of the great interest shown in the novels, the early essays of 1938–40 are not particularly interested in language.[8] The essay 'New Words' conjecturally dated 1940 in *CEJL*, indicates the beginning of a serious attempt to come to terms with exactly why language causes as many problems as it does. Here the writer's desire to eradicate inaccuracy and misunderstanding particularly after observing the manipulation of propaganda during the Civil War, sets him toward an absolutist and nominalist course. He begins with the statement that 'no new words are deliberately coined except as names for material objects' (*CEJL* II 3), or the suggestion that having a word for a thing permits definite communication, and notes the need to 'invent a vocabulary . . . , which would deal with parts of our experience now practically unamenable to the idea' (*CEJL* II 3). But as the argument proceeds the reader discovers that these statements, however indicative of the writer's wishes, have initially been set up to be argued against. The writer is fully aware of the restrictions. He notes that when dealing with concrete objects, 'we find that words are no liker to the reality than chessmen to living beings' (*CEJL* II 3). He says that most 'waking thoughts' of conscious thinking exist

> as a kind of chessboard upon which thoughts move logically and verbally; we use this part of our minds for any straightforward intellectual problems, and we get into the habit of thinking (i.e. thinking in our chessboard moments) that it is the whole of the mind. But obviously it is not the whole. The dissolved un-verbal world belonging to dreams is never quite absent from our minds. (*CEJL* II 4)

Language through which people touch each other is an interface, not a medium. It marks the limits rather than the extent of communication. Any serious attempt to verbalize leads to a rationalization of conduct 'more or less dishonestly'; individuals are unalterably isolated from understanding each other fully. While 'the art of writing is largely the perversion of words', and is a necessary perversion, the writer assumes that this must exist in tension with a straining toward honesty. He makes a casual statement that 'the less obvious this perversion is, the more thoroughly it has been done', and this will provide the basis for subsequent discussions about individual involvement. In most cases lack of apparent deceit is a matter of habitual tricks of speech and neglect. But in some cases it is due to a careful manipulation of the appearance of the familiar, which builds the strongest foundations for negative propaganda. The writer falsifies himself when he cannot control the deceit of his words: intentionally when words trap him into patterns through their conventional shape and structure, and unintentionally because the reader's interpretation varies.

Having shown himself fully aware of the process of deceit involved in any artistic creation, but here specifically creation with words, the essayist moves on to 'normal speech'. In doing so he shifts from to the issue of pure communication, in other words, to attempts at pure expression and here his absolutist tendencies begin to surface. He wants words to convey meaning more reliably, and suggests that one must change existing words and invent new ones if this is to occur. The idea that one has a responsibility to dominate language and not let it impose upon you is a reiteration of the presentation of language in *Down and Out in Paris and London*. The passing over of all that he learnt about the restrictions of a stance of imposition in both *Wigan Pier* and *Homage to Catalonia*, though, indicates just how far the essays lag behind the novels. Ironically in the light of the preceding anti-rational argument of the essay, the writer here views control exactly in terms of rational argument itself, claiming that people have a detrimental, instinctive belief 'that any direct rational approach to one's difficulties [with language] . . . can lead nowhere' (*CEJL* II 8).

Not surprisingly his solution at this point is contradictory. He says that to talk about definitions is 'futile'. What is needed is, 'to *show* a meaning in some unmistakable form' (*CEJL* II 10), for the 'now nameless feelings that men have *in common*' (*CEJL* II 11). But the 'unmistakable' betrays him: just as the conclusions to the early novels indicated solutions that were unsatisfactory because they were general, the writer here is hankering after a generally applicable standard. Not until he realizes that the key is for each individual to make his personal evaluation clear and open to public reassessment, will he resolve the conflict between the analogical activity of showing the 'nameless' which implies the inexpressible, and 'unmistakable' which implies the definite.[9]

The major change in his attitude to these ideas takes place during his work for the BBC from August 1941 to November 1942. 'The English People', written in 1943, provides an excellent contrast to 'New Words'. It discusses the contemporary make-up and potential for change in the English language, and it also presents a full example of Orwell's evenhandedness, generosity and vulnerability to misinterpretation. The essay begins with a discussion of current power-worship trends in British politics. The writer notes that the English never oppose theory with theory but with a 'moral quality which must be vaguely described as decency' (*CEJL* III 13). In earlier works the comment would have been praise. But the weakness of private decency in the face of totalitarianism has made him suspicious of it here, and later he becomes even more critical. This decency is a result of never following theories to their logical conclusions, never even assessing the method of that logic, never really trying to get to grips with the problem.[10] It is for this reason one finds the dismissal of 'decency' in *Coming Up for Air*; it is not usually an active trait but one of acceptance. But the persistence with which the essayist portrays here its positive aspects, as well as his reluctance to indicate the negative, has left the essay interpreted as being in praise of decency.

The writer proposes that the two main elements of the English language are the large size of its vocabulary and its simplicity of grammar. These allow it enormous range of meaning and tone, as well as compression. But at the same time these elements may contribute to very different developments: 'It is capable of subtleties, and of everything from the most high-flown rhetoric to brutal coarseness . . . It is the language of lyric poetry, and also of headlines . . .' (*CEJL* III 24). It is the ease with which the English language may be debased that makes constant individual attention to it essential. While this essay is a long way from the absolutism of 'New Words', the writer again tries to place his faith in something definite: here, the spoken word, and speech becomes the writer's new obsession providing the background to the theories of 'Basic English'.

Basic English as opposed to political jargon is the focus for the discussion of language in a series of essays of the later war years, specifically in an article written in April 1944, 'Propaganda and Demotic Speech'. While he specifically takes political language to task, the 'dead metaphors', for example of Communist literature, are symptomatic of a much wider range of language misuse including pamphletese, official English, scientific jargon and American slang. But as he notes in his 'As I Please' column of 17 March 1944, more serious than these conscious 'rhetorical tricks' is the characteristic of Communist phraseology which consists of 'ready-made metaphors', of 'crudely translated phrases, and from force of habit . . . [we] come to think of them as actual English expressions . . .' (*CEJL* III 110). 'Propaganda and Demotic Speech' comments that the same unthinking language is found in the journalistic techniques of 'bloodless dialect' or 'an inflated bombastic style with a tendency to fall back on archaic words' (*CEJL* III 135). These language devices themselves derive from habit, and in turn instil carelessness in their listeners.

Another 'As I Please' column of 2 June 1944, says that ordinary people remain 'undisturbed by obvious lies, either because they simply forget what is said from day to day or because they are under such a constant propaganda bombardment that they become anaesthetised to the whole business' (*CEJL* III 165). Stressed again and again is the lack of attention to meaning: 'people capable of using such phrases have ceased to remember that words have meanings' (*CEJL* III 110), 'language of this kind is used with an astonishing indifference as to its meaning'. A later essay in *The Tribune*, February 1945, reiterates the criticism on a more general scale, noting that if a metaphor moves far from the original meaning it loses the power of concrete illustration, and that 'People who are capable of this kind of thing evidently don't attach any definite meaning to the words they use'

(*CEJL* III 332). It is important to note the similarity of these linguistic details to the techniques of fantasy literature, since both are concerned with reducing the active consciousness of their audience.

The failure of language to remain concrete severs it from 'clear, popular, everyday language' (*CEJL* III 135) and the essayist claims that the average person has 'fantastic misunderstandings' of abstract words. Everyday language or Basic English is much closer to the concrete. Its essential difference from political language is that the latter is based on written English and the former on spoken. However when the writer moves into the technical aspects of Basic English he is unable to define with the kind of detail that he achieves in his study of political language. He suggests that the rules of spoken English should be studied and deduced so that the ordinary person can learn them. Orwell claims that Basic English would act as a 'corrective to the oratory of statesmen and publicists' (*CEJL* II 210), and even adds albeit with some caution that 'In Basic, I am told, you cannot make a meaningless statement without its being apparent that it is meaningless'. What the desire for Basic English indicates more than anything else is a concern for the language individuals should use not only for their own sakes, but also in relation to a popular audience to avoid the errors of the mass magazines. It is as if the writer's work on propaganda for the BBC, and his observation of encroaching totalitarianism highlight the two-way process of communication, and the responsibility of the individual in both speaking and listening.

Indeed the clearest idea of Orwell's theory of Basic English is found in his own speech. Having taught himself to cut the purple passages from his novels, he now teaches himself to simplify his language. The text of a Schools' broadcast made in 1945 is an excellent example of his procedure. The typed text is adjusted with handwritten revisions, clearly noting the kinds of amendments he had in mind. For example, the opening general statement originally read 'Anyone who invents an . . .'; but this is changed to 'Obviously if you invent . . .' moving away from the abstract. He concretizes experience, altering 'I've been suffering from bad headaches lately' to 'I had a bad headache yesterday'. The vocabulary changes are all in the direction of simple, shorter, more anglicized forms, for example: 'notoriously' becomes 'supposed to be'; 'pervaded by' becomes 'is'; 'highly indignant', 'angry indeed'; 'facilities', 'chance'; 'sequence', 'chain'; 'arrested', 'stopped' (*BA* 8/6/45). The changes provide an exercise by example in cutting out jargon and excess, and making an account more immediate. Granted the broadcast was for sixth formers, and Orwell may have been concerned to avoid boring them; but that would have been his point: there is no need to bore your audience. To interest them one does not need to cheat by simplifying concepts, but to adjust one's vocabulary and syntax to the needs of the audience.

The connection between speaker or writer and listener or reader, moves the essayist to a full understanding of the double-edged and arbitrary nature of absolutist theories. 'Politics and the English Language' (1946), refines on the technical elements of language in terms similar to those of 'The English People', but it now stresses that a relationship with words is not one of definition by them or imposition of meaning onto them. The effective factor is conscious choice:

> This invasion of one's mind by ready-made phrases . . . can only be prevented if one is constantly on guard against them . . . one can choose – not simply *accept* – the phrases that will best cover the meaning and then switch round and decide what impressions one's words are likely to make on another person. (*CEJL* IV 137-8)

The essay characterizes modern English language as lazy, passive and insincere leading to vagueness, imprecision and staleness. The words cease to be chosen, and cease even to be selected for their significance. The criticisms all add up to an accusation that writers do not want to take the time and trouble to find the precise and clear expression, that they get pulled into the ambivalent and vague, and having done this have to dress up their language with deceptive techniques. In his words: 'A mass of Latin words falls upon the facts like soft snow, blurring the outlines and covering up all details. The great enemy of clear language is insincerity' (*CEJL* IV 137).

Orwell places the root of the problem in a current belief that a struggle against the debasement and abuse of language is 'sentimental archaism' (*CEJL* IV 127). The idea had been generated out of the concept that language was a natural growth, but while Orwell denied this concept he did not have the simplistic idea that one word equals one thing, and that language is totally defined by man. In fact he saw the progress to such a possibility in the sciences as an appalling limitation that would narrow and restrict the fields of research. What he stresses instead is that full recognition of this externality leaves one with a responsibility to get as close as possible to the appropriate word. Without this care man ceases to consider language as something with which he interacts.

Positive and Negative Stances

During the period 1940 to 1946 Orwell begins to concentrate on the elements of choice and interaction for a valid stance within language. At the same time he gathers together ideas about restrictive political language and its relation to the manipulation of history and truth. He recognizes that the techniques of negative propaganda gain their singular control by the unperceived reinforcement of the absolute by the arbitrary in the dominant medium of language. The control first isolates the individual from actuality thereby denying him access to personal interpretations of history and truth, and hence depriving him of any possibility of evaluation. Without value the individual is reduced to living within a private fantasy that is structurally analogous to the political; he is therefore in a position to be deprived of any individuality at all as the political is imposed upon him. Conformity becomes the only option.

While all forms of party politics attempt this, an early article, 'Literature and Totalitarianism' (1941), notes that a totalitarian state in particular,

> isolates from the outside world, it shuts you up in an artificial universe in which you have no standards of comparison. The totalitarian state tries, at any rate, to control the thoughts and emotions of its subjects at least as completely as it controls their actions. (*CEJL* II 136)

Later essays develop a more complex understanding of this mechanism for isolation. It is a fallacy to believe that one can ever be free in one's own private terms, within a totalitarian state (*CEJL* III 132). Here he spells out the need for public and personal interaction saying that:

> The great mistake is to imagine that the human being is an autonomous individual . . . Philosophers, writers, artists, even scientists, not only need encouragement and an audience, they need constant stimulation from other people. It is almost impossible to think without talking . . . (*CEJL* III 133)

Totalitarian systems enforce a separation and isolation not only from fact but also from other people. The only possible individual identity in the system depends upon complete autonomy, on complete severance from others. There is either an enforced oneness of mind with society, or total separation from it. Either way the interaction generating social responsibility and personal political convictions, cannot exist.[11] The separation that Orwell wants between personal and party politics can now be seen not only as a practical split in terms of the individual retaining his integrity, but also as a positive element in its own right, maintaining the fight against totalitarianism by ensuring that party politics changes and grows. But the point is that totalitarian systems do not simply deny active choice and enforce passive acceptance: they create an attitude of mind that seeks acceptance and avoids engaged consciousness.

The isolation necessary to effect control through the arbitrary and absolute strategy that underlies the system is made possible by various modes of restrictive rhetorical stance analogous to restrictive language. Not surprisingly the first focus of these essays of the early 1940s is on Hitler. Hitler's power derives from being a demagogue among the unemployed, a speaker with a susceptible audience who can employ the force of his personality. Secondly he recognizes the strategic value of asking for sacrifice, not offering comfort. It involves the audience if not in the argument at least in an action and implies an identification between them, a brotherhood (*CEJL* II 2). Elsewhere Orwell notes Mosley's effectiveness in Britain through a combination of personality and force (*CEJL* I 73), and he insists on the falsity of the idea 'that propaganda *without* a display of military strength can achieve anything' (*CEJL* II 110). In 'Notes on the Spanish Militias' the writer observes that the appeal to party loyalty, strength of personality and force itself, are techniques which are respectively less and less effective (*CEJL* I 319).

Orwell picks out the specific aspects of negative rhetoric that allow it to function. He comments that there is more 'suppression than downright lying' (*CEJL* II 345) since omission gives less cause for argument than falsified accounts that may be exposed. German propaganda is inconsistent and 'deliberately so, with utter unscrupulousness in offering everything to everybody' (*CEJL* II 413). Here he implies that this is 'sound' propaganda in terms of whether it will effect persuasion. He suggests that most people are so 'politically ignorant' that they would not notice the inconsistencies, hence it would serve its purpose. The linguistic twists of German propaganda are observed almost with glee and discussed overtly in his own propaganda broadcasts. He notes, for example, the use of 'liquidation' as a 'polite name for murder' (*BA* 12/12/42) and refers to 'strategic withdrawal' and 'elastic defence' as equivalents for retreat. More sophisticated techniques are found in remarks such as 'We have successfully increased the distance between ourselves and the enemy' – which make retreat appear strategically chosen not enforced. He suggests that in using such statements 'the Germans are preparing their home public for bad news' (*BA* 19/12/42). Inconsistent information is a characteristic extended to the detail of wartime reports, but the technique is not simply a war strategy, for 'people in totalitarian countries are expected to have short memories' (*BA* 9/1/43).

What Orwell is beginning to note is that the rhetorical stance essential to war strategies is morally questionable when used in governing the day to day action of the state. It is the similarity between justified strategic war propaganda and unethical political propaganda that brings home the dangers of both. The latter is dangerous because it is rarely recognized as propaganda, yet the situation in peacetime is not serious enough to warrant such evasion. Yet he also comes to recognize that even in war strategies a code of practice should be observed (*TI* p. 9). The question of expediency as opposed to dishonesty which is initially viewed as a question of the separation between two different strategies of propaganda, is increasingly viewed more as a question of difference in degree as Orwell perceives the similarity in the stance of the two. At the same time this perception throws forward the problematical situation of the individual who is creating this linguistic propaganda for the state.

As a propagandist himself, Orwell begins at the BBC with 'broadcasts which I believe can be really helpful and constructive at a time like this'

(*BA* 1/2/42). His own broadcasts are clear, simple, almost self-effacing. As far as possible he creates an ethos not of authority but of involving, by consistently undercutting and understating, with phrases such as 'not expect too much' (*BA* 21/11/42) or 'I don't care yet to predict . . .' It is as if he does not perceive that these strategies, however technically acceptable, are still weighting the argument. They cannot protect his integrity.

After three months working for the BBC, a diary entry for 27 April 1942 laments the performance of British propaganda as confused, rather than effectively inconsistent, and blames it on lack of information from the government. Without sufficient background reported events can come across looking more like imperialism than victory (*CEJL* II 424). At first he assumes that whatever is said, one looks for 'hidden motives and assumes that words mean anything except what they appear to mean . . .' (*CEJL* II 423). Later on, he recognizes that British propaganda has been hampered by its attempts at consistency and has needed 'to tell lies about some vitally important matter, because to tell the truth would give ammunition to the enemy' (*CEJL* III 170); but he adds that in the case of propaganda cover-ups in the Spanish Civil War 'some all-important lessons were not learned, and we are suffering from the fact to this day' (*CEJL* III 170). In other words what kind of an ethos does one create for oneself even in terms of war strategy?   In resolving the problems this raises, Orwell also resolves the contradictions in his reversal of attitude toward the war in 1940. A distinction is proposed between nationalism and patriotism, the former being a matter of 'competitive prestige' and the latter of defence. In separating between the two the essayist defines far more clearly the hitherto vague reasons for the justification for the use of negative rhetoric in war propaganda, and condemnation of its use elsewhere. The primary aspect of nationalist thought is rational inductive analytical logic. The nationalist 'start by deciding in favour of something . . . and only *after* this would begin searching for arguments to support his case' (*CEJL* III 364). From this starting point arise three characteristics of nationalism: obsession, instability and indifference to reality. Obsession is figured forth in a rigid nomenclature which renames objects and events as if to remake them in the image of their thought.

Nationalists always try to impose their language on other people. Instability is a constant factor, for the individual's mind must be able to shift and change with the inevitable shifts in political outlook. As a result 'the object of his feeling is changeable, and may be imaginary' (*CEJL* III 368). Related to this is an indifference to reality which permits the acceptance of change. The writer notes that 'All nationalists have the power of not seeing resemblances between similar sets of facts . . . Actions are good or bad, not on their own merits but according to who does them' (*CEJL* III 369). Orwell calls it 'transferred nationalism' or 'attaining salvation without altering one's conduct' (*CEJL* III 369) because personal choice is unnecessary. The habit of mind necesssary to maintain the logic of nationalism must include:

> facts which are both true and untrue, known and unknown. A known fact may be so unbearable that it is habitually pushed aside and not allowed to enter into logical processes, or on the other hand it may enter into every calculation and yet never be admitted as a fact, even in one's own mind. (*CEJL* III 370)

Again, the process is one of doublethink. The danger lies not in the stage that history or 'fact' can be altered, although nationalists do live 'in a fantasy world in which things happen as they should' (*CEJL* III 370), but in the ultimate stage of totalitarian propaganda which aims at convincing its users 'that they are actually thrusting facts into the past' (*CEJL* III 372). Once a person has mastered this process he enters a world of fantasy with 'dreams of power and conquest which leave no connection with the physical world' (*CEJL* III 372). The world is one with Hitler's monomania. It is seductive and habit-forming. One needs constantly to fight it in oneself, to employ that 'moral effort' (*CEJL* III 380).

Orwell is not just indicating a possibility. The same diary entry of 27 April makes clear that he believes that many thinking people are giving way to this habit of mind. He says:

> I feel that intellectual honesty and balanced judgement has simply disappeared from the face of the earth. Everyone's thought is forensic, everyone is simply putting a 'case' with deliberate suppression of his opponent's point of view, and, what is more, with complete insensitivity to any sufferings except those of himself and his friends . . . What is most striking of all is the way sympathy can be turned on or off like a tap, according to political expediency . . . (*CEJL* II 423)

To return to the line between political and war propaganda with the distinction between patriotism and nationalism in mind: it is clear that Orwell is not naïvely idealistic. He has spent much time complaining about the British inefficiency in propaganda, about the need for inconsistency in order to be effective. His conclusions on his experiences as a propagandist are not made lightly. However, in the end only a complete recognition of and guard against negative rhetoric is advocated. The essayist warns:

> dishonesty and cowardice always have to be paid for. Don't imagine that for years on end you can make yourself the boot-licking propagandist of the Soviet regime, or any other regime, and then suddenly return to mental decency. Once a whore, always a whore. (*CEJL* III 227)

The BBC itself is called a 'mixture of whoreshop and lunatic asylum' (*CEJL* II 305). Dishonesty in terms of suppression is the worst, not only for its effect on others but its backlash on oneself for 'If you disregard people's motives, it becomes much harder to foresee their actions' (*CEJL*

III 289). His bitter conclusion on his broadcasting work is that despite all, the propaganda has been useless. There is, for example a

> [g]hastly feeling of impotence over the India business . . . the impudent way in which the newspapers can misrepresent the whole issue, well knowing that the public will never know enough or take enough interest to verify the facts. This last is the worst symptom of all. (*CEJL* II 448)

The statement belies the confidence that people would realize they were being manipulated by war propaganda, and underlines the necessity of avoiding negative rhetoric in all situations.

While political propaganda that uses but simultaneously forgets the absolute and arbitrary division is dishonest, the practical political propaganda that still manages to keep the absolute and arbitrary in view is at least sincere. The important element in an alternative positive rhetoric is the exposure and clarification of principles. One should do this personally in any interaction with the political, but the political itself should do so in its own propaganda. A late article 'In Defence of Comrade Zilliacus' comments that as a member of parliament Zilliacus may not be honest 'but at least he is sincere. We know where he stands' (*CEJL* IV 400). Here Orwell is making the distinction between honesty which is action according to personal belief, and sincerity which is action according to the practical demands of group life. The former asks for complete conviction while the latter accepts the need for some expediency. While the pragmatism of party politics cannot tolerate the honesty of personal politics, it should face it in determining the principles upon which it acts, and when acting it does at the least have its own responsibility to state those principles. They may not be reached by honest means, but the party should be sincere about what they are. Pragmatic politics still allows interaction with the honesty of the individual, and it is that honesty that keeps the paradox of absolute and arbitrary in view. Totalitarianism's destruction of the individual allows it to complete its circle of rhetorical negativity.

In these analyses both of political and wartime propaganda, Orwell is reintroducing questions about the techniques and ethical validity of certain kinds of persuasion. The conclusions of his examination come remarkably close to those of earlier rhetoricians from the classical period to the Renaissance.[12] What Orwell does is place the basic strategies of all persuasion that attempts to dominate, to control the external world by imposition, in a twentieth-century context. Although not formalized into a theory, his observations reveal a consistent approach that outlines the background for a renewed interest in rhetorical studies during the thirty years following his death. The problem is that the action of negative rhetorical stance in contemporary authoritarian states is no longer short-term either in war or peace. Limitation to the short term is a result of recognition of contradictory accounts of an event that then demands an individual assessment. Totalitarian propaganda operating through complete suppression, omission, evasion and finally eradication of possibly conflicting evidence, can control thought, history, truth and one's moral choice. Choice in effect cannot occur. There is simply selection from among a limited number of possibilities provided by the party. Such propaganda pushes the elements of political jargon to a stage under which the audience is totally submissive.

Further, developing technology has made sure that any use of suppression can approach completeness. In this age, the use of negative rhetoric by 'democratic' political parties also has its totalitarian implications, hence the contemporary need to be more cautious in its use. More than this, totalitarian propaganda aims in the end to hide its aims even from itself. Unless one always avoids negative rhetoric one can never know if one is being caught into a totalitarian doublethink; one is deprived of any standards of evaluation at all. Political parties can be restrained from such doublethink only by interaction with the personal politics of their members. But those personal politics are also subject to totalitarian propaganda. There is a double responsibility, to oneself and to one's political party, not to fall prey to negative rhetoric. And for Orwell the point at which personal politics are in most danger of becoming a victim of doublethink, is in the literary arts.

CHAPTER FIVE

Art, Propaganda and Politics

For an artist, use of negative rhetoric is the destruction of art as it has been known. Most importantly its use of language and logic would not actively engage an audience. For this reason writing and literature would also become unethical in that while they are actions themselves, they would deny and prevent any other activity. Hence art would deny its own value and in the long term would always be exposed. Until a new kind of art arises the artist, especially the writer, will either find it impossible to produce because he is isolated, or else he will compromise himself and his work. Orwell suggested that the writer would be particularly susceptible because it was the literary medium that people used most for communication at that time. Any artist using words is closer to the expression of meaning as information and opinion than an artist employing some other medium and by implication he is also closer to overt propaganda.

By 1940, Orwell connects art and propaganda because no artist can exclude meaning from his work. Hence art involves a stance and a way of evaluating , in other words a morality. The essay 'New Words' (1940), casually mentions that 'aesthetic and moral considerations are in any case inextricable' (*CEJL* II 5). But meaning here is primarily a matter of overt opinion rather than structural significance, so the morality which the essayist is referring to is tied not to the activity of writing but to the information it conveys. Such a definition provides him with a basis for a possible avoidance of meaning altogether. The essay 'The Frontiers of Art and Propaganda' (1941), returns to the topic of writing in the 1920s and 1930s. The shattering of values in the late 1920s is held responsible for the political literature which followed, since to write otherwise would have been dishonest. However the dominance of 'content' especially in the Communist political literature of the 1930s, showed that subject matter alone was not enough.

A residue from the movement, the colouring of aesthetic judgement by prejudice and belief, still exists. A later essay notes that 'The deadly sin is to say "x is a political enemy: therefore he is a bad writer"' (*CEJL* II 293). Because the word 'political' still refers primarily to party politics alone, the essayist is led to place political propaganda and art in mutual exclusion to each other. The exclusion causes a series of conflicting statements about form and meaning, art and morality. For example he says in an early comment about Tolstoy on Shakespeare that precedes his major essay 'Lear, Tolstoy and the Fool' (1941), that there will always be a 'residuum' lying beyond meaning that is pure art, and concludes that 'Within certain limits, bad thought and bad morals can be good literature' (*CEJL* II 130). In other words art and morality can be separated.

The whole question of whether art and morality are connected, of whether propaganda and literature can be separated or not, hinges on the concept of meaning. It is the writer's attitude to meaning in poetry that provides the clearest index to his ideas. Contradictions in his attitude to meaning in literature are obvious from the beginning. An early letter of 1933 suggests that apart from the creation of characters and patterns of design, the novelist should aim 'to produce *good writing*, which can exist almost as it were in vacuo and independent of subject' (*CEJL* I 126). On the other hand 'Inside the Whale' states that 'no book is ever truly neutral. Some tendency or other is always discernible, in verse as much as in prose, even if it does no more than determine the form and the choice of imagery' (*CEJL* I 506). A discussion of Hopkins's verse in 'The Meaning of a Poem', broadcast for the BBC in 1941, indicates the tension in his definition. He notes the importance of meaning conveyed by sounds, associations, and harmonies in metrical form, but speaks of that meaning as different from referential and denotative meaning. He says 'This poem is moving because of its sound, its musical qualities, but it is also moving because of an emotional content which could not be there if Hopkins's philosophy and beliefs were different from what they were' (*CEJL* II 132). Soon after, he comments that totalitarianism endangers all literature 'of any consequence' because it prevents people from feeling the truth of what they say (*CEJL* II 136). If formal meaning were indeed separate from referential meaning then totalitarianism would be powerless against it since the basis for its negative rhetorical strategy is control over the denotative relationship between word and object. But the essayist is implying that meaning related to beliefs is not simply referential but formal as well.

In a broadcast on the poetry of Yeats (1943), he says that 'The subject-matter and imagery of a book can be explained in sociological terms, but its texture seemingly cannot. Yet some such connection there must be' (*CEJL* II 271). Significantly, he puts the unresolved nature of his query on the texture of Yeats's poetry down to inadequate critical concepts, implying that with adequate terms a discussion of the interdependence could be carried out. As long as he could separate between form and content, pure art and propagandic meaning, the writer had a means of separating between private expression and political propaganda and excluding the artist from political commitment, at the same time as allowing him to comment politically (sincerely) without endangering his honesty. But it is increasingly obvious that the two are close, inextricably interdependent, if not actually taking place at the same time. The closer he comes to saying that the two aspects are inseparable, the more he realizes that the literary artist cannot write without expressing a political view.

Having reached this point, whose 'political view' is a writer to express? One of the origins of Orwell's conflicting attitudes to meaning was his distaste for simply voicing party political propaganda; and until he began to distinguish between personal and party politics, he was always to strive after a concept of pure art. After his experience working for the BBC, his observation of the dangers of totalitarianism and the growing belief that people were giving in to totalitarian habits of mind, he began to establish his distinction between the two. It is also at this time that he concludes that the artist, whatever his medium, has to express a political view. If an individual has a responsibility to interact with party politics, then so does the artist as an individual. The government depends on the artist for its propaganda, and the artist should be able in turn to influence the government; but the artist also depends on the state in financial and environmental terms. He must learn to interact with it in order to retain some control over his way of life, ability to make choices and evaluate.

Increasingly, the writer notes the correlation between government propaganda and art. He first notes the insidious control by the state over radio, cinema and theatre (*TT* 17/8/40) although he also recognizes it in fiction and predicts its appearance in other arts as well (*CEJL* III 22), and then insists on the need to resist it or at least to keep it separate from art. An awareness of government control and a means of resisting it are doubly important because with the passing of capitalism the artist will become a state employee, 'He must become either a spare-time amateur or an official'. The problem is that '(1) Society cannot be arranged for the benefit of artist; (2) without artists civilization perishes' (*CEJL* III 230). At this stage however he cannot suggest an answer. If the artist is to have a social role he will end up writing for the government, probably

> something to do with propaganda. But this is itself a kind of writing. To compose a propaganda pamphlet or a radio feature needs just as much work as to write something you believe in, with the difference that the finished product is worthless. (*CEJL* III 254)

Here his distress over his BBC work is expressed with remarkable clarity. The artist must be responsible, socially committed and involved but 'no government, no big organization, will pay for the truth' (*CEJL* III 255).

A review of Salvador Dali's autobiography is a transitional point in Orwell's ideas on art, morality and the question of whether it is possible to write well if one does not believe in what one does. The review condemns the book as 'a direct, unmistakable assault on sanity and decency' (*CEJL* III 159), but the artist himself is 'talented' and 'of very exceptional gifts'. Here the word 'decency' should alert the reader to the need for an active defence of his values; without it 'decency' is merely a sentimental *status quo*. The writer goes on to say that the average Englishmen 'are not only unable to admit that what is morally degraded can be aesthetically right, but their real demand of every artist is that he shall pat them on the back and tell them thought is unnecessary' (*CEJL* III 160). More than this, audiences apparently have difficulty with obscenity because they are afraid both of being shocked and not being shocked. They will not personally define a 'relationship between art and morals' (*CEJL* III 160), even though the ability to criticize good art as immoral is necessary because 'an artist is also a citizen and a human being' (*CEJL* III 161). In fact Orwell's analysis of Dali goes on to point out that he is supremely old-fashioned. Dali is brilliant at the representational and sentimental despite his use of ink splashes to break up the resulting whole. His work is essentially an escape, '*into wickedness*' (*CEJL* III 164), into something not part of his own integrity.

Immorality for Orwell is betrayal of self. Miller avoided self-betrayal by refusing to involve himself in politics at all in his early work. Orwell called him amoral. Similarly, party political literature is an evasion of individual responsibility, and an assumption of false power conferred by a group. An acute comment from an earlier essay notes that the 'propagandist, when he is not a lifeless hack, is often a neurotic working off some private grudge and actually desirous of the exact opposite of the thing he advocates' (*CEJL* II 306). The assumption of power to compensate for this betrayal of self is a parallel that Orwell extends out into 'The interconnexion between sadism, masochism, success worship, power worship, nationalism and totalitarianism' (*CEJL* III 221–2). The connection is based on an observation that 'the cult of power tends to be mixed up with a love of cruelty and wickedness *for their own sakes*' (*CEJL* IV 232). For literature the implication of a cult of power is an invasion of negative rhetoric that will induce a passive audience necessary to absolute control. As in totalitarian propaganda, such literature produces a 'fantasy' where things are done as one desires, might is right. And although 'The Prevention of Literature' begins by suggesting again that poetry might just elude totalitarian control because meaning is not its 'primary purpose' (*CEJL* III 67),this is followed by the later retraction that totalitarianism is 'inimical to all forms of literature' (*CEJL* IV 68).

The discussion of literature and politics comes to a head in five major essays of 1946–8: 'Why I Write' (WIW), 'The Prevention of Literature'

(PL), 'Politics and the English Language' (PE), 'Politics vs Literature' (LP) and 'Writers and Leviathan' (WL), some of which essays have already been touched on in the discussion of language, history and truth. These articles examine in detail the relationship between four reasons for writing identified in 'Why I Write' as: sheer egoism, aesthetic enthusiasm, historical impulse and political purpose; and how they affect literature and politics in the middle of the twentieth century. The interaction necessary among these aspects is achieved through specific strategies aiding positive rhetorical stance that indicate the integrity of the writer's opinion and the honesty of his presentation of events, not through the restricted stance of any one particular ideology or force of private personality but through the positive stance that informs the text.

All discussion of literary purpose in these essays is made from an understanding that literature is inevitably bound up with a political context in contemporary England. By 'politics' Orwell means two things. The first and more important is, 'the widest possible sense. Desire to push the world in a certain direction, to alter other people's idea of the kind of society that they should strive after' (CEJL I 4). The second use of 'politics' refers to party politics which are viewed as essentially timid and dishonest (CEJL WL, IV 409), a 'mass of lies, evasions, folly, hatred and schizophrenia' (CEJL PE, IV 137). There is a pressure toward conformity right across the board in party politics, which Orwell relates to their foundation in 'perfectionist ideology', and it culminates in the opposites of totalitarianism and anarchy which are, on examination, close to each other. The height of totalitarianism occurs when 'conformity has become so general that there is no need for a police force' (CEJL LP, IV 216). The two extremes fuse at the point where the greatest individual responsibility makes a man choose to lose his identity to the public will, and where the least individual responsibility has negated the possibility of personal identity and leaves all public dictates to be accepted without question.

It is this pressure to conformity that upsets the relation between politics and the individual writer. The age is such that whether he likes it or not the writer will develop a 'guilt-stricken feeling that one ought to do something about [the world], which makes a purely aesthetic attitude to life impossible' (CEJL WL, IV 409). But a more fundamental point is that 'Above quite a low level, literature is an attempt to influence the viewpoint of one's contemporaries by recording experience' (CEJL PL, IV 65). While these are political concerns in the 'widest sense', they soon run into party politics, and the party politics of the 1930s and 1940s are accused of viewing intellectual honesty and freedom as selfish and undesirable.

Orwell recognizes the necessity of effacing personality if one is to produce literature, but he also stresses the retention of an integrity. When 'sheer egoism' develops into questions of personal integrity it becomes vitally important. Integrity is the central theme of 'The Prevention of

Literature'. The essay proposes that the acceptance of any political orthodoxy will lead to loss of integrity. Discipline and group loyalty will necessarily keep questions of truth in the background, for the writer will be handed topics that he can never express if 'telling what seems to him the whole of the truth' (*CEJL* PL, IV 60). If intellectual honesty is viewed as 'antisocial selfishness' the conflict in the writer becomes one of the 'desirability, or otherwise, of telling lies' (*CEJL* PL, IV 61). Orwell argues that it is part of the historical purpose of the imaginative writer to report the response of his senses, what he sees and hears, and not to distort them. 'Why I Write' sums up his position by saying that political bias should be overtly stated for the more one is aware of it 'the more chance one has of acting politically without sacrificing one's aesthetic and intellectual integrity' (*CEJL* WIW, I 6).

The retention of integrity is also important because literature is inseparable from honesty. The argument asserts that if political pressure to conformity forces the writer to lie, his creative faculties will dry up. And Orwell proceeds to make this provocative assertion the focus for his study of rhetorical stance, specifically against the background of totalitarian control. First it is important to make clear that the word 'lie' does not refer to the process of creating fictions or to the presentation of fact and event in an imaginative manner or to the continual deceit involved in a non-representational model of language. What 'lying' involves for Orwell is any assertion of something one does not believe in. Even an imaginative writer

> may distort or caricature reality in order to make his meaning clearer, but he cannot misrepresent the scenery of his own mind: he cannot say with any conviction that he likes what he dislikes, or believes what he disbelieves. (*CEJL* PL, IV 65)

The infallibility of totalitarian states, however, is based on a system of 'organized lying' (*CEJL* PL, IV 63). Personal opinion and conviction are unnecessary since 'truth' will either be a continually shifting party interpretation or, in a more definite sense, impossible to recover. The infallible state maintains doctrines that are 'not only unchallengeable but also unstable' (*CEJL* PL, IV 66). The pressure that such shifts exert on the writer, making him continually abandon belief and conviction, depriving him of personal opinion and forcing him to lie, eventually dry up his creative talent.

The results of this extreme opposition of party political to aesthetic purpose in 'The Prevention of Literature' are intelligent, theoretical conjecture. But in 'Politics and the English Language' the writer moves into practical considerations through a reiteration of the question of integrity. Political conformity creates 'a gap between one's real and one's declared aims' (*CEJL* PE, IV 137) that leads to insincerity, and from there to vagueness, imprecision and bad writing. The acceptance of any political orthodoxy necessitates self-censorship by the writer, in order to suppress belief and reflect the party line. At this juncture party politics exert not only a limiting but also a destructive effect on the individual. The limiting effect occurs through the loss of personal conviction that leaves the writer using hackneyed phrases and idioms in order to keep to the correct opinion. Loss of conviction also encourages the writer to cloud the real issues so that he cannot be accused of faulty reasoning. The second, more destructive effect, is founded on the ability of the prefabricated phrases to relieve the writer of personal responsibility to the extent of 'partially concealing your meaning even from yourself' (*CEJL* PE, IV 136). In this manner the political party's defence of questionable issues and concealment of shifts in policy, can be disguised through the use of techniques that allow the writer to be submissive because he is deprived of any responsibility to choose either them or the opinions they express.

Getting rid of the bad habits in a language not only gets rid of worn-out meaningless usages, but makes it necessary for a writer to actively participate in the construction of meaning. In doing so his thoughts are clarified, and this is the first step to political 'regeneration'. As Orwell says, 'If you simplify your English, you are freed from the worst follies of orthodoxy' (*CEJL* PE, IV 139). Although guidelines are proposed to achieve simplicity, they are presented in negative terms as a warning, not as a prescription that might lead to yet more unthinking imitation. The final piece of advice is to 'Break any of these rules sooner than say anything outright barbarous' (*CEJL* PE, IV 139). But the most important point is to let the meaning choose the word, rather than blindly to assume the representational nature of language. To do so the essay suggests that one begin by attempting to think of the meaning visually or sensually, in material terms. Here one 'can choose – not simply *accept* – the phrases that will best cover the meaning' (*CEJL* PE, IV 138); one must actively participate. Finally, one should think of the impression that words will have on other people; one should assess the effect of the rhetorical stance. The whole process takes care, activity, and integrity.

Since these qualities have been shown to be incompatible with the conformity demanded in writing for politics, we are left asking again: should the writer even be involved in writing politically? The quick answer is that he has no choice, the age demands involvement and comment. But Orwell extends this into a consideration of how the writer can constructively come to terms with his dilemma. If he is of a small minority of people who fully believe in a current political 'line' then there will be no problem. But if he belongs to the much larger group of writers who at various moments lack conviction, then he must separate party politics as far as possible from his political writing. Orwell examines the question from the reverse side, from the reader's point of view, in his study of Swift, 'Politics vs. Literature'. As a reader, he finds himself disagreeing with Swift in political but not literary fields, and asks what is the relationship between agreement with a writer's opinions, and enjoyment of his work? (*CEJL* LP, IV 220). He suggests that in this case the writer is fully convinced of his ideas, and that it is the reader who must learn to separate between the ideas and the literary skills if he is to enjoy the work. Further he concludes that concentration on the literary will indicate the personal beliefs informing the text, and that it is these rather than opinion that lend conviction to a work. They become in effect a personal politics that may illuminate the topics of party politics.

The reader's separation of these aspects is essential. A disagreement with political topics or specific moral standards, acts in an insidious manner upon the aesthetic sense which is allied to personal politics. If a reader allows his party political beliefs to influence his aesthetic sense, then he will be basing his critical judgements on the shifting ideology of political necessity and not on personal conviction. Just as loss of the personal integrity leads to weak language and poor style in writing, so it leads to unacceptable critical judgements. Orwell notes here that 'Current literary criticism consists quite largely of this kind of dodging to and fro between two sets of standards' (*CEJL* LP, IV 221), so that political theories can fit aesthetic judgements. Later, in 'Writers and Leviathan', he becomes more insistent saying:

> every literary judgement consists in trumping up a set of rules to justify an instinctive preference . . . yet, with a dishonesty that sometimes is not even quarter-conscious . . . (*CEJL* WL, IV 408)

Literary judgements constructed in this relative manner not only lack the conviction of the critic but fail to assess the fundamental issues at hand. They result in writers with belief and without being lumped together indiscriminately, so that valid political convictions can be dismissed as belonging to a faulty style rather than being examined and discussed in terms of practical politics.

Orwell takes the question of conviction further in returning to Swift as a writer of political literature. Here we find again that he is not advocating pure attention to either ideological or aesthetic matters. He notes that some critics argue that books cannot be 'good' if they express 'a palpably false view of life' (*CEJL* LP, IV 223), yet each age produces skilful books written from many different points of view, each of which will be false to a certain number of readers. In the end he says that all one can ask of a propagandist or political writer is that he is sincere, that his views are compatible with sanity and continuous thought, and that he has 'talent, which is probably another name for conviction' (*CEJL* LP, IV 223). Sanity and continuous thought are essential for they indicate the means by which one can evaluate the work. The use of logic that they necessitate provides the reader with an example of the writer's strategy which he can follow and assess. Awareness of the logic in use makes more difficult the disguise of thought and the deception of the reader. Talent or conviction, on the other hand, provide a further means of evaluation for the reader. Here Orwell suggests that the reader will find value in the conviction of personal politics no matter how much else we disagree with. The solution he reaches is that the artist must separate his political actions which may well co-operate with the necessities of party politics, from his work, his writing. After all, as he points out, most people already separate their work from their party political activities and he is just asking for this for the writer.

In our own time of increasing politicization of all aspects of life, Orwell's next point is more interesting: that even when party political instructions enter one's work they seldom debase the nature of the medium in the way that they debase language. But it is another point that yields substance to Orwell's plea. Party political lines demand acceptance in the form of moral choice, as if political necessity automatically polarized a situation into good or bad. And Orwell denies this, says it 'belongs to the nursery', and that 'In politics one can never do more than decide which of two evils is the lesser' (*CEJL* WL, IV 413). If one realizes that political necessity should engage co-operation rather than moral conviction, then the element of conviction essential to literature becomes divorced from party politics. As it does so it justifies the separation of literature from party ideology. The writer must still react to his age by writing about politics, but he can do so as an outsider, as a recorder of events, and a more distanced commentator on the effects in which political necessities result.

Orwell came to believe that 'acceptance of *any* political discipline seems to be incompatible with literary integrity' (*CEJL* WL, IV 412). Here the key words are 'acceptance' indicating unquestioning passivity and control by the state, 'political discipline' which implies a party and expedient necessities, and 'literary integrity' which stands for individual responsibility to define personal politics and express with belief and conviction. The statement does not mean that the writer should keep out of politics as Orwell had advocated earlier, but that there should be a 'sharper distinction ... between our political and our literary loyalties' (*CEJL* WL, IV 413). The writer can co-operate with party politics in his everyday life, while rejecting orthodoxy in his writing which should be 'saner', more distanced and able to criticize than party politics. In Orwell's terms such a stance is in the end more productive and helpful than conformity. Party politics functions on short-term, negative rhetoric for expediency; personal politics involves long-term, positive rhetoric, not necessarily expedient but in the end highly practical.

'Why I Write', the first essay of the five, presents the division between the private individual and political party as the opposing forces of politics. The tension derives from the solution that is initially proffered: isolation of the two from each other which only perpetuates the situation in which one attempts to dominate the other. Totalitarianism is simply an anarchic private world become monomania and realized in terms of the public. Both are illusions to totality. Strip off the illusion and inadequacy is easily apparent: but it may not be so easy to strip off. Both conceal rather than express rhetorical stance, which encourages in others and eventually in oneself, a carelessness of thought and language. Both accept the possibility that there will be a loss of value even to oneself, if the point presented is to go across more strongly. Here the recognition of this extreme of total control through concealing rhetorical stance, gives way to the other extreme in which people pursue all possibilities of private and party politics even though they may lose themselves in those possibilities. That loss is the opposite extreme implied in such control, whether of a private world-view or of party politics. The end of total imposition is loss of one's consciousness of that imposition, resulting in the paradox of doublethink that the person controlling no longer controls, the worlds are completely arbitrary. For Orwell neither extreme will do. Rhetorical stance must be overtly expressed by bringing the personal and external in interaction with each other, refusing to isolate them and accept either their perfection or their arbitrary nature. But politics throughout the essays also provides a paradigm for the literary. Politics, as literature and art, is an enaction of the meeting between human beings and the world.

The separation between private and party politics is parallel to that between aesthetic or pure art and party line propaganda. Just as the political separation is intended to preserve from imposition, control and power, yet degenerates into anarchy and totalitarianism, so the separation in art may degenerate into the carelessness of narcissism or jargon. The ambivalence derives from the underlying separation between man and the external which is necessary to achieve objectivity, neutrality and imposition on the world which underlies the rationalist basis of most contemporary humanism. The political analogy specifically points to the restrictions that are indicated by the separation between literature and propaganda. But it is the development of the literary relationship that expands the political implications, through the relationship between writer and 'party line' which extends out to the audience. If the party line imposes upon the individual as writer he will in turn impose upon the language and its reader. But the writer in a political situation is a reader. He enacts the inclusive position of rhetorical stance which fuses writer, reader and text into the generation of value.

The Stance of Fantasy

These divisions and separations between the personal and party which propose a resolution for the interaction between art, propaganda and politics, are all very well to speak of. Putting them into effective action is another matter. In the three major essays of 1940, Orwell presents the ambivalence and confusion of his formal attitude to literary expression and politics, even though the novels written during the 1930s illustrate in practical terms many of the proposals he was later to arrive at. The same is true for the 1940s. *Animal Farm* and *Nineteen Eighty-Four* discuss the problems of literary expression in far more detail and with greater vision than their contemporary essays. But the later essays do begin to come to terms with many of the emerging changes and suggestions.

Similarly, in this study of political rhetoric and persuasion, the essayist finds it far easier to explain what he does not like about literary genres and the stances they manifest than their positive alternatives. Trying to push beyond the habits and conventions of the world one lives in means entering a strange land, nor knowing which direction to take. And Orwell was not simply criticizing the conventions of his world but the stance which had generated them. He was seeking not just to change people's means of expressing, not even their way of perceiving the world, but their fundamental belief about it. Orwell's basic criticism of his time was of its attitude that human beings could control things absolutely, enforce them into their own private definition. Private definitions impose upon other people and depend upon their submissive acceptance to succeed. Attempts at such control inevitably need negative rhetorical strategies and stance. Control by imposition is behind the persuasion of totalitarianism and of anarchism; to a less efficient extent it is also behind most party politics. But private definitions in literature breed a more subtle control, and play more intimately upon the desire for nostalgic comfort and escape.

With a few exceptions Orwell uses the word 'fantasy' to define literature being used for purposes of power and control, but what specifically does he mean and what are his alternatives? Fantasy is closely tied to escape literature and the means of creating passive audiences. The techniques discussed in 'Boys' Weeklies' and the focus of 'Inside the Whale', indicated although somewhat ambivalently the direction of Orwell's thought on such literature. They stressed the passivity, escape, the feeling of having things done to and for the reader that characterize fantasy. The writer's conclusion was that while they were definitely not to be condoned, they were just as definitely symptomatic of contemporary response and thought. In 1940 he is still hankering after a 'truth', a definite history, and the need for interaction and active involvement as an artist are not yet as predominant as they shall become. He has reached his decision concerning the essential fusion of public and private interests which parallels his recognition of the inevitably propagandic nature of art. But just as he has not sorted out the distinction between personal and party politics which leaves him confused about maintaining individual integrity in the face of totalitarianism, so he cannot distinguish between literature as personal propaganda and as party propaganda. The result is definite criticism of those who reinforce party propaganda, an ambivalent attitude toward those who avoid it completely, and curtailed attempts to define a literature of active participation.

During and after 1943, Orwell expands with growing disillusion on fantasy and escape literature. A review of a novel by Charles Reade summarizes many of the important elements, introducing Reade as one of the best 'escape' novelists. The review observes that Reade is 'in his element' with desert island stories. The work shows a fascination with 'dates, lists, catalogues, concrete details, descriptions of processes' (*CEJL* II 34–5); it concentrates on 'technical details'. Attention to technical detail is essential if the escape world is to be solidly constructed and substitute satisfactorily for the real. The main character is 'a kind of superman'; he works out how to leave the island completely rationally, step by step determining longitude and latitude and coming to a definite and satisfactory solution. Further, the moral problems are clear and straightforward: life is a 'series of tremendous melodramas, with virtue triumphant every time'.

In effect the plot is directly parallel with James Barrie's 'The Admirable Crichton'. But in Barrie's play the island is a conscious analogy for escape from social pressures, as it is in many works of this period.[1] Also in Barrie it functions as a pastoral device to comment critically upon the society that is left behind and returned to. Reade, however, 'for all . . . his eagerness to expose abuses, . . . never makes a fundamental criticism'. The persuasion used is a rhetoric of control by imposition with a negative stance behind it seeking to produce a familiarity and security for the reader. The essayist comments that there are no problems in Reade's novels, 'no genuine "message", merely the fascination of gifted mind functioning within very narrow limits, and offering as complete a detachment from real life as a game of chess or a jigsaw puzzle'. The physical, moral and social environments are totally controlled, constructed to bolster up the dominant *status quo*.[2]

A discussion of Kipling (1942), puts forward similar concepts. The essayist describes him as a 'good bad' poet which was one of Orwell's favourite classifications for literature that he recognized to be of questionable value but was entranced by. As he says here 'even in his [Kipling's] best passages one has the same sense of being seduced by something spurious, and yet unquestionably seduced' (*CEJL* II 194). A good bad poem is defined by a familiarity with and ability to back up the *status quo*. It is a 'monument to the obvious'. Specifically popular poetry is usually 'gnomic or sententious', a poetry of platitudes. In the same way that he justifies war propaganda partly because it is easily recognized as a 'line', so these poems 'reek of sentimentality, and yet . . . are capable of giving true pleasure to people who can see clearly what is wrong with them'. Again it is noteworthy that the response is connected with sentimentality. In Orwell's own novels sentimentality is the guardian of out of date feelings to which a character could escape. They were never reassessed and they protected him from having to change. Similarly, in the tradition of escape criticism including Meredith, Stevenson, Barrie, Chesterton and Lawrence,[3] sentiment is the word given to the adult fantasy, the abandonment of the demands of actuality. While Orwell notes that the experience affords pleasure and enjoyment because it relieves one temporarily of individual responsibility, in the context of his ideas about propaganda it is obviously a dangerous response to give way to without being fully aware of the implications.

The year 1940 also yields Orwell's reviews of films, which in spite of the contradictions usual for a first-time newspaper reviewer, provide a consistent approach to fantasy. The attitude goes back to the 'Mickey Mouse' world of Henry Miller (*CEJL* I 228). A film of such a world 'breaks the rules of common sense more violently than any book ever written, yet because it is seen it is perfectly intelligible' (*CEJL* I 231). This early response is allied to his early hope that film would provide a new, truthful language.[4] Later on this hope is qualified by the observation that the medium must be 'properly used' because it has extraordinary 'powers of distortion, of fantasy, in general of escaping the restrictions of the physical world' (*CEJL* II 10). The qualification is reiterated more strongly after a year or so in broadcasting when he observes that radio and film are not 'inherently vulgar, silly and dishonest' (*CEJL* II 334) but they are often put to use by people with certain aims in mind which affect the method of production.

For various and often conflicting reasons the reviewer criticizes the film industry's contempt for the intelligence of their audience (*TT* 30/11/40). Later he comes to attribute the neglect to the invasion of film by speech which imposed theatrical conventions upon it (*TT* 26/4/41). But at first the writer's own criticism is tied to a set of theatrical theories; it is only after a year of reviewing that he moves on to other issues. As if set off by a casual comment on the 'never-never land' effect of bad film-colour (*TT* 14/6/41) Orwell proceeds to discuss the fantasy elements in Wild West films. He suggests that they are popular because 'the fantasy of individual adventure. . . supplies a psychological need in a world which grows constantly more dangerous but also more regimented' (*TT* 5/7/41). The Wild West film is 'the symbol of lawlessness', 'As soon as we see a five-gallon hat we are in a dream-world where men and women are pure and there are no taxes and no policemen'. Fusing the concepts of fantasy, totalitarianism and sadism, he describes 'High Sierra' as 'the *ne plus ultra* of sadism, bully-worship, gunplay, socks on the jaw and gangster atmosphere generally' (*TT* 9/8/41). But these casual incursions into film reviewing were put aside when he started his BBC work.

When he returns to reviews and articles during 1943, Orwell's writing indicates that these concepts have become more settled into the terrain of his mind. For example he makes the casual comment that commercial amusements such as pub-going are being replaced by 'solitary mechanical ones', 'by the passive, drug-like pleasures of the cinema and radio' (*CEJL* III 43). At the same time he has begun to think of films in much the same way that he thinks of mass-produced magazines. Initially they are linked with magazines in their accessibility to manipulation by political power (*CEJL* III 22). More explicitly in an article on women's magazines, the essayist notes the escapist myth held in common with films, of 'the moral superiority of the poor' which has been evolved by a ruling class to encourage acceptance of poverty. The result is that 'By means of films and magazines you can enjoy a fantasy existence in which you constantly triumph over the people who defeat you in real life' (*CEJL* III 197). One only has to contrast the short stories in magazines with their correspondence columns 'to see how vast a part mere day-dreaming plays in modern life' (*CEJL* III 198).

The essay 'Raffles and Miss Blandish' (1944), brings the fantasy adventure of films to the closely related good bad story, here *No Orchids for Miss Blandish*. The novel is popular because 'in real life one is usually a passive victim, whereas in the adventure story one can think of oneself as being at the centre of events' (*CEJL* III 219). The popularity of this kind of writing is connected with that of American pulp magazines which are 'graded so as to cater for different kinds of fantasy, but nearly all having much the same mental atmosphere' (*CEJL* III 219). Escape is into 'cruelty and perversion' with the same worship of power found in fascism. He concludes that it is 'a day-dream appropriate to a totalitarian age'.

It is interesting that the essay so explicitly notes the sexual manipulation in the service of a greed for power. For Orwell sex has always been the element of life most closely associated with actuality, the least distorted physical experience. Given that no physical experience can be fully communicated or understood, sexual relationships provide one of the fullest analogies for the interaction with the material called for in the communication of literature, politics and elsewhere. Dorothy in *A Clergyman's Daughter* is not frigid because the author is afraid to portray sexual interest,[5] but because she is his example of someone who cannot take that final involving step. When Gordon Comstock and Rosemary finally make it in *Keep the Aspidistra Flying*, sex is the one means of communication that gets through to each one. *Nineteen Eighty-Four* is to extend the image further. There Orwell uses sex as an analogy rather than as a literal event. He comments in an essay that the explicit description of love-making in modern novels 'is something future generations will look back on as we do on things like the death of little Nell' (*CEJL* IV 484). With this observation he puts his early admiration for Miller's open description of sex in context.

He admires it for its willingness to detail actual events that other people would rather avoid, but at the same time he recognizes that without conviction it provides its own form of escape and sentimentality. Orwell uses the image positively for its implications of physical connection and the related motifs of self-loss yielding self-gain that have always been associated with it. But he also recognizes that it is the selfish manipulation of others that denies interaction in most sadism and masochism, that brings the writer to ally them with power cults and totalitarianism.

A later article on good bad books comments by implication on the significant difference between *Raffles* and *No Orchids for Miss Blandish*. The *Raffles* books, although 'escape' literature, were also works attaining sincerity from their overt lack of good taste (*CEJL* IV 20):

> The existence of good bad literature – the fact that one can be amused or excited or even moved by a book that one's intellect simply refuses to take seriously – is a reminder that art is not the same thing as cerebration. (*CEJL* IV 21)

Good bad books are serious in their 'distraction'. *No Orchids* however does not attempt to distract, its lack of good taste is directed toward manipulation rather than entertainment. That the two have identical constructions leading to a lack of cerebration, yet one entertains while the other abuses, is a case in point about the ambivalent nature of escape literature.

One of the London letters to the *Partisan Review* (1946), takes up the theme and applies it to pulp magazines. It suggests that their enormous circulations are achieved because the magazines, give 'the average reader the feeling of being "advanced" without actually forcing him to think' (*CEJL* IV 189). Another article suggests that the popularity of the press lies in inverse relation to its demand on the reader's intelligence (*CEJL* IV 62). One of these publications is described in detail: it evades any topic that could be potentially disturbing – age, work, birth, death or children. The prose style is similar to party political language, 'an extraordinary mixture of sheer lushness with clipped and sometimes very expressive technical jargon' (*CEJL* IV 235). The security against reality is an aspect he notes in childhood books and 'perhaps most of all the bad and good bad books' which create a 'false map of the world' (*CEJL* IV 242), into which the reader may retreat from this one.

As essay on 'Pleasure Spots' summarizes the physical elements of such fantasy worlds. They insist that the individual is never alone, never does anything for himself, is never in sight of natural growth, is surrounded by artificially regulated light and temperature and most of all 'one is never out of the sound of music'. The kind of music Orwell has in mind is important because it prevents conversation, discourages thinking and provides a 'return to the womb' (*CEJL* IV 80). These pleasure camps are designed to totally control one's environment, and the writer notes that 'Much of what goes by in the name of pleasure is simply an effort to destroy one's consciousness' (*CEJL* IV 81). Relaxation is needed but so also are solitude, creativity and wonder.

In an 'As I Please' column of January 1947, which calls for the recognition of conditions in post-war Germany, the trend of this criticism is explicitly tied to the dangers of passivity induced by totalitarian techniques invading language and literature. The writer says:

> This business of making people *conscious* of what is happening outside their own small circle is one of the major problems of our time, and a new literary technique will have to be evolved to meet it . . . As time goes on and the horrors pile up, the mind seems to secrete a sort of self-protecting ignorance which needs a harder and harder shock to pierce it, just as the body will become immunized to a drug and require bigger and bigger doses. (*CEJL* IV 278)

It is the need to make people conscious, to alert them to situations that they have begun to take for granted that Orwell concentrates on writing about between 1944–7. By this time he has recognized the dangers of escape literature. Fantasy may have been a natural development of an age of rationalist humanism. It describes a game in which private authority may dominate. With an increase in state authority it is reasonable to expect that the escapes that fantasy allows the private individual would become more popular. But with the introduction of modern technology and the rise of totalitarianism, fantasy is pushed into its own total private control, ultimately of power, greed, sadism, masochism and eventually monomania, a madness in which public and private authoritarianism meet to destroy others and then themselves. Unless of course they have developed doublethink: the ability to know and not know, to control and yet not control, to be sane and mad simultaneously, which implies an eradication of value.

In this discussion of fantasy literature Orwell provides a detailed background for the studies of the last thirty years of theorizing about fantasy literature.[6] His technical analysis of the literary and linguistic components necessary to create and maintain an isolated world, is one of the most perceptive and revealing to this day. He is also aware that fantasy is the motivating stance beyond a number of expressions and is not limited to one specific genre. Earlier he had called Hitler's rhetoric a fantasy of monomania made public, social and national, and recognized that there was a similar persuasive stance in government control of radio, cinema, literature and science. In terms of art, fantasy also invades a number of modes: the adventure story, and certain films, novels and magazines.

The perception of this congruency in stance led Orwell to a greater awareness of the dangers of superficially innocuous popular writing. As suggested earlier, the same attempts to control through creating isolation by suppression, omission and evasion are found in authoritarian politics and escapist literature. Not only do they have the same primary belief in their ability to gain power over others, but they use the same tactics of analytical rational logic, massive detail, jargon and ambiguous language to maintain unquestionable moral certainties and reinforce the desire for sentimentality and perfection.

But what is particularly impressive about his observations is that he recognizes the ambivalence of fantasy almost immediately. His study begins, in the early essays and articles, as do most pre-World War II criticisms, with 'pure' art. If art is pure it may have no contact with reality. As a result the escapes it provides can be treated as isolated from the external world and without value. After the second world war, primarily through the influence of J. Huizinga's *Homo Ludens* which was first published in England in 1946, theoreticians of fantasy transferred their emphasis onto literature as a game.[7] This allowed them to resist the criticisms of 'pure' art which had emerged during the 1930s, and yet retain the isolation of fantasy necessary to its non-evaluative position. However Orwell begins to think of fantasy in terms of games long before Huizinga's book was translated into English. Possibly the same political events which stimulated Huizinga's study spoke to Orwell, and in a similar way.

Huizinga never resolved the tensions within his book, which derive from the need to incorporate enough actuality into the fantasy to satisfy the reader's desires yet to maintain the essential separation from actuality that keeps the fantasy world 'amoral'. This problem has plagued other theories of fantasy ever since. But Orwell quickly came to realize that the two faces of fantasy implied in the tension bring 'sheer entertainment' too close to imposition and abuse of power. Both indicate value systems that deny that evaluation exists, they attempt to deprive their readers of assessment so that they can impose their own fixed standards.

Alternative Stances

Orwell's increasing recognition of the individual's responsibility to interact with his society and its politics, goes hand in hand with a sense of the individual artist's responsibility to manifest that interaction in his work. Up to this stage he has thoroughly described the literary techniques that tend toward a negative rhetorical stance but positive stance, apart from a simplicity of language and avoidance of jargon, is as yet uncharacterized. An article of 1941 'The Art of Donald McGill' is a quiet introduction to several of the matters Orwell becomes concerned with. On one hand McGill's postcards contain features which ally them with good bad books and fantasy; they are for example 'completely typical' (*CEJL* II 155), familiar and rigidly moral. On the other hand because they are not the product of a 'monopoly company', they make no attempt to manipulate public opinion. What they present is the 'Sancho Panza view of life', the view of a little fat man who is mainly concerned with staying alive. He is interested in the body and the belly, not in the intellect. Such figures are 'like the music halls, they are a sort of saturnalia, a harmless rebellion against virtue' (*CEJL* II 164). Elements of saturnalia and of rebellion connected with humour become central to Orwell's positive rhetoric, as does the popular appeal of the Sancho Panza figure. The writer has to be able to appeal on familiar grounds to make his propaganda effective. But he also has to break up rather than maintain those grounds through the shock and disruption of humour.

The concepts take hold quite quickly in the essayist's mind and we find a review of Mark Twain in 1943 discussing them in terms of the 'licensed Jester'. Twain was interested in the lunatic elements of character that surface when there are no external pressures to define one. Even so he did not use this humour to attack or criticize society despite its 'iconoclastic, even revolutionary vein' (*CEJL* II 326). He failed to criticize society because he held the nineteenth-century view that 'success and virtue are the same thing'. Nineteenth-century self-satisfaction, what Chesterton called the Victorian Compromise, is the element dividing pre-World War I literature from the modern. A broadcast on the Eastern Service in 1942 examines the differences between the literatures and brings it down to a comparison between Joyce and Shaw. The Victorians became so certain of life, so convinced of its stability and positive progress to a better world, that they became at the same time obsessed with the discussion of particular issues, with conveying messages and dictating opinion.

Orwell views the literature of the later nineteenth century and up to 1914, as a kind of aberration because the writers were completely unaware 'of anything outside the contemporary English scene' (*CEJL* II 200). In comparing Galsworthy's *Man of Property* with *Ulysses* Orwell decides that the former 'though he's trying to be iconoclastic, . . . he has been utterly unable to move his mind outside the wealthy bourgeois society he is attacking. With only slight modifications he takes all its values for granted' (*CEJL* II 238). In effect Galsworthy simply doesn't have any contact with anything else. By contrast *Ulysses* draws on a wide European tradition. Much of the interest is about the loss of credibility by the Church in a modern world, which is conveyed by parody. Joyce is also supremely concerned with words, their sounds, associations, patterns as well as with the implications of traditional language and genre for contemporary literature. Language and genre become parodies on meaning and communication for the modern writer. Joyce is less sure of himself and his control over words than Galsworthy or Shaw, hence his care and concern. He returns 'to the conception of style, of fine writing, or poetic meaning, perhaps even to purple passages' (*CEJL* II 237). By contrast it is claimed that Shaw would have said 'as a matter of course that the sole use of words is to express exact meanings as shortly as possible'. The confidence of it all, that language is an exact technique for conveying messages, is part of the Victorian Compromise. Yet we should remember that this was an aspect of Orwell's own attitude a few years earlier.

The following year in a further series of broadcasts, he discusses Shaw again, reiterating his role as a 'writer with a purpose' (*BA* 22/1/43). He notes that because of the emphasis on message Shaw's works tend to date; they lose interest for us. It is suggested that *Arms and the Man* wears better than most of the plays because 'its moral or "message", still needs pointing'. The suggestion relates to a comments he makes with regard to pulp magazines and 'the completeness with which they date' (*CEJL* III 73), because they are so closely tied to the grounds of their time. Dating raises questions about Shaw, about satire and about political writing in general.

Similar criticism is dirrected against Oscar Wilde. *Lady Windermere's Fan* depends on the general recognition of a strong opinion that it then runs counter to. It will 'disagree with the majority at all costs' (*BA* 21/11/43). The dependence on a particular social ground in order to satirize society produces a contradiction in effect: that one must fully understand, even support values in order to attack them.[8] The writer observes the peculiar internal irony or doublethink evidenced by the style as well. The language is witty and neat but the actions sentimental and melodramatic. Wilde's work survives because of the attention he pays to his epigrams, but also because of an 'intriguing uncertainty' as to the extent of his compromise.

As Orwell was to note, the only real test of literature was its survival through time, in other words the long-term effects of its rhetorical stance. Significantly he was to equate survival with 'an index to majority opinion' (*CEJL* IV 290), as if to suggest that the care ensuring literary survival carried in itself enduring values. The connection between popular or majority communication and the care of words is based on the belief that care ensures that the private opinion of the writer does not become despotic and personally authoritarian. If care is relaxed and opinion becomes authoritarian, the literature ties itself to private grounds and while these will initially draw the reader into the alternative world, later they will not only date but possibly estrange the audience.

There is an odd ambivalence in the works categorized as satire. Commenting on the role of 'comedians' in a review for *Time and Tide*, Orwell notes that the 'obscenities' of the Sancho Panza figure 'are only possible because they are expressed in *double entendre* which imply a common background in the audience' (*TT* 7/9/40). All shock implies initial identification in the grounds it disrupts. Identification and recognition of its absence are at the root of communication. But having said this one is immediately faced with a choice between the two, between acceptance, or questioning of it. Only then does one have the second choice, to go on to reinforce, replace or simply destroy the identification. While questioning implies either reinforcement or replacement or destruction, acceptance leads only to reinforcing, to the security of good bad books. There is of course a curious combination of questioning which reinforces all the time, actively denying that there is anything that could be changed in society. In a world less than utopian this is the ultimate compromise. Eventually, Orwell is to observe that 'All Utopia books are satires or allegories. Obviously if you invent an imaginary country you do so to throw light on the institutions of an existing country' (*BA* 8/6/45). When the direction of the utopian criticism is actually tied to that country, it is satirical and will probably date. When it exists in parallel with the actual country, using it as an example of difference, it is allegory.

Satiric humour and the simultaneous identification with and rebellion against the grounds on which it is based, become the forms for Orwell's interest during the years 1943–5. Dismissing the Victorian 'aberration' he turns to the eighteenth century. In doing so he also begins a unique and eccentric critical study of the novel, specifically the realistic novel starting with the picaresque and a moving to the naturalistic. By 'realism' in regard to novels the writer does not imply the earlier political realism. He notes the point clearly at the start of an article on Smollett: 'applied to novels it normally means a photographic imitation of everyday life. A 'realistic' novel is one in which the dialogue is colloquial and physical objects are described in such a way that you can visualize them' (*CEJL* III 244). While realism in this sense advanced technically to naturalism, the eighteenth century was far more realist in its 'attitude toward human motives'. Orwell explains this by observing a moral change between the society of Smollett and that of Dickens. Smollett lived in a world which demanded no religious or political conviction, nor 'ordinary honesty'. By Dickens's time such commitments had become part of middle-class life. There were now defined good and bad actions and motives. Smollett's disregard for the 'human dignity' conferred by such a code led him to include things 'which do happen in real life but are almost invariably kept out of fiction' (*CEJL* III 247). The eighteenth-century picaresque novel is shocking because it functions without knowledge of the Victorian code. The modern reader is jolted out of his acceptance of the various social norms he lives by, forced to re-examine them because the novel progresses as if they do not exist. On the other hand, twentieth-century attempts at the picaresque by Huxley or Waugh have to try to be shocking. They get involved in the double bind of indicating the social norm and the attacking. Their writing is satirical whereas Smollett's is radically comic.

Goldsmith's *The Vicar of Wakefield* heralds the more rigidly ethical age to come. It differs from Smollett's work in lacking psychological realism, a probability of character and plot which normally defines the novel, and there are the first indications of a tendency to dominate over the actions of characters by insisting on morally 'correct' solutions with 'one detail after the other clicking into place like the teeth of a zip-fastener' (*CEJL* III 269). But the article is used by Orwell to provide an interesting case study for the twentieth-century reader because it openly equates goodness with financial prudence. The novel combines an ethical control that the reader would expect, with a code that he would probably question. Two issues are raised: the first is that the despotic control by the author over the issues dates the work; and the second is a more subtle point that the rest of the novelists in the Victorian age assumed a similar code but did not say so openly, and asks the reader which way is to be preferred? Orwell's personal search for strategies that would maintain a positive stance, leads him to move past the fact that it is not properly a novel, because it is 'something perfectly executed after its own fashion', as a sermon or a moral tale. And his comments on the 'simple yet elegant language', the 'poems thrown in here and there' and the construction of 'certain minor incidents' indicate not only his care for language, but also his growing admiration for techniques that disrupt and reorientate the conventional strategies of the novel.

Orwell is not suggesting that writers return to an eighteenth-century style. A later review of Thackeray's work makes it clear that this is impossible. Thackeray too behaves as if he were without religious, political or social commitments, but this has become unacceptable by the middle of the nineteenth century. If there are current social standards, the humorous novelist has a responsibility to attack them or his humour becomes sentimental. In an increasingly authoritarian state the responsibility of the humorist to attack becomes ever greater. Where Thackeray's style does work well is in the isolated incidents and fragments of his writings, when he is not being a novelist with the 'factor of having to simulate real life and introduce disinterested motives' (*CEJL* III 345), to make 'in the round characters'. The shorter pieces concentrate on burlesque and caricature of mankind and social ambition; they are vignettes of behaviour that have no pretence to 'realism' at all. In other words Thackeray was willing to criticize parts of his society but not to attack the whole, but the other implication is that many nineteenth-century novels, in their very dependence on a 'realism', become too involved in the grounds of their society for effective criticism.

The one thing an author cannot do and remain a humorist is compromise. In 'Funny but not Vulgar' (1944), the essayist claims, 'no comic writer of any stature has ever suggested that society is good ' (*CEJL* III 285). Humour is defined as an upsetting of the established order without being 'actually offensive or frightening'; every joke 'is a tiny revolution' with the emphasis on 'tiny'. Modern literature is accused of not being humorous enough because it is unwilling to attack 'the virtues on which society necessarily rests'. But humour is not immoral and antisocial; it is not to degrade man 'but to remind him that he is already degraded'. Orwell concludes that 'you *cannot* be funny without being vulgar ... You cannot be really funny if your main aim is to flatter the comfortable classes'. It is possible to be simply comic in the eighteenth century because there were no authoritarian codes for the novel, but it is impossible in the twentieth. *Punch* for example has functioned for the last fifty years, 'not so much to amuse as to reassure. Its implied message is that all is for the best and nothing will ever really change' (*CEJL* III 288). It is no longer humorous, but satirical and sentimental.

Whether Orwell's eccentric reading of eighteenth-century writing is more widely acceptable in terms of literary history is not as important as the ideas it generates. It is his own age that he sees most clearly and he recognizes that there are other modes of humour that have been developed to suit an authoritarian age. One of course is satire but that too easily becomes involved with what it criticizes, another is the allegory referred to above in the context of utopia books (*BA* 8/6/45), and a third is nonsense writing. In 'Funny but not Vulgar', Orwell calls nonsense verse 'fantasy', yet he means something quite different from his earlier use as good bad literature. What he has in mind is a debunking of man as a 'rational being', and turns to a study of Lear and Carroll. Carroll makes fun of logic and Lear interferes with common sense. However the two are similar in their use of alternative worlds even though they use them for completely different purposes. Nonsense

> often depends on building up a fantastic universe which is just similar enough to the real universe to rob it of its dignity. But more often it depends on anticlimax − that is, on starting out with high-flown language and then suddenly coming down with a bump. (*CEJL* III 286)

In contrast good bad fantasy literature depends on maintaining the fantastic universe it creates. The description of nonsense verse is interesting because it allies it further with utopia literature which also invents an 'imaginary country' in parallel to the actual one. The difference is that with satire and allegory one is aware from the beginning that the alternative world is only a comment on the actual. What good bad books, nonsense verse, satire and utopian allegories have in common is the creation of alternative worlds, and yet all four use the worlds to different ends.

In effect the only humorists of the nineteenth century for whom Orwell has any time at all are the nonsense poets. In 1945 he returns to his discussion of nonsense in a review of a collection of Lear's poems. Again the similarity to the tenets of escape literature is clear: 'Lear was one of the first writers to deal in pure fantasy, with imaginary countries and made-up worlds, without any satirical purpose' (*CEJL* IV 66). For Orwell the best of Lear is not completely arbitrary, but retains an unusual logic or an abnormal means of reasoning which functions by undermining the rational process of judgement normally used in present day society. The logic does not satirize it but shows it to be useless. The verse which Orwell perceives as completely arbitrary he condemns as silly and whimsical, holding it responsible for a negative influence on children's books. It is possibly the lack of open satirical purpose so absent from the complicit humour of twentieth-century writers such as W. W. Jacobs or Barrie Paine that, along with the common use of alternate worlds, has brought nonsense and allegory to be thought of in the same terms as fantasy. Yet any reader is aware that the casual use of the word fantasy, taken seriously to define both Lear's work and say that of Charles Reade, yields an oddness and inconsistency in the parallel.

Just as Orwell searches for humorous strategies in literature that will evade complicity in authoritarianism, so he attempts throughout these critical essays, to find other modes of the novel which can reverse the tendency of nineteenth-century novels toward authoritarian control and domination. In the search, the critic is attempting to discover an historical explanation not only for the weakness of the novel but also a eans of expression for the increasing political responsibility of the individual. He repeats the implication that with more state authoritarianism there should be a greater personal attempt to interact with that state. The picaresque novel is a genre in which the individual functions in separate incidents, and the mode cannot give an account of society as a whole. The naturalistic novel arising out of it did try to account for society but in terms of the individually authoritarian view of the writer. The picaresque, as in Thackeray, only survived in fragments of journalism, disjointed non-naturalistic novels and also, although Orwell himself does not specify the mode, in the separate incidents which became the short story genre. The novel was originally 'the most anarchical of all forms of literature', a 'product of the free mind, of the autonomous individual' (*CEJL* I 518), yet anarchy in an authoritarian state eventually moves toward a private control and despotism over the reader. The nineteenth-century novelist interpreted his interaction with society in a different manner from his predecessor. He was more aware of a social responsibility but assumed that because of the stability of his world gentle criticism was all that was needed: hence Dickens's compromise arising out of a private rather than public change in society.

The difference between eighteenth-century realism and nineteenth-century naturalism in the essayist's view, is that the earlier, realistic novels achieve an individual view of personal motives, whereas the naturalist novels sacrifice this to the predominant social codes. The eighteenth-century novels could be eccentric and anarchic, whereas the later works became too tied to their surrounding convention. The coming order is specifically allied with the changing times and the rise of a new 'cautious' middle class.

When he first began writing Orwell himself saw the naturalistic novel as a suitable genre, but by 1945 he does not. A critique of Henry Miller's work written in 1946 states explicitly where the critic stands. He claims Miller has 'no power of self-discipline, no sense of responsibility' and significantly 'perhaps not much imagination, as opposed to fancy' (*CEJL* IV 134). Miller's writing is that of dangerous escape literature: the novelist announces that he has 'become God' and is indifferent to the world, and he manipulates his language so that 'the most banal statement can be made to sound picturesque, while what is outright meaningless can be given an air of mystery and profundity' (*CEJL* IV 138). Miller has no political beliefs, avoids 'real choices' and always takes care 'to stay inside bourgeois-democratic society, making use of its protection while disclaiming responsibility for it' (*CEJL* IV 135). No one could now accuse Orwell of the ambivalence of 'Inside the Whale'.

Several articles of 1945 comment on the narcissism of naturalistic novels: a characteristic closely related in a review of Dali's autobiography with self-indulgence. In a note on the narcissism of novelists the writer characterizes it in this way: 'To act with firmness and daring in moments of danger, to right injustices, to be a dominating personality, to exercise fascination on the opposite sex and to horsewhip one's private enemies' (*CEJL* IV 96). The aspects make up a private despotism of satisfied desires. Language that is too lyrical is criticized for its use of words for the author's sake not for themselves. It is suggested that the tendency is counteracted primarily by something Orwell refers to as 'probability' of character and narrative, and the creation of an integral 'texture' of words. By 'probability' Orwell indicates the need for literary devices which encourage the reader to participate in the text. Probable narrative is not fixed; its process to an ending is an invitation to assessment rather than a dictated conclusion. The integral 'texture' of words recognizes the life and materiality in language as something separate from the writer's control. Words can never be pushed into exact meaning or 'pure' sound, because they always resist manipulation. Time and again he makes the point that a writer removes himself from complete authoritarianism only by his care for words, his recognition of their separate existence.

During his last writings, of the years 1948–9, the essayist becomes increasingly preoccupied with the novel. In 1948 he defines it as,

> a story which attempts to describe credible human beings, and – without necessarily using the technique of naturalism – to show them acting on everyday motives and not merely undergoing strings of improbable adventures. (*CEJL* IV 433)

The factor of probability is important and characters should be shown in the round 'which, in effect, rules out novels in the first person' (*CEJL* IV 433). In a discussion of Gissing's work, Orwell comments that like his European counterparts, he lacks the humour, burlesque or comedy necessary to political writing. Despite the probability of his novels, his rounded characters and well-developed plots, he is an inelegant writer. But this, as with Shaw, Galsworthy and Bennett, is not so much of a problem as his narrow range of experience. In the end he has retreated even further than Dickens from society; he has 'no very strong moral purpose. He had, of course, a deep loathing of the ugliness, emptiness and cruelty of the society he lived in, but he was concerned to describe rather than change it' (*CEJL* IV 435). Dickens's concentration on the individual is similar but he is often humorous, his characters are not often in the round and he does note the ludicrous qualities of mankind.

It is interesting that Orwell had a particular blindness as far as writers influenced by religion, and particularly Roman Catholicism, were concerned. The only novelists he pays much attention to in these last years are Graham Greene and Evelyn Waugh. Yet just as with Chesterton, who influenced him enormously[9] to the extent of Orwell's apparently unconscious use of the very titles of articles to write from the same point of view on the same issues, or of his attribution of his own phrase 'good bad' books to Chesterton himself, his hatred for the potential despotism of the Church unbalances his judgement. While he recognizes that Greene's examination of moral issues is fascinating, he neglects the possibility that Greene might be exploring those very areas of non-naturalistic novels that he too is interested in; and he condemns Greene's novels as improbable and mechanically constructed in order to impose ideas of good and bad.

Toward Waugh he is more generous. Waugh is more probable despite his Catholicism and can only be faulted for his use of the first person narrator. A late diary entry shows the extent of the impairment of Orwell's judgement. Although referring also to Waugh's fascism and love for the aristocracy, he says 'Waugh is about as good a novelist as one can be (i.e. as novelists go today) while holding untenable opinions' (*CEJL* IV 513). That Orwell should describe anything out of hand as 'untenable' is startling. The remark is of course a casual private reference; but it is as if he is jealous of the ability for faith, and yet can never forgive the institution of the Church for implying that this world does not matter. He cannot see that personal faith and Church faith may function in the same kind of interaction and for much the same reason as the interaction between personal and party politics.

The Stance of Allegory

An early, undated extract from the manuscript notebook that Orwell kept during the last year of his life, discusses the main problems of the twentieth-century novel by focusing on the first person novel, which can easily become completely authoritarian and develop into the stance of fantasy literature. The similarity of the following observation on such novels, with earlier comments on escape literature is significant:

> to write a novel in the first person is like dosing yourself with some stimulating but very deleterious and very habit-forming drug. The temptation to do it is very great, but at every stage of the proceedings you know perfectly well that you are doing something wrong and foolish. (*CEJL* IV 511)

Its advantages are that the use of 'I' gets a writer over his initial shyness, that it allows him to arrive at the concept he started out with, and that '*anything* can be made to sound credible' because identification with the reader is easier. But the credibility is dangerous. Disadvantages of the technique arise from the limitation of the novel to that character. He will be a three-dimensional character amidst caricatures and the work 'cannot be a true novel' by narrowing the range of feeling to one. Further, because the narrator is not separate from the author he cannot comment, and 'even in a novel the author must occasionally comment' (*CEJL* IV 512).

Orwell says in 'Why I Write' that 'one can write nothing readable unless one constantly struggles to efface one's personality' (*CEJL* I 6). By personality he refers to the desire for personal control over the external world. *Coming up for Air* attempted to extend the form of the novel and incorporate the writer's voice, so that the reader would know the basis for the opinions in it and how its decisions were made. But the attempt did not fully succeed. The use of first person control caused Orwell to observe in a letter to Julian Symons of May 1948,

> Of course you are right about my own character constantly intruding on that of the narrator. I am not a real novelist anyway, and that particular vice is inherent in writing a novel in the first person, which one should never do . . . (*CEJL* IV 442)

The novelist, especially the first person novelist, is always in danger of imposing control without sufficient reference to his standards. The modern novel illustrates the negative characteristics of the first person technique. Only one set of grounds for reality is accepted and any conflicting set of opinions is either evaded, suppressed or denied. One point of view completely dominates the action, whether it be of the first person character or of a narcissistic narrator. The result is a culmination of the nineteenth-century movement toward naturalistic realism which gets so involved with the grounds of its society that criticism of and interaction with it become impossible.

But as Orwell has noted a novel need not be naturalistic, and his increasing interest in utopian novels examines the non-naturalistic possibilities of that genre. As he commented in a broadcast programme on Butler, utopian literature has the double-sided aspects of satire and allegory (*BA* 8/6/45). Both create alternative worlds. But the more immediate reference to actuality of satire ties it closer to naturalism, while allegory has greater scope. It is significant that he observes this alternative as one with a tradition including Swift, Butler and Zamyatin, but only partly including Huxley who is too satirical for his liking. The genre has much in common with the nonsense literature of Lear and Carroll, and is also based on the same principle as surrealism, that of creating conceptual and visual landscapes that comment by juxtaposition on conventionally accepted interpretations of the actual world.

For Orwell, Swift is a highly individual utopian writer, inspired by an anarchic impulse close to a personal totalitarianism. He notes Swift's technique of inserting a word of praise 'into a passage that ought to be purely satirical', which is 'a mark of vitality in Utopia books'. Inconsistency, disruption and vitality are linked with the non-satirical elements of utopian literature. Similarly he comments on Butler that he, 'like many other writers of Utopia books . . . doesn't fully make up his mind whether he is writing pure satire or whether he is making constructive suggestions' (*BA* 8/6/45). The two lived during different times, and whereas Swift's utopia was necessarily individual and private, Butler's is unsatisfactory because of his 'lack of interest in politics . . . he doesn't pay much attention to the structure of society' (*BA* 15/6/45).

It is the interest in politics that makes Zamyatin's *We* more successful as a novel than Huxley's *Brave New World*, despite its weak plot and other deviations from novelistic construction. Zamyatin's work is read not as a direct political satire on Russian or other contemporary politics, but as a work dealing with more general political issues. Huxley's novel concentrates on criticizing the existence of a mechanical world by suggesting that its leaders would become so apathetic that concepts of power would disappear. Orwell dismisses the suggestion and says that it weakens the novel by failing to connect with the causes of the actual political situation that exists.

Zamyatin on the other hand specifically points to the greed for power as the central motive for the political world he creates. A letter to F. J. Warburg written just before Orwell's death, clarifies the difference. *We* 'debunks the super-rational, hedonistic type of Utopia' also found in *Brave New World*, yet it continues not only to satirize it, but to suggest that it is made possible by a relegation of all other factors to 'diabolism and the tendency to return to an earlier form of civilization which seems to be part of totalitarianism' (*CEJL*. IV 486). The extension of utopian writing past a satire of individual aspects of totalitarianism, to the presentation of a landscape illustrating the source of its conceptual limitations and the negative strategies of hence controls by imposing opinion, but allegory comments by juxtaposition of the writer's values with those of the habitual world. Evaluation and assessment is only achieved if the reader himself makes the necessary connections and interacts with the literature.

The brief comments on allegory which surface from Orwell's later criticism never become a consistent pattern of commentary in the way that his discussions of fantasy do. We learn far more about literary strategies for a positive rhetoric from his development of juxtaposed analogies in *Homage to Catalonia*, his treatment of narratorial voice in *Animal Farm*, or his complex tensions of repetition in *Nineteen Eighty-Four*. But the few comments we do find indicate his growing search in contemporary literature for strategies actively involving both reader and writer to parallel the interaction between personal and party politics. The writer is no longer concerned with telling the reader something explicit, but with creating structures within which they can both discuss but also then proceed to move beyond. Failure to recognize this, failure to take up our side of the activity, severely limits the reader's enjoyment of Orwell's work.

Animal Farm, written when the writer had rejected the form of the novel but not yet turned to utopian allegorical literature,[10] is both satirical and allegorical. As a satire on the Russian revolution it is, as many critics have noted,[11] not particularly illuminating. However as an allegory containing grounds not explicitly tied to historical event it is of enduring value. Similarly, *Nineteen Eighty-Four* is satire, irony and allegory. Orwell notes that the work is not a fantasy in terms of 'a thriller mixed up with a love story' (*CEJL* IV 460), but a fantasy in terms of nonsense literature that indicates 'by parodying them the intellectual implications of totalitarianism' (*CEJL* IV 460). He wishes to combine the identification of naturalism with the distortion of fantasy (*CEJL* IV 330), to provide an alternative world not in order to supplant this one but to set it up in a commenting tension with it and encourage the reader's involvement in assessment and evaluation. *Nineteen Eighty-Four* is a 'Utopia in the form of a novel' (*CEJL* IV 475). As a utopia its naturalistic elements present a satire on the shifting truths of a totalitarian state, and it is in this sense that it is much criticized in a later age which is perhaps mistakenly more dismissive of the possibility of such a state. But as an allegory of the ease with which we lose ourselves to habitual convention, of the failure of the individual to renew tradition and of the withdrawal from a responsibility to discuss and communicate values, it is horrifyingly precise.

III   Fantasy
and Allegory

CHAPTER SIX

Animal Farm:
An Allegorical Reading

While *Animal Farm* is not utopian it does contain the twin elements of satire and allegory which Orwell thought of as the basis for the genre, and the consequent doubleness of reading has resulted in much critical controversy.[1] Constructing the simple satire of the story is a plot line of similarity with actual events, specifically with those of the Russian Revolution and its immediate consequences. There are inescapable one-to-one associations between the animal figures and specific human characters which are established by direct linear connections. These direct comparisons are didactic, and from a defining authoritarian stance that designates one figure to one character. Such naïve satire is not only resented because of its tone, but is at a fundamental disadvantage because of its logic of direct one-to-one connections. No figure or image can provide an adequate representation of an actual human being. The attempt to do so leaves the reader dissatisfied and encourages him to find fault with the work. Naïve representational satire raises objections not only because its definitive manner appears to dominate over the reader leaving him no personal involvement, but also because many readers will disagree with the narrow definitions it is imposing upon the situation it discusses.

Many readers are tempted to think of allegory as a similar associative process, which would differ from satire only by reinforcing instead of criticizing the standards being presented. But the word allegory has as its root 'allos' or 'other', and 'other' does not just imply the one thing standing for the other, which is the word as emblem or even as a restricted coded sign for the object. 'Other' in allegory is closely allied to the concept of differance in the work of Jacques Derrida. Paul de Man defines the allegorical as 'representation that leads toward a meaning that diverges from the initial meaning to the point of foreclosing its manifestation . . .'[2] In other words, allegory attempts to communicate by admitting that it cannot express what it wants to say adequately. This does not leave its technique as a negative dismissal of the ability to communicate. Instead it tries to involve the reader by alerting him to the radical difference between what is being said and of what it is speaking, of the impossibility of conveying any identity absolutely, and of the consequent need to interact with the words to achieve any communication.

The concept is not new. The stance of allegory recognizes that the external world exists outwith the control of human beings. It exercises a rhetoric or a persuasion that is positive because of its willingness to step outside often restrictive and isolating man-made definitions, in order to recognize the external. Whether that externality be theological, spiritual, material or mystical, the primary human response to the world through allegory is one of attempted interaction with it, all the while perceiving that it cannot be fully controlled. Allegory provides a counterpoise to those stances which respond to the world by attempting to control and define it within their own terms. As Orwell suggested, fantasy is an important contemporary rhetorical stance which tries to control by creating an isolated world of its own within which the inventor rules supreme. To isolate itself successfully, it needs the strategies of a negative rhetoric. Depending upon which medium it realizes itself in – the literary, the political, the historical, the scientific – its generic features will change. In literature for example the image of the island is particularly important to a fantasy stance because it provides a natural isolation from actual life. Orwell's essays studied many of the generic features of different contemporary fantasy worlds and linked them to basic negative strategies.

By comparison with the essays on fantasy and power politics, Orwell's study of modern allegory, or of a stance that does not try to control and dominate but to interact, is rudimentary. As noted earlier, his explorations were most revealing in the textual activity of his fictional and documentary writing, rather than as a specific theory. The lack of development in the essays is not surprising in terms of modern critical history; the allegorical stance has only begun to receive serious attention during the 1960s. But given Orwell's subtle use of allegory in his later novels, which indicates considerable awareness of the scope of the stance, a more telling reason emerges for the imbalance between the complex activity of his fiction and the tentative steps of his criticism.

Allegory like fantasy is a rhetorical stance. As such it is not a theory of knowledge nor a specific generic mode of expression. Although current attitudes to perception or to media affect its manifestations, it is primarily concerned with realizing a belief about the relationship between human beings and their world. For example, the generic confusion surrounding the many different kinds of literature that make use of alternative, non-actual worlds within their techniques, arises from failing to perceive the ways in which different stances structure the same generic aspects. Orwell's separation between the contrasting use of similar alternative worlds that opposes the genre of fantasy to utopia, satire and 'allegory', is based on whether they attempt to exercise power or to stimulate involvement. The distinction indicates his understanding of a rhetorical, rather than generic or epistemological, basis for the stances. It also places him in the forefront of critical studies in this area. His preliminary essays on this group of genres amount to a guide to contemporary literary activities which try to realize the interaction of human beings with the world.

But further, because the root of allegory is interaction rather than imposition, specific definitions and enumerated theories are difficult to provide. Guides to strategies that adapt and change in particular practical circumstances are about as far as the criticism can go. But fiction, which is more clearly recognized as a particular case, can present its context more fully in the activity or stance of its text. It can more easily avoid domination and control over other examples or situations because it is recognized as an analogy for them rather than a set of definitions about them. In all cases, not just in the literary, allegory establishes a process in which a human being admits that he cannot fully know the 'other', the external world. He not only admits but makes that admission the source of his experience or expressiveness. It is a process opposite to the establishing of private identities for actual things and events external to one. What allegory effects and is concerned to realize is the activity of one's lack of knowledge. It is often frightening because it throws us back on the things we do know and these are shown to be limited. Because it is frightening it is often resisted, avoided and denied.

Human beings crave and appear to need group certainties, some escapes, delusions of knowledge and authority that allow us to abdicate activity. Without them people create their own, and because these are private and not shared they are thought abnormal, insane. Societies could be said to be bound together on common grounds of escape. The catch is that without a coincident pursuit of the 'other', the escapes become rigid, unsatisfactory and technically decadent. Imagination could be described as the faculty which allows us to deal with the concept of the 'other'. If, as Orwell suggests, words and worlds fossilize through historical accretions, allegory is a device for stripping away those accretions. Allegory also strips away the accretions of the self, but in doing so it allows us to see again differently and with intensity the things other than ourselves that surround and place us.

Once allegory engages the reader or writer in activity with the 'other' or the external, it assumes the position of a positive rhetorical stance. The stance not only involves the writer in self-examination but also involves the reader in self-discovery. It does not try to lay down the exact representations of figures, events or reactions which emblematic, one-to-one definitions attempt. Instead it suggests parallel and divergent activities that often indicate directions of involvement through interpretation; and it does so by presenting the difference and radical separation which the text overtly establishes between the figure or image, and the actuality.

It is helpful to recall the different strategies that satire and genres informed by allegory, employ in their use of alternative worlds. Where genres of fantasy, such as romance, need the alternative to ensure the isolation necessary for the completeness of their desires, satire establishes an alternative world which is similar enough to actuality to propose criticisms in the contrast and comparison of the two. The problem for satire is that because its structure is dependent upon the actual it may become too tied to the very things it attacks. It may acquire a stance like that of fantasy and begin to protect and isolate the grounds it initially sought to cut away.

Allegory goes further and tries to juxtapose a radically different alternative with the accepted perception of the world. The allegorical stance challenges both writer and reader to interact with the external rather than control it by imposing upon it. Genres employing an alternative world through an allegorical stance will use its difference from the conventional to encourage a fundamental change in the way human beings participate in the world. These genres cannot help but guide the reader, but their stance attempts to stimulate him to involve himself rather than dictate his response.

As an allegory *Animal Farm* does provide a didactic element but it is actively educative rather than authoritarian; it raises questions about itself and its processes at the same time as it questions its concerns. The allegory reforms a naïve satire into a complex satirical presentation of party politics and propaganda that is based on metaphorical not associative figures, and involves difference as well as similarity. But the novel also functions as straight allegory, discussing the interaction between personal and party politics and the communication that that interaction depends on, by establishing a fundamental separation between the strategies involved within the text itself. The interaction of those strategies provides a guide to or an active analogy for the communication it is discussing. To read the work as a complex satire is rewarding. It provides a sound education in the rhetoric of politics, but its conclusion appears cynical and negative. Only if read simultaneously as allegory does it proffer a positive conclusion.

Animal Farm is openly about politics and propaganda, specifically propagandic language. As the changing political states portrayed are examined, they go hand in hand with changing methods of communication, and the method of communication defines the governing body. It is not just that a particular way of putting something across conveys the ideas, but that the kind of stance used creates the correct reception for the politics under consideration. Given Orwell's constant concern to link political language with art, it would be foolish to ignore the literary implications even if it were possible. But the writer's narratorial rhetoric continually calls attention to itself and insists on examination.

It should be remembered that Orwell was dissatisfied with the strategy of *Coming Up for Air*, which experimented with the exclusion of the narrator. The failure of that work led to his dissatisfaction with the novel in general, yet in 1943 when he writes *Animal Farm* he has not yet developed his interest in utopian literature. The main problem involved is to find a mode which is overtly fictional so that the narrator's role can be recognized and defined as a stance, yet at the same time can involve the reader in an active participation with that stance, lead him to question it. The narrator cannot simply tell the reader to be independent, or he will undercut the validity of his strategy. It is a problem of guiding without dictating, of defining and yet being defined by, of wanting to communicate something that essentially rests on the reader having to initiate the activity from his side. The 'difficulty' of much modernist writing aims at such stimulation but it has also led to charges of obscurity. In effect it often does enforce activity on the reader and may devolve into crossword puzzle solving. Orwell never forces the issue because he is more afraid of the consequences of his own dominance than of the reader's apathy. This anxiety lies behind the problems in much of his earlier fictional work; it also provokes the critical controversy surrounding the later works. In *Animal Farm* he attempts to make the strategy so obvious that it cannot dictate, but rather provide a foil for the reading. As the literary conventions used, especially that of the fairy story, intrude and gradually reverse our expectations of them, the allegory of personal interaction emerges. In order to fully appreciate both the extent of the complex satire and the activity of the allegory initiated through the narratorial stance, the following study will separate the two. I recognize that this may be a clumsy critical technique, but considering the confusion surrounding readings of the text I am concerned to distinguish between the two.

Identity and Difference

Both the complex satire and the allegory comment upon and extend each other. Initially a general analogy between animals and humans is established. But from the start it becomes apparent that the pigs are more conventionally human than the other animals. Identification with the pigs is encouraged by their assumption of human activities, especially their use of language; yet the other animals are also gradually accorded different types of human characteristics. The study of party political rhetoric in the novel focuses on the differences between the animals. Yet gradually one realizes that it is not only identification with the animals that is called for. As the pigs begin to take up more and more foolish human activities, and as the other animals are relegated to a passive role because of their inability to communicate, the reader draws back from identification. Guided by the allegorical stance of the narratorial rhetoric, the reader can perceive that the point of detachment is language. Those animals with valid standards and points of view are prevented from voicing them by their inability to communicate. Hence the pigs can take their dominant role to its totalitarian end not only because they are dictatorial, but because the others lack the means to fight back. The activity of reading that the narratorial rhetoric makes necessary, alerts us to the necessary activity of political participation. It is also underlined that the events in the book cannot be helped because of the limited nature of animals, except possibly by Benjamin the donkey, who appears to be more intelligent than the others but refuses to get involved. The point is that humans, not being so limited, have a responsibility to ensure that these events do not happen in their world. It is not a simple process of identification, but a recognition of the difference involved that suggests this positive reading.

The operation of this difference is realized in the practical effects of re-reading *Animal Farm*. Unless it is read simply as a satire on the Russian revolution and its consequences it can never be read more than once in the same technical manner. In other words, although no two readings are ever identical, the second reading of this book involves expectations radically different from the first. This results from the original expectations being irrevocably reversed by the emergence of the allegory, and from the personal involvement caught up in that reversal. A second reading involves a great deal of dramatic irony necessarily lacking in the first, and the change in this quality of reading is one of the most substantial clues to what is going on. For example, there is one's change in attitude to the pigs: after the first reading one is always suspicious of their actions instead of gradually becoming so. But more important is the change in our attitude to the 'laws of Animalism' and the construction of events. During the first reading one begins by taking for granted the 'Commandments' of 'Animalism' or the 'explanations' for past events. Only as the reading progresses do we realize that we should have tried to remember more accurately. After the first reading one pays far closer attention to those aspects. Further than this one needs the political allegory to remind one that the emphasis on our memory is only a result of the system of totalitarian domination over fact and history that is being employed by the pigs, and which aims to control the associations between things for us by supplanting memory. It brings home again the point that the animals have no recourse to the problem but that humans do.

Once the reader has grasped the interaction of satirical and allegorical elements, he has also grasped the point of individual recognition that the narrator could only make possible, not enforce. The more profound political satire that results suggests that totalitarianism depends on increased attempts to control by means of techniques that deny active interaction, and the allegory adds that the individual has a responsibility to resist this tendency and to stop it. The man and animal figuration exists throughout the tale. If one goes along with the identification, then one is automatically allied with the pigs; one accepts the implications of what they represent. But if we resist the identification, resist the image of being either pig or other animal, or the humans who are pigs at the end of the tale, then we have to take up an individual voice that is not present in the book, only indicated by the differences bodied forth through the figures.

Without the allegorical dimension, in other words reading as a simple satire, the book merely appears to state that the leaders of the Russian revolution were misguided, recreating the worst elements of the capitalist system around them. For obvious reasons this is antagonizing to Communist readers, but also the implied charges of bestial behaviour cannot have left capitalist readers content either. It is finally ironic that this limited reading can become a satire on the readers themselves: that if they do not perceive the allegorical dimension then yes, they are restricted to the animal-like characteristics of total dominance or apathetic passivity; they cannot actively involve themselves in the reading and by analogy neither will they do so in politics. But the speculation is completely un-Orwellian and rather cruel.

Language and Power

The complex satire that is created begins with the rhetoric of the Major's initial speech to the animals at the opening of chapter 1. No matter what one thinks of the ideas involved, the structure of the rhetoric here is negative in terms of the techniques that Orwell has developed and discussed in other works. The primary technique is an argument from passively accepted grounds which allows the speaker to get away with a neglect of his basic argument and establish familiarity with his audience from false premises. Although he appears to set up free choices he is in fact in total control. The detachment and objectivity the Major lays claim to by saying that he will soon die, hides the control he is effecting through the repetitions of his rhetoric. One of the first techniques of repetition is found in the use of rhetorical questions. These can often be antagonistic but here because the answer to the initial rhetorical question, 'What is this life of ours?', is clearly acceptable the acceptance is carried more easily through to the final 'What then must we do?' which precedes his 'statement of Rebellion'. The acceptance of these questions is further controlled by his tight, complete answers to them which do not encourage discussion and varied response. The second technique is the repetition of phrases that transfers a reaction to the first phrase onto the second. The assent to the first phrase, 'No animal in England knows the meaning of happiness or leisure after he is a year old' transfers to 'No animal in England is free'. There is also the repetition of key words that establishes a personal vocabulary. From the beginning the 'animals' are addressed as 'comrades', and a parallel structure of 'Man' as 'enemy' is set up. The classic technique of uniting the enemy into one is effected through the typing of 'Man' as invariably evil and cruel; in contrast, the animals are presented through personalized references that create sympathy.

Having controlled the process of his background speech the Major then also controls the following events. A vote on whether wild animals should be included in the community of animals, arises when four rats enter the barn. The Major skilfully manipulates the votes by phrasing the question that is to be voted on to say 'rabbits and rats' (p. 13) thus defusing the negative connotations of the rats alone; and secondly by forming the vote question to read 'Are rats comrades?' not 'Are rats enemies?' The weight of the word 'comrades' along with the positive phrasing used turns the argument toward them. The incident is also strategically important because it involves all the animals in the act of communal voting and solidifies the idea that they are a compact unit.

When the Major comes to his summarizing directions he says 'I merely repeat' as if referring back to a previously discussed and agreed principle. The directions reinstate the defining vocabulary with words such as the 'duty of enmity toward Man', building from the word alone to the catch-phrase, to the slogan. Yet the phrasing of the directions is entirely in terms of 'duty', of 'never faltering', of allowing no argument to lead astray. He has provided the immediate safety of established laws that precludes active involvement on the part of the animals. The account of his dream which follows (p. 14), and the rendition of 'Beasts of England' confirms the stance. His dream is a utopian vision of the past to be transferred to the future. It is carried by images of plenty, and the pastoral 'golden future time' of the song. The song itself is not there for education or illumination, but as a unifying device, playing upon the members' ability to pick up the tune quickly without thinking about the words. No matter that the Major says 'no animal must ever tyrannize over his own kind'; the authoritarian progress of the speech, discouraging participation and discussion, the forming of a set of directions that insist on a narrow view, and the use of unthinking populist stimulation, sow the seeds of tyranny while they warn against it.

The Major's speech also lays the foundation for the political developments which follow. Not surprisingly the three pigs who take up and apply his ideas are defined by their ability to handle language. Napoleon is 'not much of a talker' in contrast to Snowball who is 'quicker in speech and more inventive'. The only porker of significance is Squealer:

> a brilliant talker, and when he was arguing some difficult point he had a way
> of skipping from side to side and whisking his tail which was somehow very
> persuasive. The others said of Squealer that he could turn black into white.
> (p. 17)

As the initial characteristics of the pigs are developed, Snowball is recognizably the one who makes the rules, controls through talking and writing. Napoleon is the one who controls by manipulating the physical aspects of the farm, the products and their consumption.

After the Major's death the three pigs develop the negative strategies that are already present, and turn the Majors's directions into 'a complete system of thought' legitimized by the word 'Animalism'. The power that is conferred on them by doing so, is reflected in the way they run the meetings of the animals. Organization is left to them because 'naturally' it should be; they are 'generally recognized' as the cleverest. They exploit their acceptance by failing to answer the questions of other animals, dismissing them as 'contrary to the spirit of Animalism'. The key reaction to their techniques is that of Boxer and Clover who 'had great difficulty thinking anything out for themselves, but having once accepted the pigs as their teachers, they absorbed everything they were told, and passed it on to the other animals in simple arguments' (p. 18).

Most important is the fact that the pigs can read and write. This is the key to their intelligence. After the Rebellion we get a clue to the significance they attach to their ability: the first thing they do is to alter the name of the farm, acting out a common residual belief in nominalism and the magic of names. The second thing is to 'reduce' the Major's directions to 'Seven Commandments' of 'unalterable law'. Realizing that the directions can never be absolute unless treated as laws and enforceable, they write them down. In the process they reduce them: a first-time reader probably accepts the 'Seven Commandments' as complete, but the more wary reader checks and discovers that several minor points have been excluded, along with the injunction that animals are not to tyrannize over each other.

The pigs' dominance is extended as the procedures of the farm move through the first months of animal government. At the same time it is re-emphasized that their power comes from their ability to use language, and the direction of that power is toward reduction. Again it is Snowball and Napoleon who participate most in the debates and hence control the meetings. The differences between the methods of the two is between Snowball's superior linguistic ability and Napoleon's physical control. Snowball concerns himself with committees and education. But as his solution to the differing levels of literacy in the animals indicates, he is catering to their desire not to think, making it easier for them simply to memorize than really learn. Of course this itself is partly a result of the system which discourages active participation. The pigs have no difficulty with reading and writing, and neither do the dogs, nor the donkeys Muriel and Benjamin. But the dogs are slavish creatures, only interested in reading the commandments, and Benjamin claims that there is 'nothing worth reading'. Clover is intelligent but not enough to 'put words together'; and Boxer can only ever remember four letters at a time, even though he takes great pleasure in them; the vain Mollie will only learn her own name, and none of the other animals can get past 'A'. These differing abilities are direct analogies for the roles the animals play. At the top, the better one reads, the cleverer one is and the less work one does. At the bottom, the mass of illiterate animals apathetically accepts and does its duties. In the centre are the intelligent but not completely literate animals like Boxer and Clover, who cannot read and therefore must work, yet are clever enough to realize that they must actively participate and so take on a larger number of duties than the others. Significantly, the animals are now divided by the pigs into 'classes' for reading and writing that reflect their differing linguistic abilities (p. 27).

For those with minimal intelligence Snowball 'reduces' the seven commandments to 'a single maxim': 'Four legs good, two legs bad', which the sheep take up and bleat incessantly. When the birds object that they will be excluded, Snowball 'explains' that this is not so, the meaning is not really changed. At which: 'The birds did not understand Snowball's long words, but they accepted his explanation'. Explanation becomes the complement to force. When Napoleon is faced with justifying the fact that milk and apples are for the use of pigs alone, he sends Squealer with the 'necessary explanations'. These consist of a series of rhetorical questions that are not clearly connected to the argument, but whose acceptance transfers onto his conclusions. He ends with the unanswerable question 'do you want to see Jones come back?' (p. 29) The techniques are a superficial, clumsy, but effective travesty of the Major's.

So far the satire underlines the theory that language, written or spoken, is the key to political power. The other animals are limited in their use of language and cannot discuss or debate issues effectively with the pigs; and since they cannot write and their memories are imperfect, they cannot check the original assumptions and decisions they started from. If the pigs had to contend with either of these aspects they could not have been so dominant. Beyond these issues is the possibility that perhaps language should not be the only index of intelligence: that if there were other measures such singleness of domination would not be possible.

In the fourth chapter the situation extends out to whether this type of political situation can survive. Once again the key is linguistic propaganda. The Farm sends out birds to instruct the neighbouring animals in the elements of Rebellion, and in the singing of 'Beasts of England'. The song is the unifying cross-cultural point of contact, and is the one thing that immensely annoys the other farmers. At first the farmers retaliate by laughing and putting about contradictory rumours. Finally they resort to forcible attack on the Farm. It is rumour against rumour, but in the end the rumour with the more substantial backing, here that of the animals, wins out, and at the end of the battle they formalize and commemorate the occasion. Already they are getting into the habit of retaining memory through custom, fossilizing history so that they do not have to think about basic principles. Their medals, flags, the firing of the guns create an artificial, fixed sense of event, an escape which will not need re-examination. Such complacency will also make it possible to manipulate the past. The animals' political development is portrayed most clearly through the conduct of the meetings. Over the first winter on the farm the pigs – who are now 'manifestly cleverer' not just 'naturally' – set up a process whereby they make the decisions which are simply ratified by the rest of the animals. The consolidation of this process is interrupted by the incident of the windmill in chapter 5. Snowball has decided that building a windmill will allow the animals to modernize the farm and raise their standard of living, but Napoleon is opposed to the plan, saying that it will 'come to nothing' (p. 36). The matter is first raised as a casual example of the differences between Snowball and Napoleon, but is gradually turned into the main event that causes Snowball's expulsion.

During the final debate about whether or not to build the windmill, both pigs use negative rhetorical stances although Snowball's is less misleading than Napoleon's. At first Snowball defends his position intellectually and rationally. Napoleon counters with a terse statement of disbelief, to be interpreted as a command, and finally has to resort to force. In keeping with his educational policy, Snowball slips up by making it all too easy, by presenting his case too neatly or too emotively, while Napoleon does not even make a pretence at persuasion. Both exclude the rest of the animals from active involvement with their reasoning.

Once Snowball has left there are no more debates at meetings. A committee of pigs is established to make all decisions which are communicated later on to the other animals. Discussion is made impossible, partly because the animals cannot verbalize their questions, but also because the chanting of rote-learned slogans drowns them out; explanations are forestalled and there is continual threat of force. The rhetoric of Squealer's explanation when Napoleon decides on this form of government at the end of chapter 5, is first to reverse the potentially aggressive stance by making it look self-sacrificing, then to reinterpret factual occurrences, both about Snowball's heroic role in the battle with the farmers and about his plans for the windmill, so that he is discredited. Squealer clinches his identification with the animals he is speaking to by moving from 'you' to 'we' and concludes with the unanswerable question about Jones coming back. The rhetoric induces submission, and results in an unthinking acceptance of Boxer's second maxim, 'Napoleon is always right'.

The meetings finally develop a formal hierarchy of seating, with the pigs and dogs on a raised platform and the rest of the animals below. No reasons are given for any decisions. Worship of the Major's skull is introduced, and all the animals have to file past it in reverence once a week. This further fossilization of the active stimulation behind the Rebellion elevates the 'Principles of Animalism' to a rigidly worshipped and unquestioned position. While the Major's speech contained the seeds of negative rhetoric, it did actively involve the animals. The rhetoric has now devolved into a negative process for inducing passivity and submission.

It is at this crucial stage in development that the animals have to keep up their ability to question if they are to retain their freedom. The next rhetorical development, which occurs in chapter 6, concerns techniques that the pigs employ to stop the questioning process. The first example occurs when Napoleon announces that they are to start trading with humans. The decision causes protest because some animals 'thought that they remembered' this to have been forbidden by the Major. Their timid voices are silenced immediately by threats of force from the dogs and slogan chanting by the sheep. Squealer then moves in with an explanation, reinterpreting past events. Significantly, because the events are not 'written down anywhere' there is no counter-argument. Squealer himself stresses this because a more powerful argument, had they been capable of it, would have been from a discussion of basic principles.

Similarly, when the pigs move into the farmhouse (p. 47) Squealer is 'able to convince them' that it is acceptable. Boxer reacts by repeating his maxims; Clover and Muriel try to reread the Commandments. But sine the Commandment has been rewritten by the pigs, Clover accepts it. Squealer's rhetoric here consists of placing the animals in a negative perspective and Napoleon in a positive, using rhetorical questions negatively to deny reply; he redefines words as if the word could absolutely represent an event, and hence redefinition firmly justifies a new interpretation. Gradually with the support of sloganizing and threats of force, the animals get used to the explanations being provided and cease to question: when they are told of Snowball's evil a second time they accept it.

The conclusions to each chapter provide a clear index to the process. Chapter 1 ends with the exuberance of all the animals being stopped by Jones's gun. The second chapter ends with them coming to unanimous agreements, but in the third only 'the pigs were in full agreement'. The Battle with the farmers reunites the animals into 'unanimity', but at the end of chapter 5 the animals 'accepted . . . [Squealer's] explanation without further question'. The conclusion to chapter 6 portrays the animals simply accepting Napoleon's explanation about Snowball, and to chapter 7, portrays their final protests being put to an end by the bleating of sheep.

The endings of chapters 8 to 10 underline the mystification of the events and non-committal attitude taken up by the animals in retaliation, by presenting events upon which no comment is made. For example, chapter 8 ends with Muriel reading one of the Commandments, and finding that it has been adjusted. She recognizes the change, but no further response to it is given.

The form of government on the Farm depends on an enforced 'voluntarism' superintended by the pigs. As it develops, Napoleon becomes detached even from the rest of the pigs; his speech is reported rather than direct; and he comes to be referred to as the 'Leader'. Concurrently there is an increasing interaction with humans; the Farm acquires a lawyer and begins contact on a regular basis. But with external recognition comes compromise, because a propaganda of success has to be maintained to keep up appearances. This is easily effected by controlling the information to which the lawyer has access, through relatively crude devices such as filling the storage bins with sand and topping them up with barley to give an impression of large quantities of stores. The propaganda has to be maintained not only for the benefit of outsiders, but also for that of the animals themselves. Napoleon's control over government depends on his apparent strength and infallibility. As he withdraws even further into being an absolute figure he appears only on ceremonial occasions; he ceases to give any direct commands and Squealer communicates all his wishes. By displacing total control from an immediate source to a source at one remove, potential disagreements are defused, as there is no one to argue with directly. At the same time Napoleon realizes that there has to be some focus for discontent, and he reconstructs a history of the evil Snowball to bear the brunt of this guilt.

Each of the three major incidents of chapter 7 centre on techniques for displacing the animals' discontent. In each case Napoleon attempts to remove himself farther from direct communication, and the other animals become increasingly passive. During the first incident the hens are ordered to produce eggs for sale at a time when they should be nesting. They go on strike, claiming that this is murder, and Napoleon cuts off their food supply. Before they give in nine of them die, but it is 'given out' from an unstated source that they died of disease not hunger. Just as with the fictional reconstruction of Snowball's history, the new facts derive from an unknown origin. 'It was said' and 'It was noticed' become the catch-phrases that describe both the detachment of the source of information, and the uninvolved non-committal attitude of the animals. The animals become so used to the process of 'explaining' or rewriting history that they rarely protest. When they do, Squealer is there to persuade them.

The main rewriting of events in this chapter concerns the first Battle with the farmers which Snowball had led and won. Now the animals are told that in fact he was not even fighting, and this takes some persuasion. Even

Boxer tries to work out the implications of the change. His stolid questions push Squealer into the corner of saying that it is all proved 'by documents', and, he says, 'I could show this to you in his own writing, if you were able to read it'. Sensing a resistance, Squealer proceeds to describe 'the scene so graphically, it seemed to the animals that they did remember it'. Boxer's continued unwillingness to believe leaves Squealer no alternative but to say that Napoleon has stated it 'categorically', and this finally satisfies him. But such totally passive acceptance is poor negative rhetoric. The force of negative rhetoric comes from the ability to make someone think they have made an active decision, personally involved themselves, while in fact making it impossible for them to do anything different from what the speaker wants.

The final incident of chapter 7 is an example of negative rhetoric taken to its ultimate point. Napoleon orders an assembly of the animals and enters with all the trappings of medals and orders, surrounded by threatening dog escorts. The meeting has been called so that 'confessions' of aiding and abetting Snowball can be made. Here, however, they are persuaded into accepting personal guilt and sacrificing themselves because of it. Each animal that confesses knows that he will be killed, yet they are so convinced of their guilt they allow it to, or, rather, they make it, happen. It is important that four pigs are the first to confess. In the eyes of the other animals this provides Napoleon with a greater degree of impartiality. More subtly, it underlines the point that the only serious threat to Napoleon comes from his own kind. As animal after animal confesses and the 'pile of corpses lying before Napoleon's feet' mounts up, it is clear that hysteria has taken over. This final, physical example of persuasion is such an extreme reaction that the animals have lost personal values.

The animals who remain are confused because they sense that such extreme retribution is wrong. Boxer blames himself; in contrast Muriel and Clover try to work it out. Here it is again noted that one of the hindrances is that they cannot verbalize well. If Clover 'could have spoken her thoughts, it would have been to say that this was not what they had aimed at . . .' (p. 59), and later 'Such were her thoughts, though she lacked the words to express them' (p. 60). Her inability to work through the reasoning leaves her certain that the objectives have changed, but that life is still better than under Jones. As a 'substitute for the words she was unable to find' she sings 'Beasts of England'. But significantly Squealer arrives just as they finish to inform them that the song has been banned because the Rebellion is now over. Utopia has been achieved and a new song has been written to take the place of the first. The point is that no matter how illusory the utopian vision had been, the animals had not been deluded into thinking it had taken place. Squealer is now claiming that it has, and just as in changing the name of the Farm or making a flag for the nation, there is a belief that an exchange of superficial symbols can redefine the actual situation.

Throughout chapter 8 which follows the purge, Napoleon consolidates his dictatorial position. Rumours are circulated about threats to his life; the gun is fired not only to commemorate the Rebellion and the Battle but also his birthday; and an entire mythology is built up around him through proverbial sayings, laudatory verse and official portraits. Now that the immediate problem of controlling the animals has been solved, he turns to the propaganda needed for the outside world. The primary concern is now convincing the other farmers of the legitimacy of the Farm and Napoleon's power. Part of the campaign is to combine the external propaganda with persuading the animals on the Farm that they are threatened. The adverse propaganda directed against one of two farmers who is competing to buy some timber from them, not only inclines a second farmer more benignly toward Napoleon, but also provides a focused enemy for the animals. But as with all short-term propaganda continual novelty is necessary to sustain the persuasion, and after Napoleon is swindled over the timber with forged money, the farmers attack the farm and blow up the newly constructed windmill. However, residual hints that Napoleon might even have engineered the attack himself to cover up his stupidity over the forgery come strongly to the foreground.

This second Battle is in marked contrast to the first. The animals advance only 'boldly enough' and are easily beaten back until their pride and joy, the windmill, is blown up. Afterwards, Boxer's simple questions again expose the disillusionment of the animals, which has to be dispelled by Squealer's ceremonies, medals, 'songs, speeches, and more firing of the gun' to convince them 'after all that they had won a great victory'.

The incidents leading up to and concluding the Battle are enclosed by references to the Commandments which Muriel reads to Clover. In each case 'there were two words that they had forgotten' which change the meaning. Again Benjamin, who knows that they have simply been amended abdicates his responsibility and remains uninvolved. It is interesting that as the animals become more detached they pick up Squealer's vocabulary of persuasion. His examples that prove an action 'clearly' justified are simply adapted by the animals themselves to 'clearly' justify the next. They live in a world of rumours where things 'seem' to be so, and things are 'said' to happen. After a point Squealer ceases even to persuade by sophistical proof. He simply reads off statistics that appear to show the animals' lot as far better than that under Jones, and 'The animals believed every word of it. Truth to tell, Jones and all he stood for had almost faded out of their memories . . .' (p. 74). The continued application of negative rhetoric, of persuasion by omission, deception, reinterpretation backed up by force, has produced a state of constant self-deception.

The attitude allows for the next development in government which is the introduction of racism and overt priviledge. All the young pigs who are Napoleon's offspring receive special education and are kept apart from the others. The pigs are allowed ribbons on their tails; the man-made conveniences on the farm are now requirements not extras. The other animals are encouraged into 'escapes', 'more songs, more speeches, more processions, and comforting, organized weekly 'Spontaneous Demonstrations'. Animal Farm then becomes a Republic with Napoleon as President. Snowball's history is finally rewritten to prove that he was actually on Jones's side, and the response of the animals shifts smoothly from 'It now appeared' to 'In fact'. Moses the raven who had left when the Rebellion occurred returns with his dreams of 'Sugarcandy Mountain'. Although he is lying and suggesting that there is a better place beyond the utopian farm, so he also provides another unassailable escape. The animals use a subverted rational logic in their acceptance of his visions, arguing that 'Their lives . . . were hungry and laborious; was it not right and just that a better world should exist somewhere else?' (p. 77)

The focus for this stage of the politics is the injury of Boxer and the way he is dealt with. The pigs decide to send Boxer to a veterinarian in town, and the van which comes to collect him comes in the middle of the day when everyone is working. However, Benjamin sees it and for the first time breaks down: he reads its sign and tells the other animals that it comes from the glue factory. Boxer is being taken to be killed. Following their unsuccessful attempts to stop the van, Napoleon himself has to come out and ceremoniously formalize the death. The animals are 'enormously relieved' and their reaction indicates the exaggerated fiction of the parts being played. But they do not contest the claims; they allow themselves to be convinced so that they can escape responsibility. For the first time a Commandment has been broken without simply amending its written form. There is no legitimate cause involved in Boxer's killing. For this to be accepted the animals must not just fail to question but actually convince themselves; they must be able to self-deceive, to doublethink. And the efficient outcome of this incident marks the total control now wielded by Napoleon.

The final chapter rounds up the process. The central event stems from the need to reverse the animals' last illusion that they own the farm, and get them to accept it. To prepare them, Squealer trains the sheep in a new verse, 'Four legs good, two legs better'. When the pigs begin to walk around on their hind legs holding whips, the rest of the animals 'in spite of everything . . . might have uttered some word of protest . . .', but the sheep interrupt and prevent it. The situation is accepted: after this nothing seems strange. Finally, Benjamin consents to tell Muriel that the remaining Commandment now reads: 'All Animals Are Equal/But Some Animals Are More Equal Than Others'.

The tale opened with Major's speech, it concludes with the speeches of the farmers and pigs, and in contrast with the earlier speech these are reported not direct; they do not aim at inspiring a new situation but at summarizing an old. Both the farmers' representative and Napoleon proceed by a series of statements that do not even form an argument. The clichés used, the bland summaries laid forward, require no transfer of acceptance or belief from one to the other, but simply back each other up. Major's question, 'What then must we do?' at least implied that he had an answer; Pilkington's 'Was not the labour problem the same everywhere?' is a statement in the past tense which he does not try to explain. Napoleon announces that the name of the farm is to revert back to the original 'Manor Farm' and this superstitious dependence on a name concludes the exchange. The other animals have been peering in at the window, watching this declaration of 'co-operative' ownership among the pigs, and hearing themselves relegated to 'lower animals'. But they do not protest, they are hopelessly resigned to the development. The final transformation of the pigs into human beings is not surprising, simply inevitable.

Satire into Allegory

The complex satire of *Animal Farm* is built upon an awareness of the power that language wields. The interaction between politics and language does not just establish one-to-one relationships between animal characters and historical figures but creates an understanding of a particular set of rhetorical techniques that have a broad political application. Further, it does not simply criticize certain forms of government but suggests reasons for why they occur and what contributes to their success. However, what limits the tale to satire, no matter how constructive it is in its suggestions, is the sense of inevitability, of describing an insoluble problem, ending on a note of negativity and cynicism. At the same time though the reader cannot ignore the coincident tongue-in-cheek humour of the narrating voice. The melodramatized character of the elderly Clover, the formal dance of speeches with their all-too-neat structure, the final exaggerated irony, all belie the negative pattern of the satire.

What turns the writing into positive allegory is the establishing of genre conventions that are shifted and reversed. In these changes the narrator takes a positive stance that contrasts sharply with the satirical voice; and the primary and most obvious reversal is that to which we are alerted in the subtitle of the book, 'A Fairy Story'. The function of allegory depends on differences. Yet to repeat part of the earlier discussion, what is commonly termed 'allegory' is one-to-one use of representational emblems, similarities: hardly a subtle genre. The dissatisfaction with it comes from the limited and reduced nature of stance. If acted well the movements can afford a similar pleasure to that of chess, but as with chess the more significant aspects of the game lie in the battle between the players not that between the pieces on the board. Restricting themselves to those pieces and what they are capable of, the players limit the scope of their interaction and the involvement of their audience. The supposed author of this kind of reduced generic 'allegory' is limited by the overtly representational nature of his structure. It takes great skill to maintain the grounds of his alternative world and to avoid the sense of inevitability that arises from the associative links and habitual connotations that are established. At the same time simple destruction of those links can be just as reductive; something positive needs to be suggested to open out the dialogue and make interaction possible. The complex satire of *Animal Farm* is generated by the process of allegory out of a reductive satire about events in Russian history. Its positive nature is found in its broad applicability to politics and language. But it is still limited to the criticism and exposure of weaknesses, to saying what not to do rather than what to do.

However, there is also the broader, interactive allegorical stance of *Animal Farm* which removes itself one step further from the representational, by turning to literary conventions which establish the bases for difference. The writer spends much of the first chapter getting the narrator to set up the genre conventions that surround fairy stories. Yet from the beginning there is a counter-element which indicates why this particular genre has been chosen. Elements to note are the simple phrasing and the repetition of grammatical structures which create a formal rhythm in the prose. There is also use of specific constructions such as 'there was a stirring and a fluttering' or the literal use of common expressions like 'chewing the cud' that are traditionally allied to the genre. Especially distinctive is the formal and detached quality of the narrator generated by these elements. It is as if he has a specific recognized role as tale-teller, because individual style is played down. Even before the more personalized descriptions of the animals begin, these details alert and orientate the reader to a genre.

For several reasons, the convention is immediately effective. The form is instantly recognized as non-novelistic. The reader does not expect the naturalism of psychological exploration or 'round characters'. What he does look for is a formal structure for teaching and knowing, by way of a conventional and non-representational mode. From the beginning, we are involved in an expected manner, alerted to certain rules. The narrator has the freedom to state, and present 'types', without appearing to dictate or over-control. He also has a convention that encourages detachment because its formality states his stance for him. However, at the same time he is part of the narration in a manner that a tale-teller would not be. He throws forward the convention he is using with the addition of extraneous comment, such as the Major's alternative name being 'Willingdon Beauty'. The use of brackets at this particular point in itself indicates a grammatical 'aside' different from his formal role. The use of fairy story is further highlighted by the humour which emerges in applying human description to animals, which is unusual for the genre. The mare Clover 'had never quite got her figure back after her fourth foal' (p. 10), and Benjamin's cynicism is undercut by a devotion to Boxer. Neither character will regain the formal distance of a fairy story figure after such description.

These effects are generated by the unusual use of animals as the main elements in the fairy story. The effect for the reader is that he can identify with the animals because they fit recognizable types, but the humour in their human description allows one to remain detached. We see the humanity in them because of their lack of it. The two views are the key to the allegory. The fairy story genre conditions one to certain expectations, an inevitability, a certain and set ethical development of specific issues in which the 'good' get rewarded and the 'bad' punished, according to the terms of the society they are written for. Excitement, adventure and apparent change occur only to reaffirm the basis of the society. Working against this all the way through is the fact that the characters are animals not humans. As a result many incongruous and ludicrous comparisons surface which detract from the formality of the fairy story and call into question its ethical inevitability.

Over and above the interconnection of these two is the interplay of the narrative allegory with the satire. After all the Major's speech dominates the first chapter. It is an example of a rhetoric containing within it the seeds of negative persuasion. The premises of that speech establish a power-wielding, knowledgeable, acceptable identity; they evidence total control over the development of the logic; and they encourage acceptance and group participation in agreed custom. The fairy story elements of the first chapter also do this. If we are aware of the manipulation involved in the Major's speech we should be doubly aware of the negative rhetorical elements in the fairy story. In this interplay and in the interaction of fairy story and humour, the allegory of the writing may be discerned. However, on first reading the dominant note is that of the fairy story not its disruption. Similarly, it is difficult to be immediately aware of the implications of the Major's speech. Yet I would suggest that this is a positive aspect of the writer's stance. The reader's gradual learning about the negative use of language parallels his gradual recognition of the subversion of the fairy story convention. The process of learning involves the active participation of the reader, draws him into a personal assessment necessary to the positive rhetoric of the writing.

The second chapter begins with the narrator retreating to an unobtrusive position to let the reader get on with the activity of recognition, disagreement and questioning. Only following the Rebellion does the overtly humorous voice re-enter again to balance out the conventions of fairy story. The humour is an unspoken irony based on the animals seeing human things from their point of view and the reader seeing them from his. The difference in the standards being applied need not be defined by the narrator because they are so clear. For example, the pathetic comedy of the statement that 'hams hanging in the kitchen were taken out for burial' (p. 21) is obvious. But because the humour is a result of the animals' different perspective rather than their ignorance, it is not simply a reason to laugh at them but to understand them and further, to reflect on the justification for our own standards. The humour of the irony sets up possibilities of choice for the reader. During this section of the satire it is made clear that the characters are being defined through their use of language and this is also true of the narrator. But while the pigs move only to imposing a control, the narrator in contrast has the ability to focus in and out, controlling but also asking his reader to control.

During the third chapter, the narrator retreats even further, pulling back his humorous comments closer to himself. His detachment is underlined when he clearly fails to make the usual narratorial comments. As a result he is not just formally but personally detached. The techniques of juxtaposition, resonance and the downplaying of incidents that take over, require the reader to partipate; they alert him to discrepancies, to meanings other than the habitual. Whereas the narrator himself did this at first, now the reader has to do it. Yet in setting the farmers off against the animals in the fourth chapter the narrator places himself firmly on the side of the animals by involving the reader in the decisions between the two. The tone of presentation defines part of his attitude. When describing the humans he uses longer sentences, idiomatic language and limited characteristics. They are 'types' not people. By contrast the animals are presented by way of a more direct, simple and straightforward language, the logic is easy to follow and there are few clichés and generalizations.

Although the narrator is able to maintain a distance from the story, the shift in his expression when presenting animals and humans indicates that he cannot be impartial. The alignment against the humans and with the animals is not a serious compromise of stance. In the first place it is defused by the humour of the contrasts. It is further controlled by the insistence on the overt fictionality which makes the humans 'types' and undercuts the achievements of the animals by limiting them to fairy story. However, his alignment with the other animals against the pigs by making the pigs more like humans in their speech, is a more subtle and questionable stance, and the reader must assess how it is to be justified. The reader's trust in the narrator's alignment is partly derived from his involvement in the techniques which gives a certain share in the assessment. But what really leaves the question open and allows for impartiality is not what is said or implied against the pigs, but what the other animals have or lack in comparison with them. These elements are supplied purely by the reader and the possibility of involving ourselves to this extent creates trust in the narratorial stance.

Chapter 5 is a highly ambiguous chapter in which the fairy story elements become so accepted that one is right inside the convention. The narrative reports, observes and states with little intervention, and even the implicit comments of the involving techniques are excised. Here a pattern of narratorial stance is developing, in which as the narrator aligns himself with a group he adopts their linguistic expression. The more the narrator aligns himself with the animals, the less he says because they are linguistically limited. The result is an expression of the ambiguity and confusion that they feel.

It is in this chapter that we are told that the animals would have argued 'if they could have found the right arguments' (p. 40) and for the reader the stance here requires even more involvement with the animals, assessing from their actions and partial verbalizations if we are to understand anything at all. For example, it is important that the narrator refrains from commenting on the kind of logic that the animals use to work out the apparent treachery of Snowball. Boxer restricts himself to the maxim that 'Napoleon is always right' and Clover turns to the written evidence of he Commandments. If the narrator were to spell out the processes and their implications, the limitations would appear too obvious. As it is, the reader has to make the evaluations himself and realizes that it is not easy. Indeed on a first reading the importance of doing so may not even be apparent. But the narrator's alignment is carefully balanced. Only toward the end of the chapter do the pigs increasingly show in a bad light.

What is interesting about chapter 6 is the inclusion of more reported rather than direct speech from the pigs. It becomes even less easy for the reader to identify with them and to understand the significance of their words. When Squealer's explanations are reported they appear more plausible because they are at one remove, gaining a false objectivity, and they come from the narrator whom we trust. It is exactly the effect achieved by Napoleon's orders going through Squealer, or when Boxer and Clover explain the pigs' decisions to the other animals. Again the intercommentary on the rhetoric of politics demonstrates the problems involved in the narration itself and how we should not take it for granted. During the description of the second Battle, activity is restrained by the exaggerated ironic tone of the narrator. The animals are 'shocked beyond measure', and quite coincidentally the treacherous Snowball's footprints are found 'Almost immediately'. The artificiality of the response underlines the growing need to fit into the acceptable forms of expression wanted by the pigs. Not only are the other animals more personally restrained, but when they do speak they adopt conventional, easily identified modes for expression. As a whole the chapter separates more clearly between the pigs and the other animals, but also introduces more complexity, ambiguity and confusion so that it is difficult for the reader to know what to do about the separation.

The increasing identification of the narrator with the cause of the animals against the pigs carries on into chapter 7. Initially he narrates for them, and the reader, because of this, is led to identify with them. At the same time there is a growing inability on the reader's part to note the discrepancies between human and animal figures. While this used to be a source of humour and detachment, it becomes a worrying ignorance. No matter which reading is involved, a first or a subsequent, the reader will never be able to fully assess the situation. The process of confusion is stopped by the incident of the chickens during which the narratorial voice changes and quickens pace. This event may be read quite straightforwardly, and the reader can distinguish that the chickens are being killed, not dying naturally. It is reasonable to assume since the narrator is narrating for the animals, that the animals can also make the distinction. The suspicious reserve of 'It was given out . . .' backs this up. But such distinction is double-edged because one is then left wondering what to do about it, and the animals do nothing. Our identification with them is put under considerable stress, for we observe a self-deception on their part that we know they are aware of.

Meanwhile the whole fairy story genre is called radically into question: rewards are not being meted out as they should be, something is going wrong with our expectations. Indeed so much so that when the animal 'confessions' and swift retributions come, it is necessary to re-read to see if one has missed some salient point. The event fits no convention whatever. At this point the narrator moves from the discursive and patient to the immediate with short quick phrases following rapidly on one another, a quickly moving rhythm that repeats itself and resonates. To begin with we hear of a formal 'arrangement' and the confessions spill out 'without further prompting' as if organized. The confessions are mechanical, expected, using an 'and/and/and' construction. But then there is the sudden shock of 'the dogs promptly tore their throats out', the internal resonance of 'prompt' linking the two actions in a horrific manner. The next animals 'were slaughtered'; the following deaths become even less specific being 'all slain upon the spot', and finally just 'a pile of corpses'. The control of pace and formal repetition turns the efficient narration into an almost ritual account.

The chapter concludes with the transition into a 'pastoral' scene from the unreal and completely upset convention of fairy story. The transition into these rather different generic elements can be read at least three ways. In the first it can be seen as a true pastoral of reassessment in which case it could legitimately conclude a fairy story. On the other hand it can be interpreted ironically as an escape into nostalgia by self-deceiving animals in which case the reader assumes a different position but with the same knowledge; or it can be read allegorically as a failed pastoral which succeeds in analysing its failure because our knowledge is not simply greater but different in kind from that of the animals. The scene has all the elements of pastoral. It portrays a removal from society which leads to looking back at it from a detached point of view so that one can see its faults. The pastoral motifs of a country scene with the 'gilded' quality common to the genre, and the 'desirable' nature of what is being viewed, all place it firmly in a pastoral tradition. In common with classic pastoral Clover realizes that something is wrong; the situation is 'not what they had looked forward to'; and she decides to go back and correct rather than change it. 'There was no thought of rebellion or disobedience in her mind' (p. 60), times are still better than life under Jones.

It is the quality of acceptance that makes the scene potentially nostalgic. Clover's decision may be read not pastorally but ironically as self-deception, an escape into a dignified role which has been encouraged by the pigs to provide simple answers in terms of absolutes. Just as with the evasive 'act' that the animals do to cope with Snowball's treachery or the implications of the chickens' deaths, they turn to the melodramatic concepts of absolute good and evil offered by the pigs. Something, such as Snowball, is simply designated 'bad'. There is no actuality beyond the word; it just is so. The pigs use a rational logic perverted to 'prove' their case, in which personal reasoning and assessment is denied, and an ironic reading of this scene accepts that the animals go along with it.

The two stages of simple pastoral and ironic perspective are those which the reader has been taken through already in terms of this chapter itself and the narrative as a whole. To accept the pastoral reading we are asked simply to identify with the animal point of view. But this may be read as a delusion, in which case we detach ourselves, recognize the self-deception by the animals, step back from identification and criticize. Yet either way we neglect narratorial stance. The stance throughout Clover's scene is different. It neither identifies with the animals nor criticizes them but sets up a new convention to express what is actually in Clover's mind. The convention treats her as if she were human. The reader is explicitly led, held by the hand and shown, that it is neither ignorance nor self-deception at work, but an inability to speak and to argue out. We identify but differently. It is not a matter, as it has been, of being for or against; the perception of failure on the animals' part is here presented as a matter of lack not of omission. As Clover is accorded full human status, in other words, the ability to express herself through the temporary device of narratorial voice, so also is her inhumanity demonstrated.

The inhumanity lies in significant contrast to the inhumanity of the pigs, and sets up a discrepancy essential to a positive reading of *Animal Farm*. On the one hand Clover is inhuman because she lacks certain human qualities of speaking and verbal reasoning; she cannot express the values she believes in. On the other hand the pigs are inhuman not because they lack these qualities but because they lack the standards that would use them responsibly. The reader can separate himself from Clover not ironically but allegorically, recognizing that there is a piece missing and that in that piece lies the ability and responsibility to understand, protest and fight back. The animal is not unwilling but is incapable of doing so. A corollary to this analogy is that the identification of the pigs with humans is restricted to humans who lack values yet can express them. The parallel is aided by the fact that the humans in the story are consistently 'types', overt fictional devices not pretending to any 'realism'. With this background the reader is left not negatively identifying the fate of both animals and pigs with directly comparable human fates, but recognizing that each fails because they are different from humans; they lack qualities that humans can have, and humans should be able to overcome the failure.

In terms of genre conventions used in this chapter, the reader now also realizes why they backfire. The fairy story reward system for good and bad cannot operate validly in a world where values are either arbitrary or cannot be expressed. Personal responsibility in linguistic interaction of argument and discussion is not a valid criterion for animals – the fairy story inevitably crumbles into melodrama and nightmare. The pastoral, biblical 'dignity' sought after by the animals backfires into nostalgia and melodrama because they cannot fit into the good/bad system in any other way than the falsely conventional. They cannot, not will not, personally effect the necessary changes; they are nostalgic not because they abdicate the responsibility but because they cannot express it and therefore cannot take it on. They turn to melodrama with its well-defined good and bad conventions of expression because it is the closest they can get to the expression of any value at all.

On the simplest level, if the scene is read as a true pastoral, then one must be blind to the manipulation of the pigs. It implies a blindness to expression similar to that of the animals themselves, and it is extremely doubtful whether anyone would read it in this manner. If it is read as nostalgia, the reader is continuing to read as if it were a fairy story in which the self-deception of the animals leads to punishment. This reading would have to dismiss the intercommentary with the satire and all the elements of language and expression. A work cannot function as an allegory without reader participation. We have to be aware of the discrepancies ourselves before we can respond to them because the writer cannot present difference for us without defining it.

Here the vital connection with the satire is most necessary. The satire explicitly concerns rhetoric and its abuse. The reader cannot be blind to its workings unless he is reading it simply as a reproduction of the Russian Revolution. The satirical discussion of politics and language has by this point indicated that the pigs are abusing both powers, hence the pastoral reading is out. The discussion has also continually emphasized the problems of the animals with expression, so the ironic reading of simple self-deception is difficult to sustain. One is left with working out what should be going on. The barest recognition is that human beings are different from animals, have different abilities and responsibilities. What that recognition generates in interaction with the satire is unique to each reader, and provides the allegorical basis for a positive reading.

As well as being a crisis for the animals, the narrative situation is also a crisis for the reader. From this moment on he will either proceed to read the book negatively, unaware of the breakdown in conventions which present the positive allegorical elements; or he will always be aware of the further dimension involved. Concurrently, the narratorial stance will appear either cynical or constructive. The eighth chapter focuses once more on explicit fairy story techniques that may now seem incongruous. Here, repetitive structures are contained within the framework of the two rewritten commandments at start and finish, which provide the basis for a series of analogies. The politics, a new song, entrance of humans, the windmill and more chicken confessions, are all elements from previous chapters that we are seeing anew, through the gained perspective. The process of repetition within a circular action can be read as a negative cynical comment on the dead-end inevitability of political and linguistic corruption. On the other hand it can be read as a result of the lack of the animals' ability to rectify the situation, and further it raises the question of what human beings should do with their wider abilities.

The reintroduction of the fairy story elements now goes hand in hand not with the comedy of animals in their contrast to humans, but the black humour of the ridiculous things that they copy from them. This shift along with the continued ambiguity and confusion of the animals' response to the pigs, belies the conventional structure and self-deception that would underlie cynical reading. The clearest example is Napoleon's friendship with the farmers, and whether he allows the second destruction of the windmill to cover his mistake. The reader cannot know whether he does or not, and neither can the animals. The animals maintain their separation from the pigs through contrasting narratorial vocabulary. Napoleon is surrounded by formal and legal phrases while language around the animals is either uninvolved and passive or melodramatic.

The final drunkenness of the pigs combines both elements in the fairy story phrasing of 'Not a pig appeared to be stirring' along with the melodramatic 'cry of lamentation', 'with tears in their eyes' over Napoleon's hangover. The fairy story convention is only functional within a value system, and, since the pigs do not have one, they introduce arbitrary absolutes and superficial melodramatic response. The whole society is a mixture of artificial reactions within melodramatic conventions, and repressed personal expression. Again, for the animals, it is not just repression but inability. The reader is left entirely on his own by the narrator who returns to his techniques of juxtaposition and understatement. Yet now the lack of certain attributes leaves the humour against the animals rather sinister, as if someone were taking advantage of them unfairly. The reader reacts independently of the animals in this chapter; they do not understand, but we do. The discrepancies are cuttingly obvious. While it may be difficult to work out what their responsibilities are, it is not difficult to recognize that it is the human reaction that is more important and that it depends on us.

To start the ninth chapter the narrator removes himself again, gradually intruding more and more to present the melodrama of Boxer's death. Initially there are many analogies set up for the reader to actively discern. All the animals gain denser characters as if to emphasize that the melodrama is artificial, and also as if individual identity has become more important now that mass action has proved impossible. Benjamin's behaviour in particular becomes more effective and raises questions about why the events have happened. Since he is the character closest to the human reader in ability to express yet refusal to exercise expression, his activity may be some kind of hint.

The analogies gradually become more explicit. The reader, meanwhile, is alerted to changes by the great increase of analogy which asks us to assess for ourselves. The stance is moving away from speaking for the animals toward a human voice that intrudes with sarcasm and wit against the pigs. The apparent resumption of the voice when he mentions the 'dignity' of the animals alerts us immediately, and he follows it up with a clarification showing that they have no real choices. The deliberate pathos of their dreaming about warm mash is a restatement in curt physical terms of their own ambiguous and confused dreaming about retirement. Their 'spontaneous' demonstrations are organized and formal. The gradual intrusion of the narrator is not resented because he is speaking from the reader's human point of view on previously established events. Hence he uses a common knowledge that we are free to disagree with.

The chapter is then broken by the creation of the Republic and the return of Moses, both of which emphasize the animals' passivity, before it moves on to Boxer's accident. But any potential tragedy is undercut by reducing this event of greatest tension to the ridiculous. When the animals finally realize that Boxer is being taken to the knacker's yard they give a 'cry of horror'; they move 'In desperation' but 'Too late . . .' Clover tries 'to stir her stout limbs to a gallop and achieved a canter'. The pathos and melodrama is not shocking because the reader has been exposed to it previously. Here though the conventions are used as if they are habitual second-nature to the animals, not because they must conform. Accepting conventions makes response easier. If at first one is forced into them, it gradually becomes more and more difficult to resist their seductive patterns; and eventually like the animals, one forgets that they are conventions at all.

Clover's pastoral over-view of the Major's initial utopian urge, is the last important recognition of the structure in which the animals now live. Active participation has been taken out of their hands. The narrator himself is outside the melodrama, detached and observing, no longer identifying with the animals. Neither does the reader identify. Writer and audience recognize the powerlessness, and the point made by intercommentary with the satire is that it arises from the animals' inability to express. The further point is that our recognition of their ineffectiveness makes us responsible for action.

The movement from fairy story to melodrama is carried out through their common dependence on authority. That the fairy story usually claims a magical or external source of authority whereas the authority of melodrama is man-made and man-imposed, is an interesting parallel that stimulates criticism of the latter toward a questioning of the former. But more obviously here the man-copied authority of the pigs is oppressive, negative, destructive and self-corrupting because it retains the elements of determinism and inevitability that the fairy story places beyond man's power. It is totalitarian. Melodrama is the genre of response within unquestioned man-made convention. It may be habitual as in the animals' reaction to Boxer's accident, or it may be actively destructive as in the responses demanded by the pigs. In both it is confined, not able to reason and assess, donning what is available. Anyone capable of a more active expression finds it unsatisfactory. The flickering in and out of fairy story and melodrama is a means of bringing to the reader's attention the inadequacy of all unquestioned convention including the one the narrator is using.

The final chapter begins once more in a narratorial detachment calling for the reader's involvement. The fairy story elements are present but now inextricably mixed up with the melodramatic response of the animals. Narratorial stance is not of a tale-teller within a society re-telling a story that backs up the cultural norms, but of a distanced narrator using fairy story conventions to comment on corrupt authoritarianism. The melodramatic elements that surface in the description of Clover during the final scene remind the reader of the inadequacy of the convention; but for Clover the ludicrous is unperceived. For the animals the fairy story becomes nightmare because the source of authority, the unassailable utopian vision, dissolves and is transferred to the pigs' new superiority. For the reader there is an additional question in the transformation of pig into human. Since they can do so because all their actions are implicitly human, humans are at the same time made pigs. The ambiguity of the situation is an essential strategic device that undercuts a negative reading. As noted earlier and as the text continually points out, these humans are not complete. They are limited 'types' who are as lacking in humanity as the pigs and the other animals. It is their lack that creates the ambiguity of their status.

Determinist and inevitable qualities of fairy story are brought back in full force during the opening paragraphs of the chapter. Recurrent motifs, lists and repetitions underline the pattern. The switch from a humour generated from animal and human contrasts, to the more barbed comedy of their similarities is continued in Squealer's lists of responsibilities to 'files', 'reports' and 'minutes'. Extensive use of and/and constructions in, for example, 'neither pigs nor dogs produced any food by their own labour; and there were very many of them, and their appetites were always good', sets up the lack of actual connection between events in favour of the implied. The forced conjunction is emphasized by the liberal use of semi-colons. Three years previously in *Coming Up for Air* Orwell had tried to do away with the semi-colon. They, and colons, make it possible to omit the defining connections between separate parts of a sentence. Here he uses the device to point out that omission.

In relation to the bureaucratic jargon of the pigs, the animals' vocabulary continues to be vague and confused. Among themselves they retain the stirring phrases of the opening fairy story atmosphere. They are proud of owning the farm; they have a utopian belief that 'some day it was coming'; they use biblical phrases and allusions to stress that 'they were not as other animals'. The formal construction and use of recognized rhetorical devices such as balanced 'If/If/Then' statements that repeat and lead to their central belief that 'All animals are equal', indicate their dependence on classical convention. Many elements are directly from the Major's speech and their use here indicates what can go wrong with utopian visions, what was negative in his opening speech. His insistence on a unity achieved through acceptance denied the possibility of the animals learning how to reassess the situation. The promised utopia was another absolute that cut out concepts of bettering their lives. Because the animals did not actively participate in the direction their group was taking, because finally, they were not involved in the reasoning of the speech as well as its emotiveness, they are left with its phrases which can be repeated but which get them nowhere.

If we recall Orwell's discussion of politics and literature in the essays these are all the elements of truncated pastoral or fantasy; acceptance, self-satisfaction, refusal to question. But for the animals it is melodramatic because they know something is wrong, and gradually take on conventional responses because they cannot express themselves otherwise. The fairy story conventions that the animals hang on to are then completely undercut by the pigs walking on their hind legs, and the change in the last commandment to 'All Animals Are Equal / But Some Animals Are More Equal Than Others' (p. 87). The reader no longer experiences this as a reversal of expectation, but as a reinforcement of his different knowledge. Detached response is encouraged by the direct, knowing address 'Yes, it was Squealer' from the narrator about the pig on his hind legs.

Despite the undercutting that we perceive, the animals continue as before once their brief protest is thwarted by the sheep. When the humans come to visit, the animals are as afraid of them as they are of the pigs and stick closely to their usual jobs. They cannot understand the implications of the final scene between the farmers and the pigs, which centres on their linguistic similarity, but the reader can. Here he is faced with the idea that the pigs are actually human and vice versa. There is no longer contrast or similarity between the two, but identity. The linking concept of politics and language provided by the intercommentary with the satire, is that within these conventional authority-assuming speeches the other animals are recognized as 'lower animals'. Since the reader has spent much of his response identifying with these animals the definition is sinister rather than humorous. But one can evade the reflexive comment on the lower classes that is also contained in the concept. The narrator's third person reporting of the speeches indicates the detachment of the scene. And it all takes place in the comfort of a room, behind the glass of a safe compartment; it could be one of Orwell's train carriages.

By transmitting the scene through the 'old dim eyes' of Clover, the stance is trusted because of our response to her and because any perceived discrepancies are theoretically out of the narrator's hands. We also recognize her inability to understand which underlines our responsibilities. The resonance back to the phrase 'it did not seem strange' for anything to happen after the pigs had started walking on their hind legs, alerts the reader. Here something is again 'strange'. We question what this final change could possibly be, and although something 'seemed to be melting and changing' (p. 91), neither we nor the animals can identify it. Following this brief reminder of the animals' helplessness, the narrator reasserts himself and we discover that the pigs have become human. The final comment that it was 'impossible to say which was which' notes the ambiguity and confusion that the animals feel, at the same time as separating the reader from that confusion for he is aware of the implications. It is the separation that occurs through recognition of the differences that allegory conveys, and passes one back to the satire on politics and language with the hope that those differences will be taken up and learned from.

CHAPTER SEVEN

Nineteen Eighty-Four:
Interactive Stance

The problems in Orwell's earlier novels have concerned narratorial voice. They have been questions of validity and how validity affects choice of genre and the modalities of that genre once it has been chosen. The essential difference that makes the allegory of *Nineteen Eighty-Four* possible, depends primarily upon a device of combining utopia or dystopia with the novel – as Orwell put it, 'A Utopia in the form of a novel' (*CEJL* IV 460). It uses the 'fantastic' but not the negative strategy of adventure story or thriller (*CEJL* IV 468) that is closely related to the allegorical stance in Orwell's literary criticism, as well as the naturalistic (*CEJL* IV 330).

The narrator as a recognizable persona in the overt manner of all Orwell's previous writings, has virtually disappeared: there are few direct comments being made. But stance is not defined even primarily by direct comment, and what *Nineteen Eighty-Four* presents is a writer who finally recognizes and is confident of this. In this work stance is defined by the combination of the utopian and the naturalistic novel. In other words, it is realized in the genre chosen, and through the modifications made to that genre mainly by irony and allegory. We do not need to know what values the narrator stands for, but how he goes about searching for and presenting them. The reader's guidance to the stance of the voice relies almost entirely upon the generic intercommentary, of the topics within the text and their intercommentary with the textual structures, and specifically in the presentation of repeated motifs.

A key lies in the presentation of the central character. The reader's identification with and separation from the character is an index to what he is learning, and is controlled by the stance of the narrator. The mixed genre of novel and utopia provides these points of identification and separation for the reader through awareness of the strategies of irony and allegory that underpin it. The strength of the book derives from the narrator's ability to bring the natural and the utopian very close together through irony, at the same time as making it possible through allegory for the reader to separate them. It is an active demonstration of the power of doublethink which fuses the two into the most complete strategy for acceptance, along with the only remedy: discussion and interaction.

Nineteen Eighty-Four is an allegory about the negative stance of fantasy: but is the device valid? It appears that there is considerable initial disagreement on this point. *Nineteen Eighty-Four* is viewed through conflicting assessments as brilliant, or negatively pessimistic. Negative readings of it see only the enclosed world it puts forward without recognizing that identification with this world is only the first stage; the reader's separation, discussion and assessment must follow. While the world of *Nineteen Eighty-Four* is obviously fantastic to us, it is not so to the central character – hence the two aspects of utopia and novel. But the narrator presents the utopia in a probable context; he leads the reader to believe in the character's delusion, and thereby denies that the fantasy is obvious and safe. He brings the two very close together. In genre terms he indicates that they can be intermixed, that the authoritarian techniques of fantasy can mix with the 'naturalism' of the novel. The possibility of such a mixture then extends to the topic of politics and language, suggesting that such total tyranny may also occur in actual life and would be created, effected and maintained through a control of the linguistic medium.

The Active Reader: Establishing the Grounds

Throughout the first seven chapters the narrator is concerned to create a relationship with the reader that will establish the grounds for identification with and separation from the character. As in the earlier novels, the writer uses everyday topics such as sex, language and memory, as a focus for the reader's activity. But in *Nineteen Eighty-Four* the reader is directed toward interaction not by direct comment from the narrator but by the rhetorical stance which is experienced through the narrator's use of genre. The identification between character and reader that the topics generate, leads directly to an appreciation of the irony in the writing; while the separation of the two indicates areas of radical difference and lack that allows for allegory, and it is in a series of resonant images, figures and dreams, that the allegorical surfaces. The novel is devised on movements centred around the images, that are repeated each time from a different point of view. Both the central character and the reader must follow and assess their development without being told what is lacking from them or how they are interacting, and difference in response locates the allegorical reading of the text.

Part One of the novel presents a gradual withdrawal of the guiding narratorial voice to the recognized strategies of conventional genre, and the reader can only slowly separate or identify between the narrator, Winston and himself. In the end the very difficulty of defining the reader's sightline is parallel to Winston Smith's difficulty in defining his. The narrator is faced from the beginning with the problem of providing sufficient material for identification, but also clarifying the separation. Throughout the first chapter the narrator concentrates on the detail, the physical background and the explanation of Winston's world, at the same time interspersing this with shocking images within his mind. It is a process of familiarization and defamiliarization. There is for example Winston Smith's London, with familiar echoes of the post-war city, yet there is also the realization that for Winston, that is all it is: the city has no past and no future. He sees London in an entirely foreign way. Just so, the resonant images of the 'ninth three year plan', or eleven o'clock in the morning for remembering, or the images of the Jews all familiarize through the irony of their recognizable situation. At the same time, however, they are all slightly skewed and disorientating. 'Eleven o'clock' is the hour for the 'Two Minutes Hate', when the citizens remember their enemies rather than their dead (p. 15). The Jews are shown both as the enemy itself (p. 15), and as the almost necessary victims of war (p. 12).

The narrator comes out of this as an observant, clear, apparently factual reporter, someone whom the reader can trust. He is set up as non-interfering, a narrator who establishes the figures, the images and events, which require involvement from the reader. For example, comparisons are provided which we must complete, but although we are involved, it is difficult to conclude upon an interpretation of what we complete. As a result, the situational irony takes on a double focus. It not only points to Winston's lack of perspective and our superior knowledge, but there is a gradual breaking down of that superiority by reorientating the reader's ideas of his own actuality, and undermining his bases for assessment. Gradually, the process ends by familiarizing the reader with shock itself, and in this way makes Winston's perceptions more acceptable.

The process of becoming familiar with shock becomes more significant as we get to know Winston, particularly through his writing. Here there is an alien mind, raw shocking edges, confusion and disorientation, all very different from the simple ironic discrepancies in, for example, the eleven o'clock 'Hate'. There is his account of a film showing the bombing of a ship and the surreal image of 'a child's arm going up, up, up, right up into the air' (p. 12). The shock of this crude, macabre image and Winston's apparent endorsement of the, applause that the cinema audience gives it. This is followed by his scrawl of 'automatic' writing, and the hysterical but very

No morals/values with which to judge himself.

No way to judge himself

personal account of his fear of being shot. His three writings indicate aspects of Winston which are not available in other ways to the reader. In the first example, we see his conventionality, and in the other two, his attempts to consciously or unconsciously get past the slogans of his world. And there is the curious fact that he does not write down the one thing that he sets out to describe.

Other indexes to his character and context are found in certain key topics. There is his distorted historical perspective, his confused memory, the blatant sadism of his attitude to women and to Julia in particular, and the religious passivity of his reaction to the Party. Yet Winston is a sympathetic character despite his apparent cruelty and unkindness, when he is set against the background of his society. He is a character struggling for self-expression in a world dominated by the Party which aims to control expression. It is this aspect that is extended in the second chapter. The Party evidences most of the aspects of Orwell's views on negative rhetoric. Again there is the double focus of hating Big Brother because of his control, but knowing that he protects and therefore provides the enchantment of safety. The double focus is underlined by the ambivalence of O'Brien's relationship with Winston. Neither Winston nor the reader can know which side O'Brien is on. Winston himself vacillates and the reader cannot know whether his diary writing is self-expression or controlled by the Party. On the one hand Winston believes that 'uttering' through his private writing will provide him with identity, but in effect it is like being on the sea-bottom, 'lost in a monstrous world where he himself was the monster', isolated. This is set against his comment that 'it was not by making yourself heard, but by staying sane that you carry on the human heritage' (p. 30). Yet without discussion how can he know he is sane? This again was Flory's problem. It is the double-sidedness of writing as communication and self-expression, the double-sidedness of isolation as both madness and sanity.

We recognize the irony of this through our own identification with and separation from Winston as a character. Our sympathy derives from our own disorientation which is parallel to Winston's, and results from the narratorial technique that involves us at the same time as it cuts away our bases for assessment. What becomes apparent from the identification and the initial irony is our radical difference from Winston because of his historical and physical context. Winston's problem with self-definition cannot be solved by our own standards because Winston does not have access to those standards. We are left with the intangibility of something not known, and by corollary we are left with a separate response from the ironic which is to do with the differences, rather than with the similarities between the two worlds, his and ours, not just with ignorance or loss, but with lack. In this way Winston's cruelty and unkindness are seen as part of his distorted view. They are not inherent. Basic to *Nineteen Eighty-Four* is the possibility of learning, that values are assessed actively, not simply

Cruel by our own standards / prevailing attitudes

'natural'. Having recognized this, the reader then has to assess what it is that Winston is lacking. But further than this, the very possibility of learning, of value as an activity reflects back on the reader to underline his own areas of 'lack'. The exercise of *Nineteen Eighty-Four* is to have us assess from the difference what it is we are.

Through the third chapter the narrator moves us on to a study of the ways in which we usually define ourselves, such as dreams and the subconscious, memory, suffering, and the experience of tragedy. These means of definition each raise problems when faced with Winston's predicament, that caution us to be wary of the ease with which we accept them ordinarily. The study goes hand in hand with an abrupt change in narratorial focus, into a presentation through images and figurations of Winston's mind, here not conscious but dreaming.

The first dream, about his mother and sister in a sinking boat, is interrupted and followed by his inability to remember how the situation ended. He just has knowledge of the event of a sacrifice by his mother and his sister, and this in itself is dangerous, because assessment is removed making acceptance of necessary sacrifice inevitable and impossible to learn from. Yet as he emerges from the dream to sort out its implications, Winston's reaction is that his mother's sacrifice was 'tragic and sorrowful in a way that was no longer possible'. His mother had a concept of loyalty 'private and unalterable'. He comes to an appreciation of the importance for individual humanity, through a response to these images. They 'tore at his heart'. He 'perceived' them and was 'suddenly struck' by them. The primary images are of darkness, glass, mirror, water; conflated they become of things that not only hide and reflect, but also transform. Winston's dreaming mind becomes the demonstration of a process of discovering value or standards through the perception of figuration, a figuration that frightens and tears at his heart, but also illuminates. Next comes the dream of the 'golden country', which is still vague, but closer to reality as if his consciousness now imposes and intrudes further. The 'golden country' introduces Julia, stripping off her clothes as a perfect gesture that 'seems to annihilate a whole culture' (p. 33), the culture of the Party. Winston's attitude to her here is aggressive. Yet the connection of her gesture with Shakespeare and an older world is double-sided for it was that world that created the Party in the first place. This is a realization accessible to the reader, but Winston himself does not push forward toward it.

At this point the dream is interrupted, and Winston is woken up by the telescreen. As he exercises he mulls over the function of memory, and its dependence on deductions from evidence and conjecture from image. Here he presents the image from his memory of going into the tube, the underground, as a child. But the main point is the enigmatic statement from an old man also sheltering in the tube: 'We didn't ought to 'ave trusted the buggers' (p. 36), and the need for interpretation. It is impossible for

Winston to interpret the image, because memory has a totally different role in his world, and this is clarified by the opposition of 'actual' memory to 'official' memory that is set up as he goes along. We are told that Government memory functions by treating the past as alterable and yet not altered at the same time. History is always absolute. It can always be changed to fit in with present Government policy. In fact it has to be able to be changed in order to remain absolute. Now we have seen this discussed in Orwell's essays, but always with the proviso that it is impossible. Here, through society's acceptance of 'the lie', Government memory passed 'into history and became truth' (p. 37). Being able to accept the alterability of the absolute is the key to 'doublethink', the theory behind the Party's control of identity. The final outcome is the ultimate subtlety:

> consciously to induce unconsciousness, and then, once again, to become unconscious of the act of hypnosis you had just performed. Even to understand the word 'doublethink' involves the use of doublethink. (p. 38)

In this manner short-term political fantasy discussed in the essays can be maintained and controlled and the question of how the individual defines himself within the state becomes more complex. The only alternative here appears to be the establishing of a private, individual fantasy to counteract the official. This, for the reader, is the first hint that O'Brien's Brotherhood, that elusive and potentially saving organization of individuals, may be just as isolating as the Party.

Against this background, the values Winston struggles to perceive in memory and in his dreams are themselves questionable. The two images comment upon each other. The first dream is a brave perception of the value of individual suffering that makes Winston himself suffer in the perception of it. The second image is less deeply perceived, an individual gesture allied with the past and against the State. It is destructive rather than constructive. The first dream indicates the shallowness in the perception of the second, and the latter coming from an older world responsible for generating Big Brother, points back also to the limitations of private tragedy. What is being indicated here is that tragedy and suffering are not sufficient to the definition of human identity. Within a rational humanist world, they perhaps go some way, but that world has also always made the tyranny of oligarchy possible. They do not relate outward enough to include society as a whole; they remain too close to the possibility of an enclosed, private fantasy.

For the reader, the ironic direction here is the recognition that Winston previously lacked the humanist values of tragedy and suffering. Yet the differences between our world and his, that make the irony possible, also undermine our confidence in it and in our superior knowledge. In the allegorical direction, through the intercommentary of images, the reader recognizes that there is something more, the possibility that the gaining of values which we possess already may still be inadequate to the situation. The possibility that both we and Winston lack the something necessary to deal with the State as it exists.

At this stage in the narrative, with so much emphasis being placed on the difference of Winston's world, what becomes important is the detail of the functioning of the State within which Winston lives, so that we can assess the viability of its control of memory, history and thought. In chapter 4 the narrator begins by examining the role of words, specifically literary words, in providing identity. He starts with the process of Winston's job in propaganda at the Ministry, and involves the reader directly by flattering our ability to understand what Winston is doing. There is the casual reference to his 'rectifying' not 'altering' information and a matter of fact tone which downplays the implications of Winston's actions. And there is a sense of inevitability about a phrase like 'it was therefore necessary to rewrite' (p. 41). The reader is lulled into an acceptance, and is possibly not even alerted by Winston's destruction of previous evidence 'with a movement as nearly as possible unconscious' (p. 42). Everything is presented in exactly the same low key tone so that it only gradually dawns on us that Winston's job is to do the very thing he fears the most, to make history a 'palimpsest', to aid the Party in control of information, instruction and entertainment.

The entire process points to the ironic and satiric aspects of Winston's life within the Party. This is made more pertinent by the ease with which we initially participate in Winston's job ourselves, and only gradually recognize the implications. But there is a great deal left open. We can never be entirely sure if Winston is simply doublethinking in order to cope: if he were it would not mitigate his actions, but it would alter our perspective by presenting the dangers. Secondly, the satire against Party control of information is double-sided. It does illustrate the negative effects, but it also indicates their success. The presentation of this in the text is without judgement or comment. The reader must assess for himself. We cannot just dismiss Winston as weak, because we come to understand the charm of what he does. We follow the detailed logic of his mind in his conjectures on how to change references to the disgraced 'Withers'. To falsify/rectify adequately, the speech has to be rationally consistent, and Winston assesses and rejects the possibilities open to him, before concluding that the only satisfactory end is 'a piece of fantasy' (p. 48).

He rewrites from 'a ready made' idea; Comrade Ogilvy could be brought 'into existence' with a few lines of print and a few faked photographs. This indicates first of all the fantasist's role of creating something out of nothing, and second, the basic rule of working outwards from an acceptable and habitual situation to the fantastic so that the reader's apprehension of the difference between his actuality and the fantasy world is not disturbed. Ogilvy's life is simply stated, with odd details to provide the look of truth; finally 'Comrade Ogilvy, unimagined an hour ago, was now a fact' (p. 50). The reader watches the process of fantasy creation, carefully integrated with a background of threat to Winston. And we are quietly reminded by the interchange of the words 'fact' and 'forgery', that we cannot assess upon our own standards because Winston's are so different. We are made aware of the danger of the process in this different political state, and yet we also know how close our own is to his, and this awareness reflects back on to us and our own world.

The entire process makes State control of identity through writing appear quite possible. The narrator now moves on in chapter 5 to present the complex technicalities of the structure and effects of negative rhetoric in language and literature. The didactic structure of Winston's discussion in the cafeteria of the Ministry with the Newspeak linguist Syme, is relieved by running tension and humour that involves the reader in comparing the two men and their attitude toward language. Syme speaks obsessively of the 'definitive' eleventh edition of Newspeak that will reduce the language to an absolute minimum. Verbs and adjectives and qualification will be excised. The concept of opposites as differences rather than inversions, will go. Ultimately the reductionism will make unorthodoxy impossible because 'there will be no words in which to express it' (p. 54). The ideas in Orwell's essays are here taken to an extreme and within a context that makes their occurrence plausible and their danger actual. No thought will exist, for 'orthodoxy means not thinking – not needing to think. Orthodoxy is unconsciousness' (p. 55). Winston's reaction is to point out a neighbouring table in the canteen, where a man is speaking entirely in Newspeak and making a noise 'uttered in unconsciousness' (p. 56). Syme recognizes the nonsense, jokingly calling it 'duckspeak' but failing to perceive the irony of his recognition. The irony here is one that Winston himself recognizes; Syme is far too conscious to be considered orthodox. But he fails in turn to apply that recognition to his own consciousness of 'altering the facts', even though the reader should be aware of it.

Yet the situation is not only ironic but also allegorical. It asks the reader to find out what is different about Winston's situation. In the same way, as Winston continues to think about Syme's situation, he allies himself, Syme and O'Brien in their probable fate as dissidents to be eliminated and excludes Julia from this 'instinctive' reaction. The reader should be aware of this as a possible blindness, but is not. There is a dramatic irony here against the reader as well, because Winston is wrong about Julia and wrong about O'Brien, yet we initially trust his 'instinct'. The ambiguity generates a method of actively assessing each and every moment we identify with Winston, but we have to keep that identification in perspective. If we identify and allow that to dominate our reading then we are shocked by the failure of Winston's judgement and the shock is educative and revealing, on an ironic level. If we identify and yet at the same time recognize *does W recognise that he is also ultimately doomed?*

Winston's failure to draw the parallel of unorthodoxy with himself, his later failure of judgement will reaffirm our assessment. The text does not present an enforced reading, but simply one with different outcomes, both of which underline our responsibilities as readers.

The examination of the Government control of our identity, our history, memory, language and literature, is finally extended to our sexuality. In *Nineteen Eighty-Four*, the topic of sexuality is an analogy which begins as a sado/masochistic, power/pain dichotomy that illuminates both the function of the Party and the effect it has on the minds of its adherents. The development of the sexual element from authoritarian romance-sex, then into a humanist interrelationship where it provides a different perspective, and finally into a profound awareness of the physical which belies the whole concept of 'reality control' by language, is one of the main figures by which the book may be read. The discussion of sex begins in chapter 6 within two remembered experiences that Winston writes about, with a prostitute and with his wife. At first the two are mixed up together in a Prole versus Party opposition that underlines corresponding oppositions between sex and repression, rebellion and submission. This opposition is elaborated on in the role of the Party, which is 'to remove all pleasure from the sexual act'. Because the Party cannot control sex, it degrades it. Winston recognizes this, but he does not understand why. To him 'it seemed natural that it should be so'. He has no other means of assessing, and allows the Party views to govern his attitude. His behaviour toward his wife is patronizing, he thinks of sex with her as breaking down a 'wall of virtue', she herself is 'submissive', making him authoritative. Sex for him is rebellion against the Party. At the start he says that what gives you away is 'your own nervous system' (p. 66), and that it is essential to control it in order to confound the Party. But as he controls his sexual urge by turning it into a vicious act of rebellion, he is simply reaffirming the Party standard. Winston has no other concept of what to do. His appalling experience with a prostitute, who turns out to be an old woman with nothing in her mouth 'except a cavernous blackness' (p. 70), indicates that something is out of phase with his attitude.

Significantly, by writing down this experience, Winston tries to 'black out the memory that was tormenting him' (p. 66). The reader should immediately be able to read the negative implications. He is trying to to evade, not face, a challenge. The writing is parallel to the sexual experience being referred to: it is an attempt at conscious repression, not expression. The Party controls so effectively because it reduces its adherents to a rebellion that is the same as its tyranny, an isolated non-communicating exercise of power.

The differences between the reader and Winston are all too clear. Winston views the Proles from a Party point of view. He views sex from a repressed attitude. His idea of rebellion is simply submission to the Party's ethic of power, and his attempt to express is really an attempt to control by imposition and eradicate. Starting from the sexual, which the reader can most easily relate to, the narrator illustrates the totally circular world in which Winston lives. The only things that can escape it are his bôdy, his ineradicable memories, an image of an empty black mouth and, could he but recognize it, the writing itself.

The Active Reader: The Search for Identity

Up until the seventh chapter, the narrator has been situating and placing Winston, presenting the reader with the similarities and differences that generate the identification and separation with his world and the background for the ironic and allegorical readings of the text. The narrator now proceeds in this seventh chapter, to illustrate Winston's own process of finding out about the situation. He starts by looking for a means to identity in the factual and the physical, and their effect on history and memory, but most of all in the existence of other people, other identities which by difference from oneself throw personal characteristics into relief. These 'proofs' are at the same time the safest arbiters of the actual and the most dangerous seductions to private fantasy and private control of actuality.

The first thing Winston is concerned about are the contrasts between the Party and the Proles, especially that Party members have no way of contacting each other while the proles can speak freely. The detailed life of the proles is strongly reminiscent of the poverty snare studied in *The Road to Wigan Pier*. The working class is encouraged to construct 'a whole world-within-a-world' (p. 73) so that it does not look outside and its concerns are divided and without direction. Winston proceeds to analyse the make-up of such State-induced fantasy first in terms of an extract from a child's history book (p. 74). It has all the hallmarks of negative literary fantasy. It uses meaningless adjectives, emotive references, inclusive repetitions of 'we' and 'all'. There is alliteration and cataloguing to stick disparate aspects together, and there are vague and unprovable statistics. More generally, it exerts a control over the visual, and is full of details and prevarications. As a propagandist he recognizes the patronizing tone, and is sensitive to its control, but 'How could you tell how much of it was lies?' (p. 75)

For the reader the extract is ironic because we know it to be untrue. But the important aspect is Winston's reaction, his recognition of a questionable rhetoric and his desperate question, 'it *might* be true' (p. 75). The only evidence to the contrary that exists for him is the intuitive 'mute protest in your own bones', his sense of a discrepancy between the Party ideal and the reality. Party propaganda 'was like a single equation with two unknowns. It might very well be that literally every word in the history books, even the things that are accepted without question, was pure fantasy' (p. 76).

Having stated his dilemma he goes back to the one piece of 'concrete, unmistakable evidence' that he had once held in his hand: a photograph proving three men as solid Party members who were subsequently discredited. Soon after their confession Winston recalled seeing them in the Chestnut Tree café, but even then the 'facts and dates were growing blurry'. The narrator now creates a feeling of absolute stasis. There are short, straight sentences with little variation in rhythm and sound; there is detailed observation and no movement. It is 'the lonely hour'. Actions occur 'uncommanded', and there is 'the yellow note' of the jeering telescreen. This unnerving choice of words and phrases is followed by the enigmatic stanza from the telescreen. To underline his helplessness at this point the reader should note not only the vigilance of the telescreen picking up his heartbeat, but also his conjectural 'perhaps' concerning the fate of the photograph. Even to have touched it is of great importance to Winston in the face of the Party's final command 'to reject the evidence of your eyes and ears' (p. 82), and believe that 'two and two made five'. Winston here turns to the existence of O'Brien as if calling upon him to back up his belief, and with the feeling that 'he was setting forth an important axiom, he wrote: Freedom is the freedom to say that two plus two make four. If that is granted all else follows' (p. 82).

Winston's description of the image of the three men and his following examination present an interesting pattern for his search for self-identity. Through the image the reader perceives Winston's active and assessing mind being stimulated and transformed by resonant figures in a discussion with himself. But on the other hand the examination which ends in his private aphoristic slogan on freedom, is a specific definition for himself set up as if to counteract the Party definition. It is something that he constructs and controls in the same way that he remakes O'Brien from an ambiguous figure into a certainty, someone on his side. In our position of ironic knowledge we can see Winston's total catchment into fantasy by his construction of a private world in answer to the Party's. Yet the allegory generated by a discussion of the images of the Chestnut Tree café in which the reader also becomes involved, asks for the recognition of a positive alternative. The radical, multi-faceted nature of the images reflects back onto the reader's own 'world-within-a-world', reminding us of the necessity for continued assessment.

The final chapter of Part One provides the transition into Winston's active search for self-identity, which makes up the following section. The reader watches Winston go out into the world of the proles, away from the Party control of actuality he is used to inhabiting, to look for the facts that he thinks he needs to rediscover his history. But his frightening limitation is demonstrated. Hemmed in by his own prejudices, he cannot communicate with the proles. He cannot ask questions which they can answer, or if they do, he cannot understand the significance of what they are saying. The narrator moves the reader in and out of familiar situations that he will recognize, but that Winston misunderstands or misinterprets. When the reader asks why the discrepancy exists, he can perceive that it is not only the ironic result of Winston's ignorance, but a more radical separation and difference. For example, a bomb attack that occurs on his way home, ends with the shocking image of a severed hand, which Winston casually kicks into the gutter. Throughout he is cool and rational, detailing the situation and noticing, without understanding, the minutiae. It is we, not Winston, who make the connection with the earlier resonant image of the severed arm seen in the film.

This dual vision occurs as the reader watches Winston making mistake after mistake, not just because of ignorance, but because of a radically different attitude to human beings. Yet at the same time, an index to the reader's identification with Winston is our hope for his success, and regret and frustration at his failure. It is partly because of this that when Winston goes back to the antique shop where he had bought his diary, the reader is willing to accept that he is finally getting somewhere (p. 95). We are invited into this attitude by the details of the comfortable interior of the bedroom above the shop, or the acceptable nature of the nursery rhyme that the owner, Charrington, recites and which is also so conventional that we do not question. We should be alerted by 'the nostalgia' of the room, the 'chopper' in the last line of 'Oranges and Lemons', and its chant-like recurrence in Winston's mind, noticeably similar to the techniques of negative propaganda on the telescreen. But we are not: at least not on first reading.

The episode closes when Winston sees Julia on the street. He is afraid and his first reaction is to kill her; again the reader notices the shocking difference. The tension of the scene circles around questions of life and death, 'the treachery of the human body': a reality experienced not through images or memory, but through the physical. Winston's decision not to kill Julia arises from his realization that in crisis the enemy is 'one's own body' (p. 103), and at the same time that the issues of crisis are 'always forgotten, because the body swells up until it fills the universe'.

The movement of Part One has been to lay out the complexity of assessment and evaluation. Both the reader and Winston have parallel problems. On a first reading, the reader has no way of knowing whether the tokens of the past are enough to provide an identity, or whether they are simply devices which seduce one into the construction of one's own private fantasy of self-definition. In retrospect we may pick up some clues, but at first these tokens seem to be especially significant because they are part of our world. The allegorical direction, however, is to indicate to us the limitations of that actuality.

Part One ends with an image of O'Brien back to back with Big Brother. They make up two sides of the same coin, underlining their ambivalence and throwing forward the questionable nature of Winston's judgement of O'Brien. The reader is allowed a perception of how this ambivalence comes about through an expansion of the religious image. O'Brien tells Winston that they will meet 'in the place where there is no darkness', and Winston interprets this as the future 'which one could never see, but which, by foreknowledge, one could mystically share in' (p. 104). But the image of darkness is firmly tied to the image of his mother and the sense of lack that must be filled if Winston is to find an identity. His interpretation of O'Brien's words implies some kind of instant solution: granted never to be realized, but somehow evading the fears and dangers of the darkness itself, and stressing a mystical future. The ambiguity of each topic treated in the novel – sex, history, and literature, politics, and finally religion, all of which could provide a means to identity – is underscored by the 'leaden knell' of the Party's slogans. This recalls the bells of the nursery rhyme and indicates their intercommentary, their mutual fantasy. It is the enmeshed ambiguity and ambivalence of the topics that controls the structure of the second Part of *Nineteen Eighty-Four*. And it is the issues of sex and the physical, areas in which Winston is most ignorant, that dominate. The sexual not only consistently keeps him in touch with dream and memory, but it also allows for a comparison with Julia: a relationship that in turn provides an analogy for comparison with the reader.

Part Two begins with a encounter between Winston and Julia, which is primarily experienced through a series of reversals set up by the curious contrast between Winston's immediate reaction and his detailed, careful mental processes. But more and more the two are confused. The carefulness breaks down. The logic moves from precise, straightforward sentences into long, intense constructions, which Winston finds himself unable to shorten, and which drift out into conjecture, losing control. This activity establishes the irony of such possible loss of control, and it is associated with the careful and delicate piece of defamation that Winston is working on, to indicate the doubleness of his mind. At the same time there is the ironic reversal of his attitude to Julia, a reversal conveyed in the confidence and sophistication of his self-persuasion that she is not laying a trap for him when she bumps into him at the Ministry. The whole event of meeting resonates with the earlier image of the chess game in the Chestnut Tree café, 'like trying to make a move at chess when you were already mated' (p. 111). The reader is allowed to consider the ease of his shift through the focus on a series of physical images, that are apparent from the moment he sees Julia falling on to her broken arm, which he feels as if 'in his own body'. The scene ends with Winston touching Julia's hand, learning it. The intensity of emotion surrounding that experience is in sharp contrast with the hand which he kicked into the gutter earlier. What is important here is the act of learning, that human interaction may be intuitive, but also needs to be learned. It is a responsibility, not an intuitive right.

The second chapter in Part Two reintroduces the quality of private fantasy and desire in a scene of truncated pastoral, whose 'pools of gold', birds and fields, recall the truncated pastoral of *Animal Farm*. Winston and Julia arrive in the country by railway carriage, that resonant image of escape. They have no intention of reflecting back on the society they have left. Winston is surrounded by a feeling of safety. He is totally dependent upon the woman. Yet there is an undercurrent of unease, suggested in the cold and 'droning' doves, the odd quality of 'fifteen' o'clock. The most immediate resonance is with the repetition of the earlier dream of the golden country. But here Winston cares about Julia. He still abuses the sexual; she is 'unresisting, he could do what he liked with her' (p. 122). Yet her own aggressiveness mitigates his authoritarianism. It is still a rebellion against the Party, but it here introduces the dawnings of some personal connection between two people.

The change is connected to the purity of the bird song.[1] Its non-intellectual music that Winston allies with Julia's belief that sex is 'an animal-instinct', is for the reader, entirely ironic because the conjecture is itself an intellectualization. Winston desires the simple and animal but cannot resist the intellectual. He desires the private but is inevitably drawn to interaction. In his ambivalence he recognizes that isolation is not the answer to the Party, yet he confines his alternative to a very private politics. Possibly the most important resonance in this episode is the elusive image of 'something strongly felt, but not reducible to definite shape' (p. 123), a 'memory of some action which he would have liked to undo, but could not' (p. 124). This image he pushes away. It is an image which stands in parallel with that of the golden country, and is linked to the earlier parallel image of his mother. But the reader cannot yet read the image. We can only know that Winston should not be trying to evade or escape it, he should not be pushing the memory away.

The next three chapters contrast Winston and Julia in terms of their attitudes. This is partly to illustrate Winston's learning process as against Julia's ignorance, but it is also to underline by analogy the learning process the reader should be undergoing as a result of Winston's early ignorance. The writer is careful to defuse both sentiment and suspense here so that the developing relationship between Winston and Julia becomes a formal 'dance', within very strict rules that set an analogy between the two people, each performing the same pattern in an entirely unique manner. The dance begins with the sexual, and transfers out to the literary and political. But here, because there are two points of view, Winston learns greater interaction; he extends his personal response and through discussion, however limited, with another person, begins to establish his values.

Julia's pure animal instinct toward sex teaches Winston more about the Party than her understanding of it. The Party is to be hated because it prevents her from realizing her private desires. She is concerned to avoid it rather than rebel against it because she accepts it 'as something unalterable' (p. 133). But Winston realizes that this attitude 'solves nothing', that she is wrong to believe that it was somehow possible to construct a secret world in which 'you could live as you chose' (p. 137). It is an extraordinary conclusion to have come to in the light of his own efforts to do exactly this. The scene presents the generation of a value by means of discussion and by involvement in analogous reactions. Julia has double standards that are kept entirely separate, but Winston is struggling to a less private sense of identity. He is beginning to recognize the connection between the personal and the political. At this point, however, he is still limited to a utopian view of rebellion.

In contrasting Winston and Julia in terms of memory and history, the narrator moves on in chapter 4 into a series of intense resonances with Part One, which also make the contrast between the reader and Winston far stronger. Winston returns to Charrington's world which contains so much that we recognize and provided so much situational irony. But this time we note the oddness of his reaction to familiar things. It is no longer 'our' world, simply because the habitual connections are no longer being made. Again the allegorical face turns toward us: the world we live in is not necessarily only as we perceive it, there is so much that we forget, and our strengthened identification with Winston reminds us how easy it is to forget.

Julia however, simply has no memory whatsoever of anything different at all. She has desires and evasions, but no concept of evaluation. The implication is that Winston's memory of something different is essential to his concept of value. But a belief, generated here by the enigmatic figures of dream, memory and nightmare, is essential before one can then transform through discussion into value. Winston recognizes, for example, that Julia's wish for silk stockings is a nostalgic desire not a valid historical memory, because it does not create awareness or assessment. However, the wish is also parallel to Winston's own nostalgic desire for an absolute past in Charrington's room. The desire is coalesced into the image of the nursery rhyme and the paperweight that Charrington had shown him on his first visit (p. 147). For Winston, the paperweight is 'a little chunk of history that they've forgotten to alter. It's a message from a hundred years ago, if one knows how to read it' (p. 147). The quotation sets out the problem for both himself and the reader, but Winston's chosen reading is that the paperweight is a 'tiny world with its atmosphere complete', and that he and Julia are 'fixed in a sort of eternity at the heart of the crystal' (p. 148). The reader may not have been able to read the limiting implications of Charrington's room before this but they are now clear.

In the final incident of this fourth chapter Julia throws her shoe at a rat, exactly as she threw a dictionary at Goldstein in the organized 'Hate' propaganda. Her response in both cases is conditioned and therefore conquerable. Both are due to evading the cause of the fear. This provides a perspective for looking at Winston, who is sent suddenly back into a nightmare where

> He was standing in front of a wall of darkness, and on the other side of it there was something unendurable, something too dreadful to be faced. In the dream his deepest feeling was always one of self-deception, because he did in fact know what was behind the wall of darkness. With a deadly effort, like wrenching a piece out of his own brain, he could even have dragged the thing into the open. (p. 146)

Again he is at a wall of darkness: once this revealed a human tragedy, once it was pushed away, and here it is clearly a self-deception. Both Julia and Winston are conditioned to certain fears; and for both it is essential to push back to the grounds of that fear.

Our reading of the unexpected parallels as well as the differences involved in the comparison between Winston and Julia, underlines Winston's complexity and blindness: that he is aware of the danger of the negative path of nostalgia, self-deception and isolation but unable to find his way through it easily. But it is not an entirely negative confusion. The intercommentary of the topics indicates that response is in fact changeable. Winston can learn through the constructive questioning of private identity in interaction with others.

In the fifth chapter the doubleness of Winston's reactions is presented as the functioning of two different rhetorical strategies within the Party system that are revealed in practice to be aspects of the same stance. The analogy poses problems of narrative presentation, because it involves a technical discussion which must not only be shown to be intimately connected to characters' lives, but also must involve the reader rather than simply inform. The fiction here is overtly a device of dialectical logic asking the reader to assess by stimulating both identification with and separation from the central character.[2]

Inside the 'heart of the paperweight', in Charrington's bedroom, the two 'gave themselves up to daydreams of escape' (p. 153), and it is those daydreams that present their strategies of interaction with the Party. Because Julia is too young to remember the possibility of an alternative party, her rebellion is 'secret disobedience or, at most, by isolated acts of violence' (p. 154). She takes for granted the simultaneous hate and acceptance necessary. On the positive side, she is far more acute about Party propaganda than Winston. She knows for example that there is no real war going on. But just because of this awareness she misses the danger in the propaganda. She takes it for granted because 'the difference between truth and falsehood did not seem important to her' (p. 155).Winston's acuteness derives from his very susceptibility to propaganda, for this makes him question fact and search for the truth. The alertness makes him try to express his fears, and define an identity for himself. His idea of an anti-Party strategy is based on group discussion and communication, generating 'knots of resistance', that will band together, grow, record and pass on knowledge; beyond this is a vague idea of O'Brien and the Brotherhood. But he cannot communicate the importance of his ideas to Julia, and hence remains isolated. His problem in contrast to hers is not that he searches for truth but that he views it as factual and absolute. Hence he does not want to twist it in order to persuade her. He feels that he cannot offer alternative persuasions, such as his memories, in any valid manner. Just as Winston comes to understand that sexual rebellion alone is too private, and that Julia's necessarily divided attitude evades responsibility to other people, so he slowly recognizes from watching Julia's limitations that his paperweight world is not a means of getting at the truth in the past, so much as maintaining the *status quo* by evading activity.

But the reader has to ask how Winston can break out of this equivalence. Winston suggests that the key is knowledge, reached through discussion because 'the Party imposed itself most successfully on those incapable of understanding it' (p. 157). But he is unclear as to how this should be effected. He only knows that one has to get very close to the enemy before understanding him. What he does not yet understand is that truth, while one needs a means of assessing it, cannot be absolute and utopian as Winston's future and past utopias are. Such absolutism only brings with it more fantasy, like the eternal present of the Party. Yet again, the question is how do you do something which lies totally outside your experience to the extent that it lies also beyond your comprehension?

The structure of *Nineteen Eighty-Four* is carefully built so that the reader is led to understand Winston's position in much the same manner that he is doing so – only we have the benefit of a second reading. The external and situational irony that made us complicit with the narrator's point of view in Part One, shifts in Part Two to an internal irony that makes us complicit in the way in which we read the earlier part. We are made more aware of our reading as Winston becomes more aware of his situation. It is the resonant images that are the key to the whole book. Their development and repetition must be followed and assessed by both character and reader, without any explicit direction from the narrator. The repetition generates in the reader a curious sense of *déjà vue*, not simply from the intercommentary of the topics, but also the intercommentary between the presentation of the topics: their logic, vocabulary and images. The intercommentary is a device to give the reader a chance to learn from something that he has failed to notice before, and to place an earlier experience of learning within a new perspective. It ensures that the reader never sits back assuming that his own assessments are final.

Before the narrative moves fully on to the central event of the meeting

with O'Brien, the reader's process of evaluation is emphasized. We are
thrown into the tensions and ambivalence of Winston's mind, and all our
abilities to weigh and assess are called upon. At each juncture in chapter 6,
of working out his relationship with O'Brien we watch Winston
rationalizing amidst his fears, and always tending toward a positive
interpretation. He always moves along to what he wants: that O'Brien is a
friend. The reader should recognize the implications in his final decision to
'obey O'Brien's summons' (p. 160), and the acceptance and fatalistic
attitude that this blind obedience speaks of. Here too, because Winston has
learned about the negativity of passive acceptance from Julia, the reader
can begin to assess the extent of his self-delusion.

In Part One, chapter 3, Winston dreamt and learnt from his dreams,
hovering between a dream mentality and a consciousness which provided
the foundation for a discussion with himself. In the next chapter of Part
Two, chapter 7, the dream quickly becomes memory, as if his memories
perform the function of connecting dream to the conscious world, and at
the same time dreams harbour otherwise lost memories. The dream itself is
'too complex to put into words'. It is interesting that these internal
revelations are different from the conclusions that he overtly reaches with
Julia. It is as if transferring them to words has called him into another habit
of thought and trapped him. The reader plays in this gap between the
narrative-presented Winston, of dream and memory, and Winston's
thoughts and conversation. Within the differences the reader is able to
assess.

The first indication for our reading is the transformation of the
paperweight from an enclosed, limited and safe world, to a world of
'interminable distances'. The past can trap, but may also release. This is
followed by Winston's sudden recognition of the similarity between the
gesture of an arm made by his mother in his earlier dream with that made by
the Jewish woman in the film. Here he is making this connection overtly
for himself. The second indication is the recognition that the dream or
memory had been 'deliberately pushed out of his consciousness' (p. 162).
This recalls the dark wall of evaded memory but also the revelation of his
mother on a boat that occurred when he first pierced through the darkness.
Again, at first this was a discovery that the reader witnessed and that
Winston was not consciously recognizing, but here he is far more aware of
the nature of the revelation.

This memory of the dream seems to have dredged the earlier image
closer to consciousness as if providing it with some kind of basis, some
kind of accessibility: that accessibility is a picture of Winston himself as a
child, his poverty and hunger and his selfish cruelty. We need to see him as a
child out for his own ends, even at that time 'ashamed' of stealing food
from his sister. The implications of that act are contained in the gesture of
his mother's arm here, which is directly parallel to that which the Jewish

woman made on the boat in the earlier image, and speaks to him of the death of his sister because of his theft, and also of his mother's contrasting care, her nobility and purity because her standards were 'private'. He says, 'It would not have occurred to her as an action which is ineffectual thereby becomes meaningless' (pp. 165–6). Hence the importance of the gesture of her arm, and the value residing in the care that it indicates in the relationship between human beings.

Winston moves explicitly to spelling out the Party's denial of value in feelings, and concomitant denial of the basic alternative: power over the material world. The Party denies both emotion and fact. Yet before the Party came to power, loyalties were private, 'What mattered were individual relationships' that gave value to non-functional gestures. This recognition on Winston's part is direct repetition of the earlier learning experience, but here Winston is fully aware of the process and for the 'first time in his life, he did not despise the proles' (p. 166). In effect they possess something that he has come to value. Unlike them he has to 'relearn by conscious effort' the value of human interaction. The process has been occurring slowly since the beginning of the book, but whereas previously it left Winston confused, now it appears to clarify his situation. However, the reader notes that immediately following this understanding, Winston remembers 'without apparent relevance' kicking the hand into the gutter. He still does not know why that image arises, but we do. There are still differences between our outlooks due to his lack of awareness.

Winston and Julia conclude that whereas the Party can alter fact it cannot alter feelings. Indeed Winston goes so far as to say 'You could not alter them yourself, even if you wanted to' (p. 168). Yet he has just demonstrated that feelings can be learnt. He has moved from inhumanity to humanity as an absolute. His interpretation of the image of his mother sets up the past with humanity, feeling and privacy, as against the eternal present of inhumanity, no feeling and the Party. And while there are many positive elements within this private, absolute humanity, ultimately it is unsatisfactory within the context of his world. In the account of his memories, considerable weight is placed upon his mother's ineffectiveness, her lethargic sense of inevitability and fate. Yet he never pursues this, even though it is an element from the earlier image of tragic suffering not only as a counter-action to the Party but as somehow responsible for its present situation of power. The process has underscored the action of the images in generating value; but he never follows up the negative side of the images, only the positive.

O'Brien and the Brotherhood

At last, in chapter 8, Winston meets with O'Brien. The reader has been prepared for the religious element in this episode, but also warned.

Previous religious images have been to do with obedience to the Party or 'the sanctuary' of the paperweight world. Curiously it is as if Winston is peculiarly ignorant with regard to religion, with the implication that religion is one of the most difficult areas to assess. What the reader perceives throughout is the irony of the situation, all the conventions that we recognize, but Winston cannot; the catechism, the wine and wafer, the sermon. There is a huge middle ground of experience open to both the reader and Winston, which Winston defines positively, evading the dangers in his situation, but in which the reader can recognize a negative rhetoric.

There is a conventional initiation, couched in authoritative terms: 'You will receive orders and you will obey them, without knowing why' (p. 175). The enforced ignorance and blindness here only underlines that the Brotherhood is a counterpart to the Party, especially since Winston and Julia are asked to be prepared to hurt, maim and kill, to throw aside the newly learnt human care and ultimately to throw aside each other. There is an insistence on isolation, denying the discussion Winston thought he would achieve, and that goes hand in hand with not acting 'collectively', with the glorification of self-sacrifice and with a dependence upon a possible future. All of these are utopian delusions that only mark private fantasy rather than Party fantasy. And finally there is O'Brien's recitation of O'Brien's rhetoric, with all the hallmarks of a negative political strategy, that constructs him into an authority figure, who is eventually to be blindly worshipped. The key here is 'Oranges and Lemons', because Charrington did give Winston the last ominous 'chopper' line, but when O'Brien ends with Shoreditch, Winston is satisfied. He accepts that the line is the last one. He accepts the direction of O'Brien's rhetoric only as positive.

But the reader's ironic noting of Winston's inadequacy throughout this scene should lead further to an allegorical reading that underlines the alternative need for assessment, especially since O'Brien's rhetoric plays directly into the Party's hands by suggesting only an alternative authoritarianism rather than a radical questioning of its grounds. The Brotherhood does not break the circle of enclosure necessary to maintain the system, and in its own way actually justifies the existence of the Party.

The discussion then moves inexorably on to the overriding concerns of politics and language which take negative stance to an extreme. The chapter which follows, Chapter 9, incorporates large passages from Goldstein's book *The Theory and Practice of Oligarchical Collectivism*, which O'Brien has given to Winston. For many readers this is an annoying or destructive section akin to the political section of *Homage to Catalonia*, but similarly, it is vital to a reading of the book. The bases for evaluation that the Book, as Winston comes to see it, provides are found partly in the analogy between Winston's state of mind as he reads and the stance of the Book itself, but mainly in the reader's response to both.

We should be alerted to the rhetoric of the Book itself, since there is a clear analogy between its political persuasion and that of the Party. There are two aspects being presented in this section. The first is an extension of the devices and effects of negative rhetoric from politics to language, on the part of the writer into his work. The second is a study of the kind of reader perception that makes this possible. What is clear is that no one is without responsibility. One cannot simply foist the responsibility of negative stance onto the writer. It is also the concern of the words themselves and of the reader.

The politics of Goldstein's book are introduced ambiguously as 'the theory and practice of oligarchical collectivism'. It is presented in a neutral manner, and the reader does not know whether this is to prove positive or negative, the politics of Big Brother or of the Brotherhood. But as we read we recognize a more formal restatement of all that we have experienced in Part One. The narrator introduces the first chapter, 'Ignorance is Strength', but then shifts immediately to the third, 'War is Peace'. By placing this later section first in the reader's reading experience, he can validate an air of having already justified several of the concepts. He can create some anticipation of matters that have presumably already been presented in the book, and can set up conclusions which ask for explanations and encourage the reader to accept that these explanations have already been made. Following this up by a full recapitulation of the first chapter, he can present a logical progression, confident that the reader knows the conclusion and that that conclusion will appear to verify the type and direction of the logic. That chapter 2 is missing completely provides the narrator with a way out of explaining anything. But further, we are told that the second chapter is entitled 'Freedom is Slavery', and this is the focus to Winston's confusion that in avoiding the Party he must retreat to an isolated individualism. It is the problem containing the solution to the crises, to the balance and interaction of the personal and the political which is the question of *Nineteen Eighty-Four*. Its obvious omission here indicates its vital centrality.

The politics of the Book summarizes what has gone before. For Orwell readers, for example, the chapter entitled 'War is Peace' restates the discussion on the Superstate mentality in his essays. The illusion generated by continuous war denies value to history and eradicates reality or any external factors freely impinging upon the personal. It is referred to as 'a kind of daydreaming' (200). The Party's slogan that 'Ignorance is Strength' is demonstrated as essential, since without ignorance, the illusion would collapse. The Party system places Big Brother at the top, as infallible and omnipotent, and the system itself is an adoptive oligarchy denying all individual elements and directed toward mind control. Technically, mind control aims at 'crimestop', or stopping short of disagreement with the Party by instinct, by ability to fail to grasp analogies, by unquestioning acceptance of its step by step logic. Mind control also aims at 'black-white', which is the ability to hold mutually contradictory interpretations as standards from one set of facts, thereby applying no evaluation. Mind control also aims toward doublethink, the ability to negate and recall the existence of knowledge at will. Doublethink denies history, denies memory, and denies value. There is hence no means of making an individual assessment, one has total control only because one is totally arbitrary. Individuals, like the Party, must both be infallible and corrigible, must act and delude at the same time.

For Orwell, political fantasy, like literary fantasy, requires a creator who can totally control the world for the citizen or for the reader. The reason that the Party goes beyond present forms of authoritarianism as the Book says it does, is that people are trained through doublethink to control and delude themselves at the same time, making absolute and endless tyranny possible. It is not entirely clear how this is effected, but the suggestion is that it depends on a fluctuation between the individual controlling and then turning to the collective for an extension of his delusion. In other words, there are no complete 'individuals'. Control is always being effected on the deluded private person by someone else within the collective oligarchy so it never breaks down. What is clear is that it demands not loss to gain self, or gaining of self through group identity, but the destruction of any sense of self whatsoever: a process that *Nineteen Eighty-Four* calls 'madness'.

The narrator has detailed in concrete terms the needs of this negative political rhetoric, and the reader should look now at the rhetoric of Goldstein's book itself. It is important that Winston's reaction is initially surrounded by the imagery of pastoral escape, of a utopia that has no intention of returning to criticize the world: he sits down to read the book not as an object, but as a proof of the luxury and freedom he enjoyed in Charrington's room. The room is illustrated with the vocabulary of 'bliss' and 'eternity', 'comfort and safety'. The Book 'reassured him. In a sense it told him nothing that was new, but that was part of the attraction' (p. 201). But his response is one of an odd dissatisfaction. The sense of rereading returns, but is not at the end so reassuring. Winston reiterates the earlier statement in his diary that 'he understood *how*; he did not understand *why*' (p. 218).

Earlier this same conclusion was an indication that Winston was mad. But he denies this now, and says that 'There was truth and there was untruth . . . sanity is not statistical' (p. 219). Yet the possibility that he is making a profound advance away from his pursuit of absolute truth is left ambivalent and contradictory because the Party itself counts on the existence of truth and untruth, the arbitrary and the absolute in order to manipulate. And his claim that 'sanity is not statistical' resonates far too strongly to be disregarded with his claim that 'two plus two equals four' was a code to absolute truth. This last claim with its complex resonances, is made against the background of pastoral imagery and safety. Finally

Winston and Julia fall asleep evading any further pursuit of the implications. He is caught into a doublethink. He has chosen only the desirable.

The Book itself induces a passive, accepting, self-deluded state through specific rhetorical strategies that could come straight from one of Orwell's essays on negative devices. It has an assertive voice, false connectives, transferred acceptance. Its overall pattern is to confirm and reassure, not to stimulate into questioning. Julia who is less susceptible to propaganda, reacts immediately with boredom and sleep. Winston's reaction is more intensive, probably because he admires the undoubted skill of the writer. And it is integral to the narrator's purpose that we perceive both the boredom and the negativity, as well as Winston's catchment into it. We have to experience this if we are to understand the 'why' which leaves Winston dissatisfied. The reader has to understand what Winston does not, has to see the difference between him and ourselves and recognize the allegorical dimension. Self-delusion is the ultimate aim of negative stance in both literature and politics, to achieve total control through the totally arbitrary, and this is made absolutely possible here by doublethink, which is the ultimate irresponsibility. While the reader has an ironic view of Winston's entrapment into doublethink, the differences between the reader and Winston underline our responsibility to pursue those evaded, omitted, and hidden implications that negative rhetoric tries to disguise.

The final chapter of Part Two provides the pattern for self-delusion moving to breakdown that leads into Part Three. The scene opens with the familiar warmth and normality of Charrington's room, and a reiteration of private fantasies. This is interrupted violently by the police, who repeat the concluding lines of 'Oranges and Lemons', and smash Winston's paperweight. The ease with which these tokens are destroyed is important for the reader's later distinction between images of desire and reality. These images of private fantasy are significantly different from the images of dream and memory from which Winston has learned to generate value and find some human caring. The two types of image are not unconnected for images in themselves are ambiguous. But Winston chooses to read them differently and in doing so illustrates the importance of audience interaction.

The withdrawal of the guiding narrator has made it necessary for the reader to become objective about Winston for himself. But the intercommentary of topics and their presentation is so extensive by the end of Part Two that their initial ambivalence and confusion begins to be clarified, their ambiguity begins to be focused into questions of stance. Although Winston is reaching a greater comprehension of his limitations, the reader is still priviledged at this stage, as the superior knowledge of irony and the allegorical discrepancies make clear. But the question, both in terms of Orwell's development of narratorial stance, and after such concentration on the use and abuse of rhetoric, is with the narrator's involvement: we need to know where he stands without being pushed into his opinion. Just as with *Animal Farm*, we do know, not because he has stated what he thinks, but because his method of going about narration is so different in effect from the other stances active in the book. He stimulates to assessment, leaves undone, leaves open, provides analogy, questions logic, presents the location of value in the images which can only be defined through our participation rather than focused into interpretation. There is no sense of lack of control, but of lack of imposition.

The first chapter of the third part progresses in a series of subtle, but clearly repeated formal structures, each parallel with the preceding. For example, in all but one case they begin with a flashback. At first, these are to an experience familiar to the reader beginning with experiences straight from a contemporary world and moving on to earlier experiences within the book itself. But they then progress toward the more unfamiliar present of Winston. Throughout the successive repetitions there are refractions in the actions performed, logics used, events and images: the reader is pointed to the difficulty of reading. Set against this background is the relationship between O'Brien and Winston that becomes a paradigm analogy for all the ambiguity. Through the reader's identification with Winston we are guided toward the possible location of value within O'Brien's system – a system which has, after all, been generated by Western rationalist humanism. And in a by now reluctant awareness of a different kind of inadequacy in that humanism, which is also in the Western reader, we are thrown out to the responsibility of finding values which will not tolerate that system.

The first chapter in Part Three begins with an immediacy, directness, and extreme formal control, that distinguishes it from the beginnings of Parts One and Two which were scene-set and descriptive. A vocabulary of uncertainty conflicts with careful and detailed observation and the inevitability of balanced sentences. There are few qualifiers, and simple a to b to c rational connections. The phrasing underlines Winston's combination of tension and confusion as he sits in the prole jail to which he has been taken. In the same way, the surrounding bustle and vivid lives of the proles contrast strongly with his reserve and distance, and this separation and distance strengthens as the narrative moves into the Party jail. The entire narrative movement is controlled by the repeated coda of 'crossed hands' on the prisoner's knee, that brings one back each time to aspects of Winston's changing physical and mental condition, the topics on his mind, and the central disorientation of his sense of time and memory. The repeated phrase does not develop into the resonance of an image that generates value, but creates an overall stasis against which are set shifting comparisons between Winston and the other prisoners which place him in perspective.

Each of the characters is shown in reaction to authority, thus setting the background to the rest of the part, which will show Winston's response. Yet these reactions, potentially isolated by the dragging, static effect of the coda are also tied to other motifs that do develop. The repetition of room 101, for example, from a whispered room 'one-oh-one' to reactions of incomprehension, then fear and finally to violence, increase the suspense but point only to the unknown, give no clue as to what is at the end of it, and therefore no basis for assessment. It is as if these motifs are running ever more swiftly toward something at the same time as the movement is kept on one spot by the repeated coda of crossed hands. Other repetitions of earlier images, such as the mouth of the beaten-up man, 'a shapeless, cherry-coloured mass with a black hole in the middle of it' (p. 237), are caught in the same stasis and sundered from resonance, left dry and isolated into the pure surreal: it is not that shock is impossible because there are no values, but that there is no means of reacting at all, because values have been severed from image, language and action.

The appalling implication is that for all the repetition of these images, for all the careful attention to detail and difference, all Winston has is his own body and mind to which the coda recalls us. The final event is the appearance of O'Brien while Winston is conjecturing about the possibility of assuming part of Julia's pain. He says he cannot know whether he would assume it, but O'Brien warns him not to deceive himself. It is a warning immediately followed by Winston's own intense pain which answers his conjecture, for, 'in the face of pain there are no heroes, no heroes, he thought over and over, as he writhed on the floor, clutching uselessly at his disabled left arm' (p. 241). The image of the arm has now become intensely personal, but its meaning is left static. There is no irony here. In separating the images from value for Winston, the narrator has denied us our own means of assessing, but the reader is closer to Winston now than at any other time because we are only given access to the same bases for assessment as he has. Further, as the fluctuation between the voices of the narrator and Winston closes up, the reader loses that identification with the narrator as someone from our own background who knows the differences from Winston. Winston becomes characterized here only through his insistence on time, history, and memory.

The formal construction of the dance between O'Brien and Winston that follows parallels the earlier dance pattern with Julia, particularly in the pursuit of questions of definition and self-identity. But here O'Brien gradually becomes dominant. He alone is defining Winston, making him 'perfect' (p. 245). O'Brien's role is to question the validity of intellectual and factual means to assessment, which had been one of Winston's first avenues toward self-identity. But, just as he failed earlier, Winston's response here is to turn to a series of images. Yet these images, although they resonate with the earlier ones, are subtly perverted. Any means to assessment are through noting differences between the subconscious underwater world Winston now experiences under drugs and the earlier one he experienced in dream. Similarly, there is the resonant golden light which was earlier associated with the country, but is here inside a wide, white corridor. In both cases, the image is left open and generative in the first instance, and is totally controlled in the second. Its possible generative values here become predetermined codes. Three other images concerning O'Brien are actually realized, and this raises the question of whether these images are genuine or implanted, generative or habitual. The point is that images of desire are never meant to be controlled fully. When they are so, and realized, they destroy rather than generate identity. Therefore, even the images lying beyond the private fantasy of Winston's room can be made fantastic.

The means by which experience of fact or image is made delusive is outlined in the presentation of O'Brien as a re-creator surrounded by religious connotations of confession and rebirth, and the doubleness of his authority both as Big Brother and the Brotherhood. The Party is not interested in act but in thought. They are interested in conversion rather than punishment. They are not out for submission and obedience, but for a full acceptance. It is a new negative stance based on doublethink or organized madness. It is the destruction of all self-identity with no interaction. O'Brien destroys Winston and re-creates him by imposing his own identity in an absolute manner that this utopian novel presents as possible.[3] For example, Winston is blanked out by pain, and O'Brien fills the emptiness with suggestions that 'become absolute truth' (p. 259). It is underlined that Winston must appear to do this for himself. But all that is happening is that relationships are being destroyed, while things remain. Active logic as the key to assessment is wiped out and replaced by the rigid connections of rationalism. The constant activity of evaluation necessary to avoid self-delusion is made impossible.

But just as the process of doublethink needs not only the absolute and factual, but also the arbitrary, O'Brien proceeds by undermining Winston's new trust in this very rational, objective, and factual basis that he has incorporated. This is significant because it indicates to the reader that these things are not fundamental to evaluation; and since most of the ironies in the book have derived from the situational discrepancies of object and fact in the physical and situational, our earlier ironic superiority is shown to lack substance as well. All Winston is left with is 'human nature'. O'Brien spells this out saying that Winston must be hollow of 'love, or friendship, or the joy of living, or laughter, or curiosity, or integrity' (p. 257). Throughout the ensuing virtuoso display of negative stance, what is surprising is that Winston poses a far more coherent and consistent resistance than the reader expects, and we are left having to sort out the resulting contradictions. When O'Brien repeats Winston's avowals to maim, torture, and kill for the Government, the reader is no longer in a position to claim superiority to Winston. In the end, Winston is 'without argument, with nothing to support him' (p. 270), but value and belief, 'I believe it, I know that you will fail' (p. 270).

Through the negative religious imagery around the Party, O'Brien suggests that its main ingredients are learning, understanding and acceptance, and these activities provide another structure for the movement of Part Three. Winston learns in the first two chapters, is now understanding and will eventually, in the final two chapters, accept. What Winston and the reader are overtly understanding in this chapter is the way that the Party operates, that there must be an active acceptance of power not as a means but in itself, not as a temporary submission but as a long-term acceptance to sustained negative rhetoric. Furthermore, the Party must have suffering to prove the existence of its power.[4] Therefore, there must be individuals to exercise power on through pain. The individual is promised immortality and perception by fusion with the Party, and the first thing to go are the humanist values which, like sexuality, are transposed into the Party. The circular nature of the Party's demand for complete loyalty and therefore no individualism, yet need for individuals to exercise power upon, becomes self-supporting.

But what the reader also learns is the questionable nature not only of the Party, but also of the private individual. Both are mutually destructive, separate and isolated units. They sustain each other, just as pain sustains power and vice versa in a sado-masochistic symbiosis. The whole structure recalls the question about the private nature of the mother's value, the suffering for a reward in which one destroys part of one's self to more fully realize the goal. But in doing so, one makes over that goal in one's own image. It is the paradox of mutilation of both self and other. In that image there is the suggestion of a selfless activity of exposing self and the possibility of realizing it in a difference rather than a destruction. The paradox that results is that in so doing, one defines oneself further.

This doubleness of reading becomes available to the reader in the final exposure of Winston's battered and tortured body during chapter 4 of Part Two. O'Brien notes the connection between mind and body which links the mental degradation to the physical. But Winston reads this in reverse, pitying his body, wanting to help it, to apply his new humanist values. For the reader, the paradox is that this susceptibility does eventually destroy Winston. It is a reading that lies beyond the government of Winston and O'Brien, outside Winston's new humanism, and perhaps outside the reader's own comprehension, in an allegory of the unknown.

It is Winston's care for his body that finally induces him to try to accept O'Brien's system. As his body begins to mend, he accepts that sanity is statistical. He has no care for distinctions of time and memory, 'he accepted everything' (p. 278). But into this creep indications of a problem. He concludes an argument, but ends with 'only – !', or works through a situation to 'except – !' The possible problems are the 'submerged wreckage' of thoughts that are then pushed down. It becomes apparent that he is consciously training himself in crimestop and doublethink, and the precise and formal structure of the prose presents the balance of his delicate manoeuvres.

The chapter culminates in an image of the golden country, here fused with the sunlit corridor and total confession. But Winston wakes from the dream screaming Julia's name. In amidst the now broken prose which he desperately tries to control, Winston confesses 'he had hoped to keep the inner heart inviolate' (p. 281), and to retain an integrity of feeling. The earlier surprise that the reader may have felt at Winston's strength of resistance is here turned to respect for the depth of his integrity, for our expectations of his smooth acceptance are reversed. There is something more beyond it.

O'Brien's entrance and recognition of Winston's feeling underlines the different kinds of interdependence at work. O'Brien may need Winston to exercise power over and make into the same as himself, but Winston needs O'Brien to define his difference. O'Brien's recognition of the feeling is Winston's proof of an external reality for it. Winston is then taken to room 101 and threatened with the rats that are to be let loose on his face. But the reader reacts not only to the classic construction of suspense within the narrative, but also to the image of the dark wall and the unknown beyond it. From the beginning of the novel the image has indicated something feared and evaded. At times it has transformed Winston's recognition of standards and given him access to values otherwise totally beyond his experience, but not without considerable personal jeopardy and reassessment. Yet at other times it has located the terror lying beyond experience in the complete unknown, a terror arising from evasion, and the failure to take up the activity of evaluation. The reader is not to know which way the balance will fall. And Winston, in his evasion of fear and evaluation here, in his reaction to the rats, and his sacrifice of Julia, responds in a way difficult to criticize within the standards of humanism.

However, the very extremity of his sacrifice indicates the value of feeling as the most reliable index of personal identity within this world of separated private and party interest. The earlier identification with Winston and his entrance into a world of humanist values goes together with our awareness of the limitation of those values when they are restricted to the private within O'Brien's system. Here when he is faced with the rats, that identification produces a desire for his ultimate resistance, a hope that his human feeling will work to protect him even though it has been shown to be inadequate to break the power/pain world of O'Brien. It is our own desire and it indicates our own possible evasion.

But to be aware of this reading denies the evasion. The image of the dark wall is not just an image of fear within a specific system. It is an image of the stance of allegory. It throws the reader out into the unknown as it threw Winston out, not just generating but also transforming. Here we are thrown out toward the necessary activity that will stop O'Brien's system. Just as that system is something absolute and therefore different from anything we have known, to ensure its defeat we have to search for the entirely different. In doing so we may even find ways of stopping the temporary manifestations of it that surround us in pragmatic terms, and providing an alternative. An ironic reading will stop at the point where Winston's humanist values are shown to be inadequate. Such a reading will inevitably be limited to the pessimistic. But it is not Winston's newly found values that transform his outlook, and help him go beyond the aspects within experience. It is his way of evaluating.

The final chapter of *Nineteen Eighty-Four* illustrates Winston's total acceptance of O'Brien's system as it returns to the tempo of the earlier sections. But here the reader knows why Winston is inadequate and curiously it is also our own inadequacy. The analogy is carried by a reiteration of the image of the Chestnut Tree café. This final scene is an exact duplicate of the previous one in which Winston was searching for some radical or significant difference between his given world and actuality. There neither the reader nor Winston could interpret the scene, but here, after the process of the book which pulls the pieces together, and allows us to assess, Winston perceives nothing, while we do. We have taken on his discriminating role. The structure is again one of a dance, but here between Winston's thoughts and the interruptions of the telescreen. There is no longer even a generative conflict with O'Brien, but a controlled conflict with a false communicator. The game of chess he plays is associated with reports of war, both are conflicts as games. There are no real opponents, merely counters of established weight being moved around. We are told that in this chess game white always mates, and for the new Winston this is an emblem of the Party's omnipotence and perfection. The reader recognizes the falsity involved, and the contrast with Winston's earlier knowledge. When the telescreen announces victory, Winston realizes that it had happened 'as he had foreseen' on the chess board. The coincidence of apparent reality with his own thoughts excites him enormously, as if he has finally participated in the game. He has been allowed to win, to control reality himself. The dance has ended.

Significantly, he can no longer distinguish between memory and reality, nor can he define reactions or values. 'Feeling', the earlier key to his standards, has been scrambled. Winston now responds with a 'violent emotion, not fear exactly but a sort of undifferentiated excitement'; or he has 'an extraordinary medley of feelings – but it was not a medley exactly; rather it was successive layers of feeling, in which one could not say which layer was uppermost . . .' (p. 290). He is left without an ability to differentiate in terms of value. Just as the image of chess presents its controlled quality of game alone, so the 'golden country' is fully realized and allowed only its controlled aspects of fulfilled desire and confession. Winston's final conversion leaves him:

> back in the ministry of love, with everything forgiven, his soul as white as snow . . . He was looking down the white-tiled corridor, with a feeling of walking in sunlight . . . The long-hoped-for bullet was entering his brain . . . He had won a victory over himself. He loved Big Brother. (p. 298)

All that is now left, having destroyed himself and achieved full acceptance is the desire for death. But whereas earlier death was either through private suffering or public extermination, Winston now looks on death not even as an active reward, but as the ultimate acceptance. The possibility of death being a positive act of contemplation is not even thought of.

Winston is now a useless bureaucrat who meets with others like himself to discuss notes to footnotes on obscure papers. These men have 'extinct eyes, like ghosts fading at cock-crow'. They are the dead in life, who come to life only when they hide their betrayals from themselves and fade back into corpses when they recognize them. In the same way Winston recognizes his betrayal of Julia and accepts it as an index of his inhumanity. The recognition triggers off the telescreen jeer, 'Under the spreading chestnut tree / I sold you and you sold me', and the tears well up in Winston's eyes as they did in Rutherford's, in the earlier café scene. There is an initial parallel that should make the reader read the image again: that betrayal should have such power to destroy means also that loyalty and trust must have some value. But further than this, what is questioned is why betrayal should have the value it does and similarly why its guilt should have the strength that it does.

An Allegorical Reading: Images, Figures and Intercommentary

The point of the analogous levels of reading is that one should not be simply aware of the alternatives involved in each image, but should be able to assess why the alternatives exist and to evaluate them. The naturalistic elements of the novel provide the common ground necessary for irony. It may be a positive irony generating an awareness of the reader's greater knowledge, of his unique situation and resulting in an assessment of that situation. Or it may be a negative irony building on and manipulating that common ground to reinforce our prejudices, as in *Burmese Days*. There is considerable positive irony in the reflection of the inadequacy of Winston's humanist values back upon contemporary Western perception and knowledge. The irony derives from the fact that none of the values usually accepted as residing within the topics of sex, history, memory, and religion, is actually effective in the political and linguistic world proposed by the novel. Within the naturalistic form of the novel, the narrator can impose most of his ideas. As Orwell has pointed out, the novel can be a vehicle for the 'narcissism' of the writer, and he can get trapped within his own grounds, failing to question his environment. It is from this aspect of the genre that Orwell as a writer of fiction is trying to break. Negative readings of *Nineteen Eighty-Four* concentrate on the irony and the naturalism, They are inevitably pessimistic because the final ironic direction is to indicate the inadequacy of the humanist standards people accept. But they are also negative because they see the author only as an imposition, forcing a view which implies the uselessness of history and memory, the authoritarianism of religion, and the futility of sexual relationships and the physical, since the final betrayal is by Winston's body. The response is parallel to that which reads *Animal Farm* merely as a satire without taking the point that animals and humans are not equivalent, that because of their difference humans can prevent the situation that the animals get into, which is the allegory of the work. Just as in *Animal Farm*, the active reader of *Nineteen Eighty-Four* needs to establish the differences that make the allegory possible, and while it is not so easy, since there is no clearly posited alternative rhetoric to the Party's, the differences do arise from the textual use of the utopian genre that Orwell studies in the work of Swift, Butler and Zamyatin.

For Orwell utopian literature, like the nonsense literature of Lear and Carroll, was based on an ability to comment by the juxtaposition of radically different created worlds, with the standards of the habitual world. And it is the juxtaposition of the utopian and naturalistic within the novel, analogous to the juxtaposition of the world of the novel with our external, habitual world that generates the allegory, for in the juxtaposition the reader can perceive difference. Learning about their double-sided nature as either transforming to value or as habitual convention, the reader participates in the emerging allegory and recognizes that value resides within the interaction that transforms toward humanism, rather than in the standards of the system in themselves.

The commentary functions between the text and the topics themselves and the literary structures presenting them, specifically the repeated motifs and images. The images from the dream and memory of the central character transform the factual importance of history into a method of assessing and evaluating the past, not as an absolute either private or Party, but as a source generating personal activity. The image of the dark wall, and of Winston's mother focused this activity, presenting it as allegorical, transforming value from the activity itself, rather than its end. At the same time, sexuality is transformed from the authoritarian into the desirable and then into self-loss, love and trust, through the linked images of the underwater boat and the golden country. These images transform by providing Winston with experience radically different from his everyday life and in which he faces their implications squarely at cost to his selfish dignity and isolated private individualism. He learns to have 'feelings'. Religion is a transitional topic in the novel. It is shown primarily as absolute and authoritarian through the controlled image of confession, in the golden country within the Ministry, and is only briefly glimpsed at the end as a question of trust. One can find the religious allegory only by questioning what is missing: it is not generated for either reader or character.

The explicitly changing topics of history, memory and sexuality, affect Winston's life in a way that he is more able to assess than those of politics and language. Although he is surrounded by politics and language, he finds it far more difficult to recognize the manner in which they impinge upon his life. More than this, they are placed within a utopian background that presents them as unchanging and complete, without the analogical strategy of the images that could invite others into activity. However, the intercommentary of the initial three topics increasingly indicates to the reader that the latter two topics also lack something. In terms of results and ends it is never explicit what language and politics lack, but it is clear that within O'Brien's system they are without any means of generating value in their process. The reader can evaluate them in terms of their stance even if he cannot judge their end product.

And of course the actual stance of the writer in *Nineteen Eighty-Four* does propose this alternative, positive stance, by the manner in which he juxtaposes the genres and generates allegory. The difference involved in the presentation of language and politics is found in the relationship the reader has with the narrator, which is analogous to the relationship set up in the development of the images. In each case, interaction is initially what helps to transform the images, establish a radically different attitude to the topics; but in Winston's case the interaction ceases, becomes enclosed within itself, habitual, and finally, as in the last chapter, dead to the revelation of difference by image.

The reader's identification with Winston, initially interactive, remains interactive. We can read the images of the final chapter as disturbing and out of place, whereas he cannot, and this is because our response to the character is effected through the narrator as well. The reader has a narrator who consistently stimulates toward a questioning of language, who through teaching and interaction between reader and text in looking at the personal topics, establishes a stance that is analogous to an alternative language, an alternative politics: of communication, response, and discussion in the public. The interaction essential to Winston's first learning process is stopped, but the reader goes on.

The mixture of utopia and novel places Winston within a world where these accidents of language and politics are actual. As noted, for the reader, Winston's world placed beside our own may lead to ironic pessimism, and a recognition only of the common factors. As he fails we fail with him. Yet at the same time it is too easy with this reading to say that his world is untrue, that absolutes do not exist, that there is always the possibility of escaping the situation and the dangers can therefore be dismissed. This is indeed what happens with the defenders of fantasy: the claim that such absolute control is not possible and therefore we should not worry about it. In *Nineteen Eighty-Four*, by means of the utopian within the naturalistic, it is suggested that such dismissal only evades the implications. Instead of mitigating totalitarianism by saying that it is just a more extreme authoritarianism, the author posits its basis in an absolute and asks us not only to view the inconsistencies, but also the similarities. We are asked to recognize the interdependence of private and party worlds, and further, to recognize the need to pursue a means for obtaining a personal and public interaction in order to move toward an alternative.

As with the earlier novels it is a question of narratorial stance, of expressing value without imposing it. Here, the value of value lies not in itself but in an ability to both generate and stand up to constant reassessment. The reader does not know what specific outcomes the narrator is advocating, but he does need to know how he goes about searching for them: by the choice of genre and its modality, here the ironies of naturalistic and utopian informed by the allegory of their juxtaposition. In the end the work is a discussion of the public and private separation, and the negativity that it leads to. As in the earlier novels, the author uses the topics of sex, religion, language and literature, memory and history, and politics, because they all generate values through the choices they make necessary in everyday life. In *Nineteen Eighty-Four* the reader is directed toward necessary interaction in the topics not by direct comment from the narrator but by his rhetorical stance, his use of genre and pursuit of value.

The point is that there is no conclusion given. Whereas such conclusions were ambiguous and distracting in earlier works, here the answer lies in Winston's process of learning. The process is analogous to our own learning about Winston's similarities with and radical differences from us, at first in the absence of our standards and then in the limitations they have which throw us out into our own unknown. The narrator's skill, the strength of *Nineteen Eighty-Four*, is in bringing the reader so close to identification yet retaining the possibility of a separation, which is also a separation from those contemporary standards which we may have taken for granted. It is a dance that defines our individuality by difference. Winston is sucked into a conflation of identification and separation, into the loss of evaluation and the madness of doublethink: into fantasy, a dance of conformity in which he devours himself.

The topical conclusion posited by the allegory is at risk of being contemporary and temporary. Doublethink resides in absolute tyranny, which is manifested as a physically realized fantasy. But that absolute system is so similar to the authoritarian, especially totalitarian states, that closer and more dangerous implications of them may be revealed. Further, the Appendix on Newspeak is placed at the end of the work, as well as being footnoted from chapter 1. Its enclosing of the text within the confines of language allegorizes the topical political conclusion. Its style is ambiguous for it presents the narrator as either in the past or in the future of the events of the book, providing a signal warning for alertness. Having read the book we cannot assume that it is past, nor can we know it is in the future. The aim of the narrator is to help us to think and evaluate by providing situations asking for active rhetorical response. The abiding allegorical text is that doublethink is the loss of value through manifested and realized fantasy. *Nineteen Eighty-Four* is an allegory about fantasy and the only answer to the negative strategy of fantasy lies in the difference between our worlds and the posited world. It is in our interaction between them rather than any result that Orwell's elusive community of mankind resides.

Discussion

In my introductory chapter I suggested that many of the readings of Orwell's work restricted what he had to offer by placing him within a social, historical and philosophical framework that he would have questioned. The dominant, rationalist mode of much contemporary thought generates a series of dualisms that arise from its separation between fact and value, and to read Orwell's work within these dualisms is unsatisfactory: not only for the practical reason that works are not as interesting or stimulating, but also because Orwell himself was trying to move beyond the separation, to combine description of the world with his personal interaction with it so that the activity of the writing would engage the reader into active evaluation.

Orwell's development of fantasy and allegory was not toward a specific solution or end for his writing, but toward ways of reading. They are based on fundamental attitudes to the external world that body forth, among other things, our beliefs about whether we impose upon the external, treat it as different, or with the absurdists, as unalterably alien. They are beliefs that express themselves in various rhetorical stances, which describe the interaction of human beings and that external world. Fantasy in Orwell's terms, as in those of many critics of fantasy writing, is a stance encouraged by rationalism. But Orwell went on to outline the negativity that arises from the all too easy breakdown of the activity of rational logic into restrictive, dualistic systems. In contrast, allegory is a stance that is helped by strategies that expose their own grounds, assess themselves and their limitations, and is most positive when it provides the opportunity for going beyond those limitations.

Just because fantasy and allegory are rhetorical stances they apply to all disciplines. They inform philosophy, politics and art as analogous activities. It was the perception of the extreme fantasy in the politics of totalitarianism that alerted Orwell to the strategies conducive to negative stance in literature. And in searching for a valid personal voice in literature, he posits the basis for a positive stance in contemporary politics. But fundamental to stance is its immediate activity: a political event or a piece of writing may be read in a number of ways, but I would suggest that Orwell is saying that fantasy and allegory are two predominant activities in the twentieth century. The controversy surrounding him as a writer indicates that his own work was just as subject to both readings, but it is also the basis for suggesting that he did achieve the positive voice for which he was searching, that his clear transparent prose did indeed conceal a complex and enigmatic writing that stimulates discussion far beyond the limitations of the grounds of contemporary politics and art.

Bibliography

Bibliography, with abbreviations, of texts by George Orwell
All quotations taken from his writings in this commentary are from these editions, and the page numbers follow the quotations in brackets.

AF   *Animal Farm*, (London: Secker & Warburg, 1945)

BA   *British Broadcasting Company Archives*, 1942–6

BP   *British Pamphleteers*, from volume I, *From the Sixteenth Century to the French Revolution*, ed. with R. Reynolds, (London: Allan Wingate, 1948)

BD   *Burmese Days*, (London: Victor Gollancz, 1935)

CD   *A Clergyman's Daughter*, (London: Victor Gollancz, 1935)

CEJL   *The Collected Essays, Journalism and Letters of George Orwell* volumes I to IV, eds. S. Orwell and I. Angus, (London: Secker & Warburg, 1968). Throughout this commentary quotations from this collection are followed by volume number in roman numerals and page number in arabic numerals. For example, such a reference might read: *CEJL* I 26, meaning Volume I, page 26. Occasionally, where a major essay is continually referred to, its title will be abbreviated and will precede the volume number. For example, a reference from 'Writers and Leviathan' might read: *CEJL* WL, IV 410.

CUA   *Coming Up for Air*, (London: Victor Gollancz, 1939)

DPL   *Down and Out in Paris and London*, (London: Victor Gollancz, 1933)

HC   *Homage to Catalonia*, (London: Secker & Warburg, 1938)

KAF   *Keep the Aspidistra Flying*, (London: Victor Gollancz, 1936)

1984   *Nineteen Eighty-Four*, (London: Secker & Warburg, 1949)

RWP   *The Road to Wigan Pier*, (London: Victor Gollancz, 1937)

TI   *Talking to India: A Selection of English Language Broadcasts to India edited with an Introduction by George Orwell*, (London: George Allen & Unwin, 1943)

TT   *Time and Tide*, 1940–1

Bibliography of and abbreviations for frequently cited books

CC   N. Wheale, 'The Case for Comstock', unpublished essay
CCE   R. Williams (ed.), *George Orwell: A Collection of Critical Essays*
        (Englewood Cliffs: Prentice-Hall, 1974). The essays are:
        (1) R. Williams, 'Introduction'
        (2) T. Eagleton, 'Orwell and the Lower-Middle-Class Novel'
        (3) R. Hoggart, 'Introduction to The Road to Wigan Pier'
        (4) L. Trilling, 'George Orwell and the Politics of Truth'
        (5) E. P. Thompson, 'Inside Which Whale?'
        (6) S. Greenblatt, 'Orwell as Satirist'
        (7) I. Deutscher, '1984 – The Mysticism of Cruelty'
        (8) J. Calder, 'Orwell's Post-War Prophecy'
        (9) C. C. O'Brien, 'Orwell Looks at the World'
        (10) G. Woodcock, 'Prose Like a Window-Pane'
CCS   F. Gloversmith, 'Changing Things: Orwell and Auden' in *Class Culture
        and Social Change* (Sussex: Harvester Press, 1980, pp. 101-39)
CF   A. E.Dyson, *The Crazy Fabric: Essays in Irony* (London: Macmillan, 1965)
CH   J. Meyers (ed.), *George Orwell: The Critical Heritage* (London: Routledge
        & Kegan Paul, 1975)
CS   G. Woodcock, *The Crystal Spirit: A Study of George Orwell* (London:
        Jonathan Cape, 1967)
ELI   J. Wain, 'George Orwell', *Essays on Literature and Ideas* (London:
        Macmillan, 1963, pp. 180–213)
G   L. Brander, *George Orwell* (London: Longmans, Green, 1954)
GO   T. Hopkinson, *George Orwell* (London: Longmans, Green, 1953)
GOL   B. Crick, *George Orwell: A Life* (Harmondsworth: Penguin Books, 1980)
GOR   P. Lewis, *George Orwell. The Road to 1984* (Heinemann Quixote Press,
        1981)
IEB   M. Fixler, 'George Orwell and the Instrument of Language', *Iowa English
        Bulletin and Yearbook*, 9 (1964, pp. 46–54)
LH   C. Pawling, 'George Orwell and the Documentary in the Thirties',
        Literature and History, No. 4 (Autumn, 1976, pp. 81-93)
LME   A. Sandison, *The Last Man in Europe: An Essay on George Orwell* (New
        York: Barnes and Noble, 1974)
O   R. Williams, *Orwell* (Glasgow: Collins, 1971)
Or   E. M. Thomas, *Orwell* (Edinburgh: Oliver & Boyd, 1965)
OF   R. A. Lee, *Orwell's Fiction* (Notre Dame: University of Notre Dame Press,
        1969)
OL   A. Zwerdling, *Orwell and the Left* (Newhaven and London: Yale
        University Press, 1974)
OLS   J. Atkins, *George Orwell: A Literary Study* (London: John Calder, 1954)
OT   P. Stansky and W. Abrahams, *Orwell: The Transformation* (London:
        Constable, 1979)
PGO   R. J.Vorhees, *The Paradox of George Orwell* (Purdue University Studies,
        1961)
RGO   J. Meyers, *A Reader's Guide to Orwell* (London: Thames and Hudson,
        1975)

RM   C. Small, *The Road to Miniluv: George Orwell, the State and God* (London: Victor Gollancz, 1975)

RT   B. Bergonzi, *Reading the Thirties: Texts and Contexts* (London: Macmillan, 1978)

SGO   C. Hollis, *A Study of George Orwell: The Man and his Works* (London: Hollis and Carter, 1956)

TMS   S. J. Greenblatt, *Three Modern Satirists: Waugh, Orwell and Huxley* (Newhaven and London: Yale University Press, 1976/65)

WGO   M. Gross (ed.), *The World of George Orwell* (London: Wiedenfeld & Nicolson, 1971)

Notes to the Text

Introduction

1. See I. Murdoch, *The Sovereignty of Good over other Concepts* (London and Henley: Routledge & Kegan Paul, 1980/70) for a broad discussion of the history of the separation between fact and value in Western philosophy since the Renaissance.
2. See particularly notes on negative rhetoric in the work of K. Wallace, 'The Fundamentals of Rhetoric', in *The Prospect of Rhetoric* (Englewood Cliffs: Prentice-Hall, 1971); R. Scanlon, 'Adolf Hitler and the Technique of Mass Brainwashing', in *Rhetorical Idiom* (New York: Russell and Russell, 1966/58); and W. Brandt, *The Rhetoric of Argumentation* (Indianapolis: Bobbs-Merrill, 1970); but also see work on positive alternatives by, for example, W. Booth, *Modern Dogma, a Rhetoric of Assent* (Chicago: U of Notre Dame P, 1974).
3. For example: F. and B. Christensen, *Notes Towards a New Rhetoric* (New York: Harper and Row, 1968/67); H. M. Davidson, *Audience, Words and Art* (Ohio State UP, 1965); P. France, *Rhetoric and the Truth in France* (Oxford: Clarendon P, 1972); and L. Hunter, *Rhetorical Stance in Modern Literature* (London: Macmillan, 1984).
4. Science predominantly uses a negative stance even now; see T. Kuhn, *The Structure of Scientific Revolutions* (London: U of Chicago P, 1962/75); and R. N. Giere, *Understanding Scientific Reasoning* (Holt, Rinehart and Winston, 1979) for a recent application of the stance.
5. C. Manlove, in *Modern Fantasy: Five Studies* (Chatham: Cambridge U P, 1975), concludes his study by noting the in-built failure of fantasy construction.
6. Two other excellent studies of fantasy strategy either do not perceive these implications at all, E. S. Rabkin, *The Fantastic in Literature*(Princeton: Princeton UP, 1976), or evade them as in W. R. Irwin, *The Game of the Impossible* (Chicago: U of Illinois P, 1976).
7. For example M. D. Springer puts forward the word 'apologue' in *Forms of the Modern Novel* (Chicago: The U of Chicago P,1975); Northrop Frye speaks of

'modern romance' in *The Secular Scripture* (Cambridge: Harvard UP, 1978/76), and E. Honig specifically distinguishes a form of 'modern allegory' in *Dark conceit* (London: Faber and Faber, 1959).

8. P. de Man, *Allegories of Reading* (London: Yale UP, 1979),p. 76; see also F. Kermode, *The Genesis of Secrecy* (London: Harvard UP, 1979).

9. This is a phenomenon noted by such widely different writers as M. Foucault, *The Order of Things* (London: Tavistock Publications, 1970); and Iris Murdoch, in the essays collected in *The Sovereignty of Good*.

10. *O*, p. 89.

11. *SGO*, p 47; *GOR*, p. 18.

12. *SGO*, p. 71; *CCS*, p. 106; *CCE* (10); *CS*; *PGO*; *WGO*, p. 80; *O*, p. 71.

13. *WGO*, p. 138; *OF*, p. 109.

14. *SGO*, p. 145; *CCE* (6), p. 110 or *OL*, p. 91.

15. *TMS*, p. 62; *RM*, p. 108.

16. *G*, p. 171; *OF*, p. 109.

17. *Or*, p. 71; *CCE* (10), p. 175.

18. *OF*, p. 107; *RM*, p. 103.

19. *Or*, p. 72; *OL*, p. 93.

20. *ELI*, p. 181.

21. *OL*, p. 143.

22. *O*, p. 46.

23. *Or*, p. 28; *CS*.

24. G. Orwell, *CEJLIV* 442.

25. *RM*, p. 80.

26. *OL*, p. 147.

27. This comment becomes particularly revelant in view of R. Barthes's development of then concept of 'seam' in *The Pleasure of the Text* (London: Cape, 1976).

28. *CS*, p. 173.

29. *RM*, p. 20, or *Or*, p. 37; *G*, p 92; *GOR*, p. 13.

30. *LME*; *TMS*.

31. *CCE* (7), p. 127; *Or*, p. 38, or *GOR*, p. 13.

32. *RM*, p. 212, or *OL*, p. 191; *CCE* (10), p 164.

33. *RM*, pp. 15, 23 and 105.

34. *LME*, or *CCS*, p. 122; *OF*, p 65.

35. *CCE* (4), p. 72; *CCE* (5), p. 81.

36. *OL*, pp. 147 and 151; *Or*, p. 70.

37. *OL*, pp. 193–7; *RM*.

38. *ECI*, p. 181; *OL*, pp. 158 and 185.

39. *CCS*, p. 102; *GOR*, p. 27, or *CCE* (3), p 46.

40. *Or*, p. 37; *CCS*, p. 103; *CCE* (9), p 158.

41. *CS*, p. 224; *CCS*, p. 122, or *CCE* (10).

42. *CCE* (3), p. 38; *GOR*, p. 8, or *OT*, p 157.

43. *LME*, p. 75, *CS*, p. 53, *CCS*, p 104, *CCE* (2), p. 15, *CCE* (3), p. 36, or *O*.

44. This is the burden of R. Williams argument in *O*; and of the essays in his collection *CCE*: see pp. 83, 119 and 158. *O* has become one of the most influential perspectives on Orwell's work in recent years.

45. See *RWP*, p. xxii; *SGO* p. 88, or *CCS*, p. 123.

46. *OL*, p. 15.
47. *CCE* (3), p. 50.
48. *LME*, p. 6, or *CCE* (4), p. 68.
49. *Or*, p. 100; *LME*, p. 11.
50. For example see *Or*, p. 28 and *CCE* (5), p. 86; *CCS*, p. 102.
51. *Or*, p 101; *G*, p. 85; *ECI*, p 187.
52. *CS*, p 50; *PGO*, p. 58.
53. *CS*, pp. 279–80.
54. *RM*, p 105.
55. *GO**, p. 7.
56. *CCS*, p. 102, or *TMS*, p. 48.
57. E. Said, 'Tourism among the dogs', *The New Statesman*, Jan. 1980, pp. 93–4.
58. Much psychological hay has been made of this separation, see *GOL*, pp. 27–8 and *RGO*, p. 18; but as B. Crick also points out, Orwell himself appears to have been easy-going about it, *GOL*, p. 234.
59. F. Gloversmith for example reads the fact that Orwell himself published a poem presented in *KAF* as written by Comstock, as an indication that Comstock's verse must be taken seriously, *CCS*, p. 104. See also *SGO*, p. 75, or *OF* and *GOR*, p. 4.
60. *CCE* (7), p. 128.
61. *RM*, p. 160; *OL*, p. 102.
62. See *G*, chapter 7; *RM*, p. 64; *CCE* (2), p. 24.
63. *GO*, p 7; *G*, pp. 21 and 22; *OL*, p 147.
64. *CS*, p 279.
65. *G*.
66. *CCS*, p. 116; *Or*, p. 26.
67. *GOL*, p 280.
68. *O*, p 30.
69. B. Crick, 'The Road to 1984', *Times Literary Supplement*, 3/6/77, pp. 685–6; and B. Crick, 'When Orwell Wrote for the Observer', *Observer*, 9/11/80, p. 27.
70. E. Crankshaw, *Times Literary Supplement*, 26/12/80, p 1456; J. Symons 'Such, such were the pains', *Sunday Times*, 23/11/80, p. 45; and H. Spurling, 'Nailing a dead fish', *Times Educational Supplement*, 5/12/80, p. 21.
71. G. Orwell, CEJL I 4.
72. *CCE* (3).
73. *OL*, p. 85.
74. Orwell's ability to involve the reader is noted by Woodcock (*CCE* (10)), p 166); but the conscious attempt not to dominate has been misread, as in for example Hoggart's introduction to *RWP* (*CCE* (3), p. 45) when he notes that one often agrees with Orwell's arguments but that one is rarely 'illuminated'.
75. *CCE* (8), pp. 152–3.

Chapter 1

1. It is interesting that D. Geroge, reviewing *DPL* in the *Tribune* during 1941, only half recognizes the ironic melodrama and rather timidly suggests that Orwell might have been copying Georges Ohnet or Marcel Prevost, *CH*, p. 48. W. H. Davies in the *New Statesman and Nation* so misses the point of the melodrama

that he tries counter it with his own factual evidence of the sale of pornographic postcards in England, *CH*, p. 43. During the 1930s French literature and pornography were being made almost synonymous by the flood of Olympia Press books – not that the reputation was new.

2. Although the reader is referred to as 'he' throughout the commentary, it is to be taken as indicating both 'she' and 'he'.

3. A. Zwerdling complains that the book lacks ideological consistency because the reader does not know the narrator, *OL*, p 165, Yet it is this search for consistency that itself causes dissatisfaction with the work.

4. R. A. Lee in *OF*, which is one of the best studies of Orwell's writing to date, examines with lucidity the question of communication.

5. W. Booth in *A Rhetoric of Irony* (Chicago: U of Chicago P, 1974) examines in detail the different ironies arising from the different responses to the initial rejection of literal meaning. These primary assumptions and the mode of their rejection become the description of ironic figures.

6. For example *The Times Literary Supplement* review of *BD* criticises the book for its portrayal of the conventional older type of Burmese people rather than the new. Other reviewers praise the book for its realistic portrayal of the people and life of Burma, *CH*, pp. 51–3.

7. For example see R. A. Lee, *OF*, p. 8.

8. See T. Eagleton, *CCE* (2), p. 15.

9. T. Eagleton in *CCE* (2) suggests that because Dorothy enters 'low-life' only through loss of memory and not through conscious choice, she therefore is not required to question her previous history. But in effect she does exactly this. She becomes acutely aware of the way language structures the past, makes history. Part of the narrator–character relationship is to indicate the ease with which she forgets this initial awareness, and the criticism may well arise from the writer's insufficient distinction between the two.

10. Even R. A. Lee says that Orwell shows a resignation before the external tyrannies of the world, *OL*, p. 25; this perception of the character's passivity is often used to stress the author's negativity and insufficiency as in *RM*, p. 60.

11. See L. Brander, *G*, p. 93.

12. See G. Woodcock, *CS*, p. 106.

13. The fusion is made for example by C. Small in *RM*, by L. Brander in *G* and by T. Eagleton in *CCE* (2), and particularly by F. Gloversmith in *CCS*, p. 104.

14. Yet this loss of objectivity is clearly a central source for dissatisfaction in the novel; it appears to disturb T. Eagleton *CCE* (2), pp. 24–5, possibly because the relationship is still not sufficiently well-defined.

Chapter 2

1. Although as B. Crick points out, Orwell thought it unlikely that it would be included in the Left Book Club selection, *GOL*, p 279.

2. For example, F. Gloversmith says that the detail of the Brooker's house, 'evinces Orwell's defensive self-distancing' and suggests that it is a 'baffled response' *CCS*, p. 111, that leads into his distinction between the northerner and the southerner. Because of the concentration on Orwell himself as the author,

Gloversmith does not consider this blatantly heavy-handed treatment a device to indicate the narrator's ignorance, but a serious statement of his beliefs. On a different point, but again because of a lack of consideration of the difference in narratorial voice, L. Brander in *G* cannot understand the narrative bridge of the courting birds between chapter 1 and chapter 2, and accuses Orwell of no logical progression.

3. In effect, the different readings of this joke are a fascinating index to readings of the book as a whole. Among others, it has been interpreted as the story of a journey to a place that never was (*G*, p. 113) indicating that although he could go so far, the solution always eluded him; it has been presented as an example of Orwell's callous misunderstanding of class structure in the juxtaposition of seaside jollity and forbidding inland town (*Or*, p. 21); and as an indication of his superficial attitude to the working-class, reducing their problems to the idea that Wigan Pier was where you went if you couldn't afford Blackpool (*GOR*). All the readings have point and validity, but their very range indicates the complexity of response to Orwell and of the writing that generates that response.

4. For an example of a contrary view, see F. Gloversmith who says that Orwell claims that the working-class is quietist because of a long-standing lack of sound education (*CCS*, p. 121).

5. See F. Gloversmith, *CCS*, p. 111. Much criticism has been levelled against Orwell for failing to criticize industry because of strong 'liberal humanist' tendencies; but while he does neglect the economic questions of capital (*LH*, pp. 88–9), he does not dismiss them and wishes to extend the field into other areas affected by class issues.

6. For accusations of idealism and sentimentality see *CCE* (3), p. 41; or of middle-class ignorance see *CCS*, p. 121; and for a note on the superficial change in the narrator see *OL*, p. 130.

7. In contrast, F. Gloversmith suggests that this omission shows a dismissal of the intellectual attitude of the working class (*CCS*, p. 119); R. Williams says that the omission indicates Orwell's political point – one of evasion of things that do not fit his view (*O*, p. 52).

8. A surprising number of critics have actually read this to mean that Orwell thought that working-class habits were 'better' than middle-class, for example *CCE* (3), p. 44, or P. Toynbee, *Encounter*, 1959, also in *CH*, p. 117. B. Crick once again puts the suggestion into reasonable perspective, quoting from a letter from Orwell to Gollancz that tries to re-state his position on several of these issues, *GOL*, p 344.

9. The number of people reading the book as partly or mainly a 'factual autobiography' is legion, although these readings are becoming less common. See for example D. Goldring in *CH*, p. 108, or P Toynbee in *CH*, p. 117.

10. R. Hoggart notes Hopkinson calling it Orwell's 'worst book' and Brander saying that it was 'his most disappointing performance' (*CCE* (3), p. 34); at the time of its publication W. Greenwood said, 'I cannot remember having been so infuriated for a long time' (*CH*, p. 100); more recently it is the centre of F. Gloversmith's rather panic-stricken criticism of Orwell's entire work. He calls it 'a rather unintelligent assault on intellectuals and on political theory' (*CCS*, p. 115).

11. R. Willliam's main criticism of *RWP* is that it puts forward a fictional and sentimental version of England as a unified country, held together by acceptable compromise; and that this leads to the hope that the working class would simply become middle-class: an idea behind 'revisionist' British Labour Party essays of the 1950s and 1960s (*O*, p. 84). It is an interesting reversal of Toynbee's accusation (1957) that Orwell denounced the middle class for not becoming working-class in *CH*, p. 117; and R. Hoggart is probably the most perceptive when he suggests that the coalescence of middle class and working class into one 'bland' consumer would have horrified Orwell (*CCE* (3)).

Chapter 3

1. The catalogue of adjectives that surrounds *HC* is warming but slightly embarrassing. Glancing through the entries in *CH* one sees 'integrity and independence', 'honesty and sincerity', 'heart of innocence', 'a patently honest man', 'truth and decency', 'truthful', 'faith', 'trust', 'moving', 'supremely good and honest'. Although this legacy has turned against his other works, *HC* has survived remarkably unscathed; those who feel they cannot praise it usually leave it alone. The main criticism is of Orwell's naïvety and innocence, as if the critics cannot accept that he understands the practical situation. P. Mairet, reviewing for *New English Weekly*, claims that the interesting part of his book is Orwell's unwitting portrayal of the 'ideological war' (*CH*, p. 129); S. Spender writing in 1950, is still trying to undercut Orwell's account by playing on his 'innocence' (*CH*).
2. See for example *O*, pp. 55–57, for an account of Orwell's supposedly chance affiliation with the Communist Party during his early days in Spain.
3. This in contrast to the suggestion that he was critical of the revolutionary militia in a wholly negative manner, preferring instead the practicality of the Communist 'line' (*O*, p. 57); early in his military education this is indeed so, but the process of the book is to indicate the limitations of the latter and the long-term effectiveness of the former.
4. L. Trilling points this out firmly in his introduction to the book, in *CCE* (4).
5. Here one comes to the most serious allegations that Orwell's 'plain reportorial style coerces history, process, knowledge itself into mere events being witnessed', E. Said, 'Tourism among the Dogs', *New Statesman*, 18/1/80, pp. 93–4; but this rests on a naïve assumption about what 'plain reportorial style' is, and what it is supposed to achieve.
6. While *HC* itself usually evades these accusations, a dominant view is of the man as having little understanding of human relationships (*GO*, p. 7), or a 'bleak' attitude to 'human individuality, friendship, affection. ..' (*CCS*, p. 107). B.Crick carefully documents the many oddly abusive remarks that people slanted against the memory of Orwell, see for example, *GOL*, pp. 420 or 525, wisely refraining from concluding on their relevance; but it is more difficult to understand how this response translated to the literary text.
7. Although R. Williams manages to defuse the challenge by saying that the idea that the POUM and the revolution was suppressed by the Soviets was not widely held (*O*, p. 57).

8. Here I use 'significance'and 'meaning' as glossed by W. Booth in *A Rhetoric of Irony*(Chicago: U of Chicago P, 1974); I note this because this usage is nearly the reverse of that proposed for the term 'signifiance' in current structuralist theory.

9. For example see T. Eagleton *CCE*(2), p. 29, or those such as P. Lewis who view the novel as sentimental, nostalgic, an idyllic looking back, and fail to note the irony involved (*GOR*, p 77). For an alternative and sound assessment, see B. Crick, *GOL*, p. 376.

10. The former is the view of, for example, E. Thomas *Or* who allies the novel with the passivity of 'Inside the Whale' as does T. Eagleton in *CCE* (2), p. 33 who also notes the lack of solutions; R. Lee points out that the solutions lie within the person rather than in society (*OF*).

11. See L. Brander, *G*, p. 152, C. Small, *RM*, p. 100, and G. Woodcock in *CS*.

Chapter 4

1. B.Crick in *GOL* rightly presents the unpleasantness of this aspect of Orwell, pp. 360–2, or 439; but he also points out his 'characteristic' attempts to make peace on a personal level with most of these people.

2. Critical appreciations of 'Inside the Whale' split down the middle as to whether it is advocating a passive attitude to the world or condemning it. R.Williams's influential book implies that Orwell is for passivity, as do many Orwell critics following his line. A. Sandison in *LME* implies that he is not;and C. Small says that he leaves the argument 'unresolved', *RM*, p. 98.

3. Orwell's other comments on Miller may be found in *CEJL* I 228 and I 400.

4. C. Small notes that the whale is a 'symbol of choice between political and non-political positions' (*RM*, p. 98); the point about the story of Jonah is that it is about the evasion of answers, not about the answer itself.

5. See B. Crick, *GOL*, chapter 12, for a sensible and detailed account of this change.

6. Orwell did, however, suggest that the one way to retain some idea of historical perspective was through the encouragement of the publication of pamphlets. Orwell also suggests that since history books are not commercially profitable, an institution such as the British Museum should be funded to print several copies of all particular viewpoints in order to ensure 'possible correctives to accepted lies'(*CEJL* III 212). An early comment indicates his belief that in this time of organized lying and restriction of expression, 'For plugging the holes in history the pamphlet is the ideal form'(*CEJL* II 285). During 1944 he still retains some confidence that individual pamphleteers are writing real history; he says that they 'are trying to write contemporary history, but *unofficial* history, the kind that is ignored in the text-books and lied about in the newspapers'(*CEJL* III 234). But only a few months later he is claiming that in pamphlets 'Nobody is searching for the truth, everybody is putting forward a "case" with complete disregard for fairness and accuracy' (*CEJL* III 289); they have completely lost their sense of distance. The conclusion is undoubtedly influenced by the state of war surrounding him. Later on his 1948 introduction to *British Pamphleteers*, while not claiming truth for the pamphlet does reiterate its importance as a 'footnote or marginal comment on offical history. It not only

keeps unpopular viewpoints alive, but supplies documentation on events that the authorities of the day have reason to falsify' (p. 15).

7. See for example *HC*, p. 30.

8. In the early work one only finds odd references such as the comment on the 'morass of words' (*CEJL* I 19) used by a certain brand of Catholicism as a barrier to understanding, or the observation with regard to Miller that the written word loses its power 'if it departs too far, or rather if it stays away too long, from the ordinary world where two and two make four'(*CEJL* I 23). But few though these references are, they contain the seeds of later, wider concerns such as Orwell's anxiety about the manipulation of large numbers of words to confuse and twist meaning with imprecision.

9. 'Unmistakable' analogy is to be effected by giving meaning physical form, and Orwell's film reviews of this period indicate his naïve enthusiasm for a possible solution within the medium. Films are offered as a means to expose the unverbal motives 'which are a cause of constant lying and misunderstanding [they] could be tracked down, given visible form, agreed upon, and named ...' (*CEJL* II 11). Although he slightly withdraws from this suggestion in the conclusion, he finishes by positing the absolutism of a 'truly expressive language of gesture alone', in which the sounds of words are not necessarily correlated to their meaning and it becomes simply a sign system, a code.

10. But I would not agree with B. Crick's implicit judgement, with Gollancz, of Orwell as an 'intellectual anti-intellectual' (*GOL*, p 310).

11. For an interesting discussion of the circularity of group and individual autonomies,the former moving to 'natural law' and the latter to 'liberalism', but neither assessing the grounds of their world, see I. Murdoch and the essays in *The Sovereignty of Good* (London: Routledge & Kegan Paul, 1980/70). Murdoch links the power of this autonomy with the combination, subsequent to Kant's philosophical writings, of the rational man with isolation.

12. For a summary of a number of these studies see L. Hunter, *Rhetorical Stance* (London: Macmillan, 1984).

Chapter 5

1. See L. Hunter 'J. M.Barrie's Islands of Fantasy', *Modern Drama* (May 1980).

2. Negative rhetorical strategies are often delineated by the figure of mathematics, see L. Hunter, *Rhetorical Stance* (London: Macmillan, 1984).

3. See L. Hunter, 'J. M.Barrie: The Rejection of Fantasy', *Scottish Literary Studies* (May 1978).

4. See Orwell's comments on film in *CEJL* II 11.

5. A number of critics, for example C. Small in *RM*, p. 48, suggest that Orwell was afraid of sexual topics and account for Dorothy's frigidity by calling it an evasion on the writer's part. The suggestion limits the reading of the novel. A. E. Dyson points out in *CF* that Orwell 'accepts sex with almost Laurentian completeness', (p. 202).

6. For an extensive treatment of theories of fantasy in the twentieth century see L. Hunter, *Modern Allegory and Fantasy* (London: Macmillan, 1984).

7. For example, see W. Irwin's detailed and perceptive study of fantasy *The Game of*

the Impossible, A Rhetoric of Fantasy (Chicago: U of Illinois P, 1976).

8. Among many others, R. C. Elliott notes the conservatism of satire in *The Power of Satire* (Princeton: U of Princeton P, 1960), p. 273.

9. Both C. Hollis and E. Thomas note, as I do, the similarity between Orwell and Chesterton.

10. It is not until February 1944 that he mentions in a letter that he is toying with a work similar to Zamyatin's *We* (*CEJL* III 95).

11. See the comments on *AF* in the introductory chapter above for a detailed account of the generic confusion.

Chapter 6

1. M. Hodgart's 'From *Animal Farm* to *Nineteen Eighty-Four*', in *WGO*, claims that *AF* is a 'point-to-point correspondence' with Russian history, p. 138. Yet R. Lee in *OF* asserts that it is neither a 'simple political allegory' nor a 'classical satire' because its levels interact thematically, p. 111. See also the introductory chapter above for other points of view.

2. P. de Man, *Allegories of Reading* (London: Yale UP, 1979), p 75.

Chapter 7

1. See L. Hunter, *Modern Allegory and Fantasy* (forthcoming publication), for an account of the transition from theories of pure art and music into theories of games and fantasy.

2. By dialectical logic is implied the argument and ordering from juxtaposed propositions culminating in analogy, that forms the basis for Plato's dialogues.

3. Most theorists of fantasy as a game state that since absolute control is not possible then the implications of negative strategies need never be taken seriously, see L. Hunter, *Rhetorical Stance* (London: Macmillan, 1984).

4. K. Burke discusses 'heresy' within authoritarian societies in *The Philosophy of Literary Form* (Louisiana State UP, 1941), p. 104.

Index

allegory 3–4, 12, 88, 92, 110, 152, 154–5, 159–80, 185, 190–2, 201, 217–26;
  and fairy story 180;
  and fantasy 3–4, 164, 224–6;
  and irony 160, 191–2;
  and nonsense 155;
  and satire 129, 154, 159–60, 164–6, 180.
analogy 71, 79–83, 89–94, 117, 146, 165–8, 187, 199, 203–6, 210–11, 214.
anarchism 72, 78, 81–4, 89–91.
art 108–16, 133–6, 142–3, 166, 225–6;
  for art's sake 111, 114;
  and morality 134, 136;
  and politics 142, 166, 225–6;
  and propaganda 108, 110–13, 116, 133–5, 142–3;
  and purity 114, 135, 142, 149.

BBC 116, 118, 120, 123, 125, 129, 130, 134–5, 145.
Butler, S. 159, 221.
brotherhood 81, 93, 128.
Carroll, L. 154, 159, 221.
Chesterton, G.K. 113, 145, 150, 157.
class 6, 17, 20, 27, 37, 47, 49–50, 53–68, 80, 94, 118, 146;
  middle- 15–17, 21, 49, 53–68, 152, 156;
  working- 47, 49, 50, 53–68, 200.
Crick, B. 9–10.
capitalism 77–8, 168.

comedy 152–4, 157.
criticism
  literary 108–15, 140–64;
  self- 27–8, 62–6;
  of Orwell 3, 5–6, 9–10, 28, 59, 109.
Dali, S. 136, 156.
Derrida, J. 162.
Dickens, C. 39, 109–11, 152, 155, 157.
deMan, P. 3, 162.
decency 33, 68, 102, 123–4, 130, 136.
documentary 1, 3, 5, 7, 14, 21, 35, 43, 46, 57, 60, 69, 94–5, 104–5, 109, 117, 163.
dream 203–8.

education 21, 28, 32–7, 42, 56, 63, 84, 113, 115, 165, 169;
  political 11, 99.
England 18, 26, 90–2, 137.
escape 26, 32, 34, 36–40, 43–6, 48, 50, 52, 56–9, 63, 69, 76, 91, 100–4, 111, 113, 136, 143–8, 154, 156, 158, 164, 172, 177, 183–4, 200, 204, 206, 121;
  literature 143–8, 154, 156, 158.
fact 1, 3, 14, 33, 44, 46, 51, 67, 83, 85, 93113, 117, 120–1, 130, 167, 198, 207, 209, 216, 225.
faith 28, 30, 33–5, 63, 67–8, 124, 157.
fantasy 3–4, 11–12, 20, 32–3, 41, 43, 99, 111–13, 118, 125, 127, 130, 136, 143–55, 160–5, 189, 192, 196–8, 200–4, 207, 210–12, 216, 223–6;
  stance of 148, 163, 165, 192, 225;